D0093623

NO EXCUSES UNIVERSITY™

DAMEN LOPEZ

HOW SIX EXCEPTIONAL SYSTEMS
ARE REVOLUTIONIZING OUR SCHOOLS

Follow us on

TurnAround® Schools Publications

NO EXCUSES UNIVERSITY™

DAMEN LOPEZ

HOW SIX EXCEPTIONAL SYSTEMS
ARE REVOLUTIONIZING OUR SCHOOLS

Special thanks to those who generously granted their permission to include their material in this book. All reasonable attempts have been made to obtain permission for the use of material quoted in the book. We regret any errors and omissions. If the owner of any material published in this book believes that such permission has not been granted, please contact us at TurnAroundSchools.com.

ISBN: 978-0-9842154-3-0

LCCN: 2009938081

Available through
www.NoExcusesU.com

Printed in China

Dedication

This book is dedicated to the six women
whose support has made all the
difference in my life.

To my wife, Lara,
it is my greatest joy to know that everything
that is written in this book
was first heard by your ears.

To my four daughters,
Sophia, Olivia, Mia, and Ava,
who remind me daily that my greatest
accolade is that of being your daddy.

And to my mother, Barbara,
who started the entire journey with
a pat on my chest, a kiss
on my forehead, and five little
words whispered at bedtime:
"After high school comes college."

I love you all very much.

About this Book

As someone who has never forgotten the challenges that teachers face on a daily basis, I want educators to find the words within these pages not only enjoyable to read, but practical as well. I, like many of you, have attended conferences, examined articles, and read books anticipating solutions to everyday challenges that I faced as a teacher and principal. Too many times, however, I was left asking, "What now?" I found few offerings of how I might actually improve my pedagogy. From the moment I began writing this book, I knew that I wanted it to be done in a format as practitioner-friendly as could be. Because of this, I focused on three strategies as I wrote.

First, I was diligent in writing in a style that might mirror a conversation between two caring professionals. Second, I began each chapter with a Key Concepts section in an effort to frontload the reader. Finally, no chapter was complete until I added a Theory to Practice section at the end. What begins with questions that teams can discuss, ends with step-by-step suggestions that schools can act upon. The Theory to Practice section acts not as a book study, but rather as a transformational guide.

It is my hope that you be validated by what you read as well as motivated to produce change that fosters results for the hundreds of very deserving students within your school.

Table of Contents

Chapter One

Key Concepts

"How wonderful it is that nobody need wait a single moment before starting to improve the world."

— Anne Frank

1

For some children, the only hope to escape a life of poverty is found through the front gates of a school that cares.

2

The humble beginnings of Damen and his family acted as a driving force for change.

3

The words "After high school comes college" shaped the author's view on education, and instilled in him a passion to influence the lives of others through the work of the No Excuses University.

Chapter One

Five Whispered Words

I had watched hundreds of children walk through the gates of our campus each day in my six years as the principal of Los Peñasquitos Elementary School, but this one child was different. At the time I didn't know exactly what led me to follow him to his classroom, but as I reflect back on that day I realize that it wasn't just one thing; it might have been many. Maybe it was the tattered clothes that he was wearing. His white tank top t-shirt and cutoff jeans, covered in dirt stains, was the most unlikely first-day-of-school outfit that someone could imagine. Maybe it was the way his mother walked beside him as his younger sister held on to her dress and his baby brother was being transported on her back, as is the custom in their Mixteco culture. Or maybe it was the butcher's bag that was dangling from his left hand, holding a sippy cup of milk and a small snack wrapped in aluminum foil. This bag that you and I throw away after so many visits to the grocery store was the only semblance of a lunch sack that this little boy had on his very first day of school. Whatever it was, I knew that I had to follow him, little Luis, to class to find out more.

We've seen it hundreds of times. Children are brought to the door of their first kindergarten classroom with much trepidation on the part of parents. Some of the children cry as they cling to their mothers, while others walk silently into the unknown as they take seats at their places on the carpet. Little Luis did neither. With a huge smile on his face, he said goodbye to his mother in his native language and eagerly responded to his teacher's direction to take a seat on the orange square with his name on it. I stood there. I watched him. I could not leave. Here was a child of poverty who could not speak a word of English, yet his bright and eager eyes told a story of hope that could fill the pages of this book. It was as if he knew that he was beginning a journey that had the potential to change his life forever. That day, Luis was a reminder of my purpose as an educator, because on that day he reminded me of … me. Forty years ago, my life started under similar circumstances. And while I would never know the depths of poverty the way that young Luis would, I do remember the times that I clearly stood out as the exception rather than the rule.

I grew up about an hour and a half drive outside the city of San Diego in the small mountain town of Julian. This one-stop-sign community has grown since we moved there in 1976 (it now has two stop signs), but at the time it was called home by a little more than a thousand people. Because of the rural environment of the town, there weren't many housing options for families who couldn't afford to purchase a home. In fact, the only available apartment we could find at the time was on the second floor of the Julian Market. It wasn't spacious, nor was it clean, but it did bring the perks that could only be found by a family who had nowhere to go but up. One of those perks was to spend each night cleaning the store in exchange for an extra $50 a month off the rent. Every night, my parents, brother, and I would go downstairs and do our best version of "whistle while you work." My mom, Barbara, would sweep, my dad, Steve, would mop, and my brother, Dan, and I were taught to arrange the cans on the shelves just right so that the labels would always be facing out. Truth be told, it wasn't long before our version of *stocking* turned into *stacking* and my parents soon realized that we weren't exactly expediting the cleaning process. But because we were doing our best, and because there was no one to watch us while they worked, my parents insisted on having us participate.

In the afternoons as the sun went down, my brother and I would retreat next door to an empty parking lot to play with a group of kids that lived close by. This was the hangout where the rule "no shoes, no shirts" did not exist. During the weekday afternoons, we would ride bikes and walk the trails throughout the small town. Occasionally we would witness a drunk who was a bit out of hand or a fight between two locals whose lives, and wives, had crossed paths in all of the wrong ways the night before. As we observed the colorful characters within our community, we grew up finding normalcy amid what by many accounts would be seen as atypical to families who valued social and academic success. As I look back, I now know that unlike Luis, I was not growing up in a cycle of generational poverty. I was experiencing an example of situational poverty. I also understand why my parents were so motivated to move us out of these circumstances as fast as they could.

My father did so by working any job that he could in order to pay the bills in the short term. He would sit on the steps of the grocery store every morning and ask the construction foremen if they needed an extra helper for the day. When asked by a contractor if he knew how to _________ (fill in the blank), he would exclaim with confidence that he was highly skilled. Electrician or butcher, carpenter or logger, my father never pushed away work. His commitment to his family was just too great to exhibit any kind of pride that might stand in the way of putting dinner on the table.

Much like my father, my mother did everything in her power to support the family. I never knew it then, but her pride was also challenged in her daily life. No example is greater than the times that we would walk to the post office on Sundays in order to get free bread, milk, and cheese. At the time, my brother and I thought that we must have hit the dairy lottery. Later however, we found out that those free handouts were an example of government welfare that my family had no choice but to partake of. In hindsight, such participation on the part of my mom and dad never skewed our pride in them. Instead, it has helped us to develop an understanding of the source of my mother's motivation to "break the cycle," as she would say, of a status-quo life for each of us. And in spite of the fact that neither of my parents was college educated, they operated with an understanding of just how important it would be for us to be. Proof of this came in the form of our nightly bedtime routine.

Every evening, no matter the circumstances that transpired during the day, the family ritual in that little apartment remained the same. My mom would tuck my brother and me into bed, read us a story, pat us on the chest, and whisper the words "after high school comes college" in our ears. These same words that my mother shared with me as a young boy just so happened to be some of the first words that little Luis would hear from his teacher on the day that he entered his kindergarten classroom for the first time. Little did I know the impact they would make on me decades later and perhaps on Luis decades from today. What started as a whisper from the mouth of my mother has now become a rally cry for educators across this country as they promote college readiness through what is known as the No Excuses University endeavor. And while you now know its origin, it is up to you to define just how far this work of promoting college readiness will go. It is my hope that you will find the motivation for this cause in this book. May it inspire you to provide never-ending hope for our neediest children.

Chapter One

Theory to Practice

Items for Articulation

- ❑ Take the time to share with your colleagues thoughts about the person or persons in your life who helped to break a chain of events that otherwise might have led you down the wrong path.
- ❑ Who is your Luis? What evidence do you have that the work being done within your classroom and school is offering ways to break the cycle of poverty for kids like him?

Items for Action

- ❑ On a blank piece of paper, create a checklist of reservations that you may have in promoting college readiness to students. For example, some may feel that students in elementary school are too young to understand, while others may be concerned that the parent community will lack support for such an endeavor. Whatever your concerns, write them down. When you are done, put the paper in a small, sealed envelope and place it at the back of the book. You'll be asked to revisit your concerns later on in your reading.

Chapter Two

Key Concepts

"Don't wait for extraordinary opportunities. Seize common occasions and make them great. Weak men wait for opportunities; strong men make them."

— Orison Swett Marden

1

Many will have you believe that the process of change is much harder than it actually is … don't believe them.

2

Acting with a spirit of mindful risk-taking is often much more productive than waiting on sloth-like research studies that may or may not exist.

3

Because of an impatient obsession to achieve academic success, the Los Pen staff chose to BE the research and find new ways to promote college readiness for all students.

Let's Be the Research

December 20, 2003. I remember this night the same way I do the birthdates of my children. Shuffling in the dark, I woke up searching for something to write on in an effort to document the kind of inspiration that seems to come only in the middle of the night. As a relatively new principal, I had learned to always keep a notepad and pen on my nightstand for times just like these, but on this night I couldn't find either. Not wanting to lose my thought, I turned on the lights in desperation, waking my wife and our brand-new baby. Immediately, I scribbled the words "Let's BE the research!" on a 4x6 lined notepad. These words, which lacked the slightest significance to my wife at the time, would eventually launch an endeavor that is changing the lives of students across the country. But before you understand their meaning, you must first understand the inspiration behind them.

In September 2002, I found myself packed into the superintendent's meeting room alongside two dozen elementary school principals from all over our district. Cabinet members greeted each of us with a hope that sprung eternal after a well-deserved summer break. In turn I, like so many of my colleagues, entered this first administrative meeting with an eagerness to welcome a new year the way a painter does a blank canvas.

As was always the case, the agenda for the morning was broken up into two distinct categories. First came the housekeeping items that brought an abundance of minutiae and ensured that our role as *managers* was secure. The second focus was based on the district's yearly strategic plan. This portion of the agenda was intended to encourage us as *leaders* who actively sought ideas and strategies in the hope that we would create greater academic and social success for our students. I had been through meetings like these on a number of occasions, and, to be honest with you, they rarely inspired me as a leader. However, on this day I hoped that the message might be different. To my surprise, it was.

The members of the superintendent's cabinet stood strategically around the room as one of our top district leaders shared the number one goal of our district. "This year, the number one initiative of our district is to promote college readiness for all!" he said excitedly.

I watched the faces of my colleagues as we all eagerly waited to hear more information. Silence. That was it. After a few brief seconds, sensing that I was not alone in my question, I stood up and asked, "What does that mean for elementary school?"

This fair question immediately received a fair response, which was, "We don't know. We haven't done the research. We're going to learn a lot more this year."

Accepting this answer as one that was more than reasonable, we concluded the meeting and went on our way.

After a year went by, I found myself in that same room, with that same group of elementary school principals. Again, the proclamation was made: "The number one goal of our district is to promote college readiness for all."

Again, I asked the same question. "What does that mean for elementary school?"

This time, the answer was different, but far more disappointing. "We don't quite know because we really couldn't find the research," said the cabinet member.

As the meeting wrapped up on that fall day, I left with a great sense of frustration over the lack of direction that was given to us as leaders. And while I found the mission of college readiness to be one that was noble, I didn't exactly believe that what my district was stating was all that creative. This to me was a perfect example of setting a lofty goal without offering a means to achieve it. It's safe to say that this likely was not my district leadership's intention, but it did nonetheless cause great frustration for me and my colleagues alike. In fact, I found myself frustrated by this lack of direction for months. Which brings me back to that early morning in December.

The clock read 2 a.m. and I was the only one in my house who was not fast asleep. I stared at the ceiling for many minutes before finally writing down those four life-changing words: "Let's BE the research!" Unlike the times where I processed a thought over and over again before writing it down, these words were immediate and demanded action. I remember thinking to myself, "Damen, get this on paper. Something big is about to happen!"

Whether it was my desire to share my inspiration or simply my need to explain why I had turned on the lights in the middle of the night, I made my wife sit up in our bed and listen to what I had to say. "Lara, Lara, you've got to listen to this. I've got a great…"

Before I could say more, she grabbed me by the cheeks, looked affectionately in my eyes, and said, "Damen, go back to sleep and leave me alone!"

I couldn't blame her for wanting to go back to sleep, but I insisted that she needed to hear me out. "No, Lara, you don't understand. I have a great idea and I have to process it with someone. Just listen."

Sensing that her attention span was not capable of keeping up with my excitement, she convinced me to take my ideas into our small home office and get my thoughts on paper. For six hours I sat at my computer writing notes, listing bullet points, and laying out a plan that I believed had the ability to revolutionize public education. Soon after 8 a.m., my wife walked into our office, took a seat at a chair, and said, "I'm ready to listen."

I won't lie to you when I share that I looked at her with tears in my eyes and said, "There's a lot to do and I need to work closely with my staff on this, but I think I just found a way to change the lives of thousands of pre-K to college students across this country."

Before I could speak another word, my wife said, "I don't know what you are going to tell me, but I can tell by the look in your eyes that you are telling me the truth."

I indeed was that morning when I spoke with my wife and I certainly am today as I write for you. What began so randomly in the middle of the night has become a systematic endeavor that is changing the lives of thousands of students, educators, and families across this country. That endeavor acts not only as the title of this book, but more importantly as a renewed sense of hope for even our most challenged students.

The No Excuses University was founded in January 2004 with the support of the Los Peñasquitos Elementary School staff. After being told by many that the most successful initiatives were ones that required validation by academics who conducted research studies on efficacy, our staff boldly decided to go about our business in a unique way. We decided that instead of waiting for the results of studies that were not even being conducted, we would become the research. Such experimental reform is often regarded as careless by those who embrace the status quo, but for our staff it's really all we've known for more than a decade. Unfortunately, I remember a time when this positive entrepreneurial spirit was all but non-existent at our school.

Chapter Two

Theory to Practice

Items for Articulation

- ❑ Think about a time when your school was told that something could not be done because of a lack of resources, research, personnel, etc. How did you handle this problem? Did you give up, or did you find a way to create success in spite of such challenges?

Items for Action

- ❑ As a team, think about one strategy, lesson, unit, or intervention that you have been putting off creating because of a lack of resources or research. Make a plan today to go forward collaboratively and implement this one idea.

Chapter Three

Key Concepts

"We are all faced with a series of great opportunities brilliantly disguised as impossible situations."

— Charles Swindoll

1

One goal changed Los Peñasquitos Elementary School: Every student without exception and without excuses will be proficient or advanced in reading, writing, and math.

2

Never underestimate the influence, both positive and negative, of a veteran staff on a new teacher.

3

The potential of an individual student is limited only by the desire for an adult to draw upon it.

FINDING POSSIBLE IN THE IMPOSSIBLE

While performing at the Lincoln Center in New York City, Itzhak Perlman, world-renowned as one of the best violinists, encountered a challenge unlike anything the crowd had likely experienced before. It has been reported that after the first few bars of his solo, the audience heard a loud twang and snap that came from Perlman's violin. The nightmare of a broken string came during the performance of Mendelssohn's Violin Concerto, a piece that many had deemed impossible to play. Because Perlman suffers from the effects of polio, a disease he has battled since he was a child, he did not get up to replace his instrument, as is the custom during such a time. Instead, silence blanketed the crowd as he paused and then began to play with the three remaining strings. In spite of such a great challenge, he played the remainder of the arrangement flawlessly. Afterward he was asked how he was able to accomplish such a tremendous feat. Perlman simply replied, "You know, sometimes it is the artist's task to find out how much music you can still make with what you have left."

Just as Itzhak Perlman found success in what others deemed to be impossible, so too must educators as they work with a wide array of students. In 1995, I started my career at Los Peñasquitos Elementary School as a one-on-one special support teacher for a student who was struggling with his behavior. I didn't know much about the school, known as "Los Pen" by those in the community, other than that it was the lowest performing in the Poway Unified School District, located 25 minutes outside the city of San Diego. Before accepting the job, I conducted some informal research and asked several teachers whom I knew around the district for their advice. There seemed to be a universal agreement that this was the place that, as one teacher told me, "Good careers go to die."

"It's the lowest-performing school in the district and it always will be," said one person.

"That's the place where all of the poor, second-language students and drug-addicted parents live," said another.

No matter how hard I tried to encourage a nice word to be said about this place, there was none to be found. Still, I accepted the position with the idea that I could always leave if I chose to do so. As I think back, it's amazing I lasted more than a day.

Dominic was a third-grade student who battled OCD (obsessive-compulsive disorder) as well as a mild form of Tourette's syndrome. Told that he was a good boy at his core, I introduced myself to him one early morning. My job was clearly defined as "Dominic's special teacher," which in layman's terms meant that I was responsible for keeping him out of trouble and on task. While many felt that Dominic made the choice to disobey the rules, the fact was that his lack of ability to process simple directions made it difficult for him to manage in the classroom without help. I soon found that Dominic had no "get to know you" phase; he immediately showed a side of himself that explained why he required individual attention in the first place. When he didn't get what he wanted, he would throw chairs and desks and he would yell at me. If he were really angry, he would hold his scissors in his hand and threaten to stab me with them. However, almost immediately after tirades like these, this third grader's conscience and tender heart would shine through. He would look me in the eyes, say he was sorry, and then on many occasions he would wrap his arms around me and hug me. As the year progressed, I found that Dominic would hug me more and try to stab me less. His academic and social success became a reason for celebration for the school, his parents, and me. As I watched him mature over the next several years, this young man, who would grow up to attend Purdue University, taught me something that would stick with me for the rest of my career: *The potential of an individual student is limited only by the desire for an adult to draw upon it.* I would soon find out, however, that this lesson was not one learned, or at least believed, by a number of staff members at Los Pen.

After finishing my work with Dominic, I was offered a position as a fourth-grade teacher some three doors down from the third-grade classroom that I worked in. Because I was a late hire, I only had two days to get my classroom ready for the school year. New key in hand, I opened the door to what would become my very first home as a teacher. A flip of the light switch allowed fluorescent attention on what was by all accounts a gloomy setting. The desks were stacked at the back of the room and the chairs were scattered in a pile without rhyme, reason, or unified color, for that matter. In fact, the chairs of this fourth-grade classroom appeared to be a size more appropriate for our first-grade friends across the hall. The textbooks were ragged and ripped, and the teacher's desk was wobbly no matter how you arranged it. Cushy teacher's chair? As my Italian grandfather would say, "Forgettaboutit!"

As I look back on that day, I realize that the lack of equitable supplies found in my room had little to do with bad luck and everything to do with the fact that my colleagues had taken the best of the best and given me the leftovers. Even though I had been the victim of this pervasive form of hazing that takes place in schools across the country, my attitude remained steadfast and spirited. One reason for this had to do with the voices that I heard across the hall from me.

I had been told for several months that the staff at Los Pen was one that could sometimes be challenging to work with. And while I did spend many months working as a long-term substitute, I hadn't been given the opportunity to truly work collaboratively with my colleagues in a way that would allow me to create an opinion of my own. As I heard the voices of two teachers in the room next to me, I immediately decided that the negative publicity must have been unjustified. I heard two colleagues who were actively engaged in lesson planning that was the model of collaboration. So inspired was I, that I reached into a bag of items I had bought at a local teacher supply store, pulled out my brand-new red lesson plan book, and confidently trotted to the room next door. I introduced myself, saying, "Hi, my name is Damen and I'm the new fourth-grade teacher. I see that you are planning and I'd like to join you."

After some pleasantries were exchanged, one of the teachers looked up from her chair and said, "Thanks for your offer, but we don't really ***team*** here; we ***partner***."

Because it didn't take long for me to translate the meaning of her message, I smiled and began to walk out of the room. Before I could take my first step out the door, the other teacher said, "By the way, your partner is right next door to you. Her name is Sandra."

A slight chuckle echoed into the hallway as I left. Even though this should have been a clear signal not to forge a partnership with Sandra, against my better judgment I opened the green accordion door that separated our two rooms.

Sandra *(whose name has been changed to protect the guilty)* was a teaching veteran of 20-plus years. It must be said that in the years since I entered the field of education, I have met many exceptional educators with 20, 30, or even 40 years of experience. In addition, I have been inspired not only by their knowledge of the curriculum but also in their ability to change and seek the best new methods of teaching possible. That said, Sandra was not one of them. In fact, one of the first things that I noticed about her was that she had stacks of worksheets lined up throughout the room. With some of them dating back to the early 1970s, the worksheets clearly did not represent cutting-edge pedagogy. After seeing this, I glanced at a lesson plan book that lay lifeless on her desk. Instead of stating the days of the week or specific dates on the calendar, Sandra's book was clearly labeled "Day 1, Day 2 … Day 180." Knowing that this likely meant that her routine was set in stone, the hairs on the back of my neck began to stand up as a signal for me to shut the door and go about my own business. Again however, against my better judgment, I looked her in the eyes and timidly said, "Hi, I'm Damen and … I guess … I'm your new teaching partner."

In an instant I watched what started as a blank stare on her face turn to frustration. Immediately she scowled and said, "Partner? Partner? I don't have a partner."

I tried to explain that our colleagues had sent me over to speak to her, but it was too late; I had struck a nerve. She continued, "I've been working here for 20 years without a partner and I'm not going to start now. I'm happy to share any ideas and you are more than welcome to copy some of my worksheets, but I'm not going to partner with you."

After her declaration, she shut the accordion door and, I can only assume, went back to her work. Rejected by someone whom even others did not wish to work with, I stood stunned. While it was many years ago, I vividly remember sitting in a pea-soup green, kindergarten-size chair in the middle of the room, saying to myself, "Damen, what the hell did you get yourself into?"

Even though I would take great joy in teaching the wonderful students who made up my very first class, I must say that I survived that year on will alone. Unfortunately, by the end of my second year, I had turned into someone whom I grew to despise.

For years I had heard excuses from educators about why some students could not learn. Whether it was because their kids were poor, spoke a different language, or had parents who just didn't care, I made it a point to turn my back on colleagues who displayed such negative attitudes. Little did I know that I would begin to take that same path. After teaching for two years, I soon discovered how hard it was to teach students with challenges, especially those who lived in poverty. After months of fighting inner frustrations, I remember being in the staff lounge and sharing with a colleague about one of my students. "What the heck am I supposed to do when this kid's parents don't even read with him at home!" I exclaimed.

In an effort to comfort me, my colleague said, "Welcome to the club."

As he said it, he took a certain sense of joy in the statement that made me uncomfortable. Later, I walked through the hallways asking myself, "Is this really a club that you want to be in?"

The answer to this was clearly "no," and I had decided then and there that I would rather give up a profession that I was passionate about than become another example of status-quo teaching. I had decided that I would pursue another line of work at the end of the year. Fortunately for me, I never had to make that choice because, in many ways, a different choice was made for me.

Jeff King was assigned as the new principal of Los Peñasquitos Elementary School at the end of my second year. I didn't know much about him, and had only heard that he was someone who was passionate about changing the reputation and results of Los Pen. So, convinced about his potential as a leader by the reputation that preceded him, I decided I needed to stick around and see what kind of changes would be made for the better. To this day, it is one of the best professional decisions I have ever made.

Jeff was bold, fearless, and sometimes brash, but he was just what the doctor ordered for a school that had been failing for decades. From the first moment that Jeff spoke to our staff, until the day that he left Los Pen some five years later and I replaced him as the principal, he never wavered from his expectations of us as professionals. With Jeff, there was but one goal: *Every student, without exception and without excuse, will be proficient or advanced in reading, writing, and math.* It was that simple. What started as an edict from Jeff's lips to our ears became a motivational mantra that still exists today. This unlikely goal, from a school where four in ten students live in poverty, stands today not because it sounds good or is inspirational. It still exists today because it works!

Los Peñasquitos Elementary School is made up of 650 students representing 35 different languages. Forty-two percent of our kids live in poverty, most residing within the largest Section 8 subsidized housing complex in Northern San Diego County. Crime levels and drug use are the highest in our district. There's no doubt that such demographics have acted as a tailor-made excuse for our school's poor performance over the years. With challenges like these, poor performance was not only acceptable within our district; it was expected. Because of this, many might suggest that setting a goal with academics at the forefront was an exercise in futility. Our fundamental belief in all students, however, would drastically change those perceptions and foster results that would make Los Pen a showcase for schools across the nation to follow.

Between 1997 and 2012, our school went from being the laughing stock of our community to the darling of Title I schools in the state of California. The staff at Los Pen worked diligently to promote academic success for every student, no matter the circumstance. As a result of their commitment, our school was ranked within the top 10 percent of all schools in the state of California nine times between 2001 and 2012. In addition, Los Pen was ranked number one out of 100 similar schools in our state for four consecutive years. While schools similar to ours were challenged to find academic results that closed the achievement gap between subgroups, each of Los Pen's five subgroups met levels of academic success that exceeded the norm. The focus of research studies, books, magazine articles, and news reports, Los Peñasquitos Elementary has created a momentum for change that is affecting the lives of thousands of students across the United States. But what others find surprising about this success is that it is grounded not on a plethora of programs and mandates that stifle a teacher's ability to use good judgment, but rather on six exceptional systems that both unify a staff and encourage an entrepreneurial spirit. These six systems are the heart and soul of the No Excuses University movement.

CHAPTER THREE

THEORY TO PRACTICE

ITEMS FOR ARTICULATION

- ❑ How many goals does your school have? Can you name them all? Is there one goal that stands out as a driving force for continuous improvement?

ITEMS FOR ACTION

- ❑ As a school, make a list of accomplishments that you would like to achieve that others would suggest are impossible. Keep this list handy, as they will help you to shape your BHAG at the end of chapter 5.

Chapter Four

Key Concepts

"He that is good for making excuses is seldom good for anything else."

— Benjamin Franklin

1

Successful schools simplify their focus.

2

No Excuses University is an organization that focuses on supporting practitioners with practical ideas that can be replicated in their schools.

3

No Excuses University is a network of schools that work together to promote college readiness for all.

4

No Excuses University is a philosophy that encourages schools to focus not on programs but instead on the creation of six exceptional systems.

NO EXCUSES UNIVERSITY

We are living in an age of "educational hoarders." From teacher to administrator, we have been conditioned to add, include, and incorporate but never encouraged to remove or simplify. This has created chaos in our classrooms and in our own minds. Our students sense this chaos and respond negatively through their behavior and learning, which is destined to produce frustrating results. The sad thing is that most educators take the knee-jerk reaction of blaming the students, when in reality it's our own fault. I have found, almost without exception, that the best schools are not the ones that consistently add; they are the ones that take away and refine their approach to teaching and learning.

Recently I made a big move from California to Texas. The amount of junk that we had accumulated in every closet and storage space throughout our home was embarrassing but not uncommon for anyone who's lived in a house for a decade with four kids. Long before my departure date, I set aside a weekend to conquer the beast that was my garage. Being the systematic guy that I am, I pulled out my cars and removed everything off of the storage shelves along the walls. (Right about now, many of you might be asking, "How bad can this guy's garage be if he had storage shelves and could park his cars in there?" If that's you, then all the more reason why you'd better be paying attention to this story!) Nonetheless, I continued to create three groups on the floor of the garage.

The first group represented items that I knew I needed access to on a continuous basis before the move. After sorting through them, I then restocked those items on the shelves that were easiest to access without climbing too high or bending over. The second pile was made up of things that were old dust collectors that we never used and that no one in their right mind would want. It was not only easy to decide to throw these things away; it was liberating! The final batch was maybe the most important of all. These were things that I carefully arranged on the floor and asked for my wife's permission before I took them to the local Goodwill. Hell hath no fury like a woman whose husband has given away an obscure 15-year-old knick-knack!

My wife, who now stays at home with our kids, used to work for many years as a first-grade teacher. Before our first daughter was born, she was sure to pack up every teacher-related item that she used throughout her career. From lesson plans to art ideas to sentence strips and math units, nothing got past her. The result, 17 file boxes that sat in the middle of my garage waiting for her approval to be sent off. You can imagine the conversation that ensued. It went something like this:

"You're not throwing those boxes away, are you?" she said.

"No, I'm going to give them away." I sheepishly responded.

"But what about when I go back to teaching?"

I treaded very lightly as I said, "Honey, if I were a principal looking for a new teacher and you were still using the same ideas and materials that you did 15 or 20 years ago, you probably wouldn't be someone that I'd hire."

As someone who is also quite practical as well as supportive of the idea of giving students the very best instruction possible, she agreed and said a phrase that I rarely hear: "You're right."

After speaking with her, I took the remaining items that we decided were not giveaways and carefully placed them on the storage shelves. The result? A ton of open space on the shelves, and a huge sigh of relief on my part. Leonardo da Vinci once said, "Simplicity is the ultimate sophistication," and I could not agree more. And the thing is, as an educator, I don't think I'm alone in that sentiment.

New ideas and programs are packed onto our classroom shelves and funneled into our daily agendas on a yearly, if not monthly, basis. From state mandates that districts must comply with, to top-down decisions that add uniformity to every classroom on every campus. These new ideas are often wonderfully supportive to the academic and social success of students, which I love, but the fact that they are add-ons and never seem to take the place of other initiatives is what we at the No Excuses University despise. And before I share with you exactly what the No Excuses University is, I want to start with an understanding of what it is not.

The No Excuses University, or NEU, is not complicated. I have found that many educators, academics, and politicians seem to be on a mission to make the idea of school-wide success appear so complicated that it creates an urgency that leaves schools running to pay top dollar for a quick fix. In fact, some consultants and educational service companies are the worst offenders, where profits take precedent over the academic gains of students. When my brother Dan and I officially created the No Excuses University, we did so with three very important expectations of ourselves. First was to offer the best possible staff development in our field while at the same time treating educators like professionals. Second, we wanted to present ideas and strategies that could immediately be put in place on any campus the very next day. Third, we never want to require our clients to buy "something else" from us at a later date in order to be successful. No yearly subscriptions. No next level learning kits that cost thousands. And no regurgitated productions of materials that are basically the same message in a repackaged form. Does this upset the establishment who thinks our model makes terrible business sense? Who cares. Our bottom line is really pretty simple: How many lives will we change before we die?

No Excuses University is not a mass-produced message intended to be thrown at educators as if they were koi fish in the middle of a feeding frenzy. Our desire is to create a coalition of like-minded individuals who seek to promote college readiness for all. Through this work, it is our hope to create the next greatest generation of citizens tomorrow by offering a quality education to our students today.

Finally, the No Excuses University is not another program. Sure, we embrace programs that can help support the achievement of our students, but we do not foolishly buy into them as if they are the savior of school reform. As you'll read, programs might produce results in the short term, but the only way for long-term, consistent, school-wide success is through the development of exceptional systems.

From our organization's commitment to the very best professional development, to our passion for creating a collaborative coalition through the No Excuses University Network of Schools, to our fight to remove our profession's dependence on programs and replace them with exceptional systems, No Excuses University seeks to be different. We choose to dream big for our students and simplify the solutions for our practitioners. Since 2006, this spirit has led us to connect with some of the greatest educators in the world and experience amazing transformations alongside staffs that have generated terrific results together.

No Excuses University: The Organization

In 2006, our organization was created and fueled only by the dedication of two brothers who had little more than a few thousand dollars to invest. Formerly known as TurnAround Schools, the No Excuses University is becoming far more than an idea; it is transforming into a destination.

In the beginning, No Excuses University was one concept among many that my brother Dan and I shared with educators for a number of years. Over time, people became so convinced by our idea to promote college readiness, beginning in elementary school, through our six exceptional systems that it eventually became the basis of our company. It is our hope that when educators ask each other for practical ideas and solutions to support student success, the response will be, "Let's go to the No Excuses University for answers."

Currently, No Excuses University hosts a number of events that share ideas from practitioners to practitioners with our six exceptional systems at the heart of their work. From institutes to annual national conventions, we are constantly on the road bringing this message to life. When educators attend our events, we view them as members of our family. They won't be given half of a Costco muffin and a box lunch to eat on the grass outside of a rundown high school campus. Instead we select upscale locations where we cater to them and treat them as professionals. We do this while keeping our prices well below our competitors' and ensuring our products are of the highest quality. And even though we enjoy touring the country throughout the year, our real calling is to someday create a No Excuses University Campus that others can go to as a destination for higher learning.

No Excuses University: The Network of Schools

Another effort that you will read more about in future chapters is related to the No Excuses University Network of Schools. This network of like-minded individuals is made up of schools that choose to apply for official NEU status as part of their desire to be a part of a movement far bigger than what might take place on their campus alone. Not all schools that have attended a No Excuses University event make the choice to apply for this status. In addition, not all schools that do apply are accepted. This network works as a collaborative coalition with three very important goals in mind under one clear promise:

Our Promise

We have no desire to participate in the politically driven or to take the easy road. We are dreamers and problem solvers who are advocates for students first. When we invest our energy in a project, we do so in a way that results in that endeavor becoming the best of its kind. We know that life is too short to listen to naysayers and the excuses that they share. Our students only get one shot at school success and because of this our clocks are set to one time … NOW!

Our Three Goals

#1 Goodbye to the Status Quo

Revolutionize K-12 public education by focusing on six exceptional systems created under the umbrella of college readiness for all.

#2 Schools of First Choice for Students

Partner with districts and charter school authorities to create and operate NEU Academy Prep Schools. Featuring a rigorous K-8 framework, these schools are bold in their approach and unique in their delivery of instruction.

#3 No Excuses University: A Campus for College Bound Kids

Build, from the ground up, an NEU Campus dedicated to serving foster children who will live and learn in a loving, college-like boarding school environment.

As of January 2013, what started as the first No Excuses University at Los Peñasquitos Elementary School in 2004 has grown to a network of more than 150 schools in 22 states that represents more than 100,000 students from preschool through college. What impresses most people about this coalition is not the size of it or how rapidly it continues to grow, but instead the fact that we don't collect any annual dues or fees for our schools to be a part of the movement. The expectations that we have of our official schools are certainly lofty, but paying big bucks every year is not one of them. In fact, the only financial requirement that we have is for schools to send a team that includes grade level representation, along with the principal, to one of our many institutes across the country. Other than that, the only other financial requirement is that No Excuses University Schools send the principal and at least one colleague to our NEU National Convention at least once every two years.

Many years ago, I sat down with a group of educators who help to run one of the largest educational movements in the world. As I sought their advice for how I might best go about growing our network, their first question was, "How much do you charge your schools each year?" When I said that we don't charge our schools dues or fees each year, one of the individuals exclaimed, "You'll never make it with a business model like that!" Since that meeting, we have added more than 100 schools to our official network and are seeing greater success than ever before. When asked for one piece of advice from people in search of accomplishing big goals, world-renowned survival expert Bear Grylls said, "Don't listen to the dream stealers." The No Excuses University Network of Schools lives according to that same belief.

No Excuses University: The Six Exceptional Systems

Before there was an official NEU Network, there was our company. But before there was even a company, there were six exceptional systems. These systems are the most important component of everything that we do as an educational organization or a business. They are the first prescription for any school's success. Everything else is a distant second.

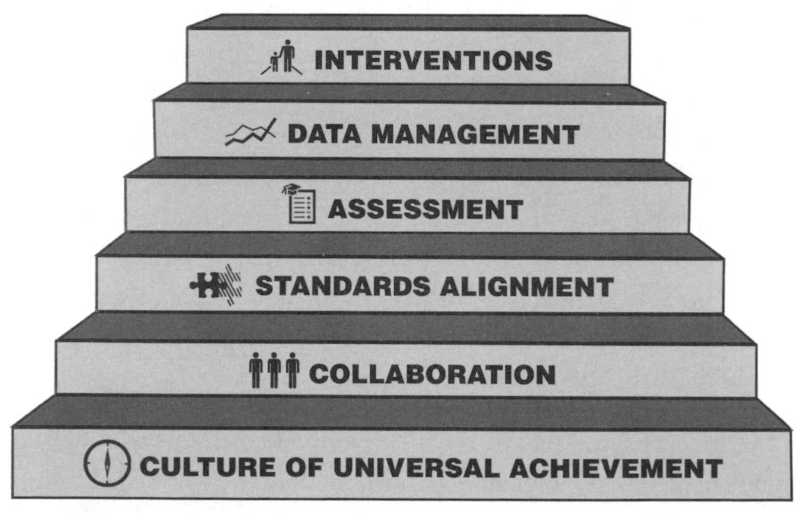

These six systems, which will be explored in detail in the next six chapters, are working to shift the culture of schools across the country as they help to generate academic results for even the most challenging demographics within a school's student population. They should be thought of as a sequential model via the exceptional staircase seen here.

It is a must for schools to focus on taking the time to create systems that are not just average, but rather exceptional before they move up the staircase. When schools exhibit a culture of universal achievement by believing in students, they collaborate around that belief. During collaboration, they align their standards as a team. As teams align standards, they need to assess the standards and manage the data. Then, and only then, can they pursue meaningful interventions with their students. Too many schools are trying to go from the bottom step all the way to the top in one fell swoop. Why? Because in their mind, "interventions" fix students. As they soon discover, their shortcuts produce few results. Unfortunately, it doesn't matter what interventions schools use; the only way to find sustainable success is to create one system at a time, get it right, and then move up the staircase. As Joe Girard once said, "The elevator to success is out of order. You'll have to use the stairs … one step at a time."

Get It Right, and Then Move On

Every spring, my wife, Lara, and our four daughters prep a patch of the backyard soil in order to grow a variety of vegetables. From the beginning, she knew very little about gardening. I would often joke with her about how there wasn't a plant that she couldn't kill. I recall her taking this teasing in stride as she attempted to plant her very first garden many years ago. Not unlike others who have gardened before, she took the typical steps during the process. She prepped the soil, designated individual sections to grow various vegetables, and ensured the proper watering for each. During this first year she planted at least 15 different types of vegetables. While she did a wonderful job of making it look like a garden, the similarity ended there.

At the end of the summer, during a time which she referred to as "harvest," a word that I assure you was used very loosely, the only plant to grow among the 15 different ones was pumpkins. That's right, pumpkins. For weeks leading up to this time, I remember her scouring the garden looking for remnants of other growth. And while there were a few sprigs from other plants here and there, pumpkins cornered the market in our backyard.

Sitting in my chair one day as the sun went down, I noticed my wife staring out on her garden. I figured that now was as good a time as any to console her for the disappointing outcome of her first attempt. As I walked toward her, I planned how to say how proud I was of her and how "these things take time." I imagined that her eyes would be welling up with tears, so the tissue in my pocket was ready and waiting. As I drew closer and put my arm around her, I was shocked by her demeanor. With a giant smile on her face, she looked at me and said, "Isn't it great?" I wondered for a moment whether or not she was referring to a beautiful bird in the trees or possibly my neighbor's garden. Again, she gave me a little jab with her elbow and questioned, "Isn't it great?" At this point I understood that her pride was in reference to her garden. Immediately, my plan to console her changed to words of encouragement and praise. Still, I had to ask, "What's so great?" She looked perplexed. "Look at all of those pumpkins. Look at how big they are and how well they grew." Needless to say, my wife's expectations for her first garden had been met. I decided that the best thing I could do was to be supportive. I went on and on about how proud I was of her and how excited I was for next year.

A year later I would grow to regret my praise as I noticed that the "pumpkin patch" had doubled in size. Again, 15 items were planted but the only thing that grew were pumpkins. This time I learned my lesson. At the end of the season while Lara was in the backyard, I took the opportunity to share my true feelings about the garden with her. While I don't remember the exact words of our conversation, I do remember that it went something like this:

Me: "Honey, I'm really proud of your hard work with the garden. I can see that you find great joy in planting alongside the girls and I don't want to see that end … however, I have to be honest with you, man cannot survive on pumpkin alone."

Her: "What is your problem with my pumpkins?"

Me: "It's not that I don't like pumpkins; it just that I don't like pumpkins that much. When you think about it, pumpkins are only good for two things, carving and pumpkin pie, and I've never seen you bake a pumpkin pie from scratch before."

Her: "But I like pumpkins."

Me: "What is it that you like so much about pumpkins?"

Her: "They are easy to grow in our backyard. All I have to do is water them. It's what I know."

Me: "I understand, but consider this. What if you take the time each year to perfect your gardening techniques so that a different vegetable grows every season. In 10 years you'll have a magnificent garden filled with produce that we can all enjoy."

It took her a little time, but she agreed. Each year she picked one fruit or vegetable to focus on. The first year, she invested the time to learn about the soil needs of corn. After that, she found just the right tomato cages that would support the growth of Roma, cherry, and beefsteak tomatoes. In her third year, she discovered how to use bamboo poles so that green beans would grow toward the sky, instead of rotting on the ground. Whether her efforts were guided by a commitment to have the world's greatest garden or just simply an extreme desire to prove me wrong, it worked. Eight years later we now harvest tomatoes used in pasta sauces and bruschetta, melons and strawberries that bring a sweet smile to the faces of my kids, and squash, corn, and green beans that last us through the summer. And, when the time comes for us to run out of these healthy treats, we always have plenty of pumpkins available. I suppose that's her small way of staying true to her gardening roots.

This conversation that I had with my wife not only changed her approach in terms of her garden, but also painted a perfect picture about developing exceptional systems. Just as my wife realized a need to take steps to ensure success for each vegetable that she planted, so too must we take the steps necessary to produce results through the development of individual exceptional systems that we create at our school sites. Schools must create systems with a focus on getting them right before moving on to the next one. Now I'm not suggesting that you put off assessing your students for three or four years while you work on your collaborative efforts, but I am suggesting that you choose one system as your main focus, get it right, and move up the staircase.

After my wife had perfected the growing of corn and moved on to tomatoes, she didn't forget how to grow corn. She fine-tuned her efforts and learned new ways to get better results, but because she did it right from the start, she has never since needed to start from scratch. As you make your upward journey, you will find that your exceptional efforts will be long lasting and far more successful than the old way of doing business. In addition, you will notice that rather than having to constantly recreate each system every year, you will simply need to fine-tune your efforts on an annual basis. Before you learn the details of each system, let me first share exactly what it is that makes a system exceptional.

What Makes a System Exceptional?

There's a big difference between average and exceptional. Average touches its forehead on the bar, while exceptional leaps over it with plenty of room to spare. The funny thing is that the way to get from average to exceptional doesn't really require us to work much harder; rather it mandates that we work more wisely as staffs. As you read this book, please use the four criteria below as they help you define the difference between average and exceptional.

Exceptional systems are created by the critical mass of the staff in a highly collaborative way.

You've seen it happen time and time again. When a principal creates a system, it stays in place for as long as they lead the school. When the "critical mass" of the staff joins together to create an exceptional system, however, it lasts far beyond the tenure of the principal. Of all the things that I am most proud of related to Los Peñasquitos Elementary School, it is the fact that even though I have been gone from the school now for several years, they have never been more successful than they are today. Was I a good leader? I think so. But I was not the reason for the school's success; it was and continues to be the result of the staff's commitment to create these systems together.

Exceptional systems find unique solutions to very important challenges.

One of the saddest things that we see in public education today are the many educators who spout off about all the things that are wrong about our industry and all the reasons for our lack of results. If given the time, they could spend hours blaming the state legislature, lack of funding, class size, and on and on. While I acknowledge that all of those things are a factor that works against our profession, frankly I'm kind of sick of hearing these complaints unless they are followed up with ideas for how to fix them. Instead of viewing our challenges with such despair, we should be seeing them as great opportunities. Every good thing that any No Excuses University school has ever done has come as a result of great, caring educators who are inspired to fix the problems that others have deemed beyond repair. When it all comes down to it, no matter your situation related to budget crisis, labor contract, class size, materials, or any other challenge that you face on a daily basis, one thing remains constant: Students will show up at your doorstep tomorrow. And they don't care about any of those problems; they just want to be taught. Exceptional systems find ways to do just that.

Exceptional systems are documented, endorsed, and reviewed annually.

If you can't write your system down on the front side of one page of paper, start over. How many schools out there have listed 12 goals accompanied by a three-page mission statement that no one can recite? How many times have you seen the result of your hard work end up in a fancy binder or colorful folder at the bottom of a pile or placed on the top of a bookshelf only to collect dust? What a shame! What a slap in the face to your hard work. Exceptional systems need to be practical and always active in our minds. Because of this, it is important that we document our plans with clarity and post them in places where we will revisit them on a consistent basis. And because the staff are the ones creating the system, they should also sign their names to them as an endorsement of the plans set forth. Endorsing your systems is not meant to be contractual in nature; it's meant to be a promise that you make to each other that says, "We worked our tails off on this and we are going to hold each other accountable to seeing it through." This kind of endorsement that is reviewed on an annual basis acts as an anniversary of sorts where you celebrate your hard work, while at the same time renewing your commitment to the future.

Exceptional systems are driven by results.

When we lack results based on clear data, our opinions are useless. I've been in the position many times as a teacher and principal where I could swear that my gut instinct was right. In matters of examining the social and emotional needs of students, it often was. But related to the academic success of those same students, it was far too often off track. The success of our systems must be measured by the results that we get; otherwise our plans are based on nothing more than educated guesses.

Exceptional systems and the staircase that defines them were created in such a way that encourages schools to take one step at a time, get the system right, and then move on. To jump from a culture of universal achievement to interventions may create scattered success, but it will never create the kind of long-term educational prosperity that occurs when schools move systematically up the staircase. As we work to promote college readiness for all, this exceptional system staircase acts as the core, the foundation for our endeavor. From the beginning of our journey, this has represented the north of our compass, supporting the travels we've made to a destination that focuses on college readiness.

Every aspect of the No Excuses University places the successful academic and social skills outcomes of students at the forefront. Our efforts strive to be reflective of this dedication through every conversation that we have and every decision that we make. By no means are we flawless in this endeavor, but we do attempt to be above reproach in our work on behalf of kids. When our conversations and decisions veer off course and begin to be about adults, students lose every time. Because of this, the culture that we establish from the start at every school site must embrace a desire to provide and ensure universal achievement for each and every student.

Chapter Four

Theory to Practice

Items for Articulation

- ❑ Are you an educational hoarder? What items and/or behaviors have you held on to for too long?
- ❑ Which step of the exceptional system staircase do you think your school is currently on?

Items for Action

- ❑ One of the best ways to reinvigorate your staff is to find clarity in your purpose. Choose one day to throw a "purge party." Get a dumpster and have your staff spend the time throwing away items in their classrooms that have the potential to create chaos. After doing so, work with your team members to create a schedule that uses your combined talents to redesign and redecorate each other's classrooms in a way that is structured for student success.
- ❑ As you prepare to learn about a culture of universal achievement in the next chapter, take the time to make a list of individual words or phrases that you think currently describes your school's culture.

Chapter Five

Key Concepts

"Greatness is not a function of circumstance. Greatness, it turns out, is largely a matter of conscious choice, and discipline."

— Jim Collins

1

The critical mass of the staff drives a culture of universal achievement.

2

Without belief, there can be no action.

3

Each staff member can practice six beliefs every day that will help to shape the school's culture.

4

No excuses begins with adults.

Culture of Universal Achievement

While working with a dozen members of a leadership team from a school in California, I came across an incident that was so powerful that it not only shaped the view of the team, but also serendipitously created an analogy that I have now shared with thousands of teachers across the country.

Just as I was offering the details of an agenda that would include topics that ranged from collaboration to small group reading instruction, one particular member of the leadership team, Amanda, begged for me to tackle a pressing issue that was on the mind of the team. As I paused, I listened to her concern that there were many staff members who were "not on board" and all of the efforts completed by the leadership team that day would mean nothing if these naysayers did not get on the "ship." Listening, I found out the following:

- Her use of the word "*many*" equated to about three people on the staff who were not on board.

- ❖ She had a concern that these negative influences would pollute the positive people on the staff.
- ❖ Finally, her concerns evolved to include not only the people on site who were not on board, but district decision-makers who hindered progress by cutting the budgets and raising class sizes.

As she wrapped up her concerns, she took what was meant to be an uplifting off-site leadership summit on a local university campus and turned it into a downer of a retreat. As the wheels began to spin in my head, I took advantage of a prop that sat outside the conference room that we were in. There in the center of a commons area was a magnificent granite ball resting above a spring of water that flowed underneath. I decided that this half art/half fountain hallmark would help begin our day anew.

As I led the team outside the door, many wondered about the impromptu field trip that we were going on. When we arrived at the granite ball, I could tell that their wheels were already beginning to turn. As I stood on one end of the ball, I asked Amanda to stand on the other side as the rest of the team observed. I asked her to spin the granite ball as fast as she could in an effort to get the momentum headed in my direction. While the water that flowed underneath allowed Amanda to create some movement, it also made it very difficult for her to produce the friction necessary to hold on. She clearly was no match for the ball.

After asking her to step aside, I requested that four team members take her place and try to do the same thing. In an instant they began to get the ball rolling. Each revolution created more speed and motivation for the small group. I then asked two more members to join in the fun. The result: a granite ball that was both in direct alignment with me and also spinning at a speed that was tough to halt.

With the ball spinning at a tremendous rate because of this group of six, or critical mass, I asked another member to stand on the opposite side. I offered the following direction to the team member: "You represent the budget. I want you to stop this momentum." As hard as the person tried, she could not. I asked another member to stand on the opposite side and said, "You represent an increase in class size. I want you to stop the momentum." He could not budge the ball. Finally, I asked Amanda to stand in the same opposing side and said, "You represent the people who are not on board. I want you to try as hard as you can to stop the granite ball." In spite of Amanda's best efforts, she too could not stop the ball. I yelled at her, "Come on, don't give up. Get your legs into it. Press as hard as you can!" She did so, but to no avail. As I watched her struggle, I also watched water flying up in her face. It was in her hair and on her clothes and was making the mascara on her eyes begin to run down her face. It was at that moment that Amanda did something incredible. Not only did she step away from the granite ball, but she went to the other side and joined with the critical mass as they continued their momentum in the opposite direction.

Why did Amanda step aside? For two reasons. First, just like a naysayer, she was uncomfortable being on the other end of the critical mass. Second, she recognized that it was easier to join in the fun than to fight against the movement of the mass. Amanda's experience exemplifies the power of a group of people who press forward in spite of the discouraging words and actions of others. Wherever I go I have found that while there are always a few naysayers who are not on board, there are far more good-natured and passionate educators who can make up the critical mass if they choose to bond together.

Unfortunately, the concerns that Amanda offered are being experienced today on hundreds of campuses throughout the country. And it's not difficult to understand how this happens. Many of today's veteran principals, teachers, and classified staff members have become frustrated by the negativity of others. This all too often leads to a negative attitude on their own part that extinguishes the fire that they entered the profession with. When this happens, you are left with, at best, a staff that is apathetic toward the future. I've been there. I know what it's like to be sucked into a toxic environment like that and behave in a manner that is embarrassing for me to even reflect upon. But through that reflection I know one thing for sure: Success is far more enjoyable than failure. Anyone who has had even a taste of what it's like to work with colleagues who inspire you, as they believe in each student, would never choose any other way to live. That kind of spirit exemplifies a culture of universal achievement and has to be the foundation for every school. So what is a culture of universal achievement?

A culture of universal achievement takes place when the critical mass of the staff believes that each student is capable of meeting academic standards in reading, writing, and math AND that the school has the power to make that opportunity a reality.

These words set the foundation of our exceptional system staircase and are at the heart of the No Excuses University endeavor. While our reading, writing, and math focus may be elementary in nature, they can easily be substituted by the most important areas of focus that you find appropriate at your level. What cannot change is the concept of whose responsibility it is to create this culture of universal achievement in the first place.

What Exactly is Culture?

The word "culture" is used often by a variety of educators wishing to shape reform efforts in our country. Their definitions, however, are not always understood and therefore rarely embraced. So, what is culture?

As someone who has helped to shape the culture of a school as well as a network of more than 150 No Excuses University schools, I can tell you that there is nothing more important than culture. To us, a culture is the flag that we plant in the ground as a declaration of our commitment to students. It firmly states what we stand for, as well as how we plan to go about our business as we make our stand. The statements that schools make about culture should be simple and easy to understand. Before we go any further, think for a minute about the culture of your school. Can you answer a confident "yes" to the following five questions?

1. Can the critical mass of your staff make a pledge that succinctly describes your belief in students?

2. If required to offer the most important goal of your school, could the critical mass of your staff do so?

3. When a colleague is down or having challenges, is there an abundance of staff members from across all grade levels and departments who would come to their aid as if they were all family?

4. If a new teacher were to show up on campus on day one, would you be able to offer an endorsement that documents and reinforces the overall culture of your school?

5. Does the critical mass of the staff hold one another accountable for results and share in the responsibility of leading your school?

After reading, you may have noticed the words "critical mass" used on a number of occasions. This is intentional, as it squashes the perception that every staff member must be on board in order to create a successful school culture.

With the momentum of a critical mass, a staff is capable of developing and implementing strategies that make for a remarkable culture of universal achievement. Consider these five questions again this time with practical answers.

Question #1: Can the critical mass of your staff share a pledge that succinctly describes your belief in students?

The Pledge: "We are committed to creating a school that knows no limits to the academic success of each student." This pledge is our purpose, vision, and mission all wrapped up in one. It is made up of 18 words that are easy to remember and thus easy to live by. Walk on the campus of many No Excuses University Schools across the country and you will meet dozens upon dozens of educators who can share it in an instant. Schools today need not document commitments that are 10 pages long and inevitably end up in a file folder somewhere. All they need to do is make a short pledge that succinctly solidifies their commitment to students.

Question #2: If required to offer the most important goal of your school, could the critical mass of your staff do so?

The Goal: "Every student will be academically proficient in reading, writing, and math." Depending on your academic level, your goal may look different, but in elementary school, there's nothing more important than supporting the literacy of a child at an early age. Regardless of where you land, the most important thing to remember about creating a goal that contributes to a successful school culture is that it be singular in nature. Too many schools use too many goals. Because of this, they forget them all and make very little progress toward any of them.

Question #3: When a colleague is down or having challenges, is there an abundance of staff members from across all grade levels and departments who would come to their aid as if they were all family?

The Family: The best thing about a good family is that you know you can depend on each other. Just as any one of you would likely rush to the rescue of your brother or sister stuck on the side of the road, staff members can also embrace a similar loyalty as they work together. From the way they collaborate to the simple act of eating lunch together, relationships that are built with a sense of caring for one another always contribute to the positive culture of a school. Staff members who think of themselves as members not of a staff, but of a family, are far more likely to support one another on a daily basis.

Question #4: If a new teacher were to show up on campus on day one, would you be able to offer an endorsement that documents and reinforces the overall culture of your school?

The Endorsement: When a staff creates a strong culture, they must endorse their commitments in writing. As I wrote in the last chapter, and will share in greater detail in Chapter 18, every time one of the six exceptional systems is created on any of our campuses, it is always followed by the staff signing their name to a document that we call "The Endorsement."

Question #5: Does the critical mass of the staff hold one another accountable for results and share in the responsibility of leading your school?

The Accountability: All of us would likely agree that cohesiveness is far better than divisiveness. That said, there is always a time for challenging one another in an effort to promote growth as professionals. The fact of the matter is that if you are not challenging each other in a way that creates a little bit of discomfort, you probably aren't doing a very good job of promoting such growth. Our role to hold one another accountable has nothing to do with catching each other when we fail, and everything to do with strengthening our culture. We must never forget that we are in a business that can thrive only when our students achieve results. Accountability ensures that this takes place.

How Do You Practice a Culture of Universal Achievement?

In spite of their best intentions, many educators will often say to me, "Damen, I love what you are saying, and I want to believe in the potential of all students, but I have to be honest and tell you that I really don't. What do I do if I don't truly believe?" My response stuns them. "Fake it. Pretend like you believe for one year. If you pretend like you believe, I know that you will see results that will validate those beliefs." How can I say this with such confidence? It's simple: When you believe in something with your whole heart, it changes your behavior. When you believe in your marriage, it changes the way you get along with your spouse. When you believe in your children, it drives the decisions that you make as a parent. When you believe in your students, it changes your actions as you respond to their needs. Because the concept of believing lacks a tangibility that you can touch and see, it's crucial that you consistently practice your belief in ways that can be seen on a daily basis. Here are six beliefs related to a culture of universal achievement that every staff can take part in.

Belief #1: Every student will be proficient or advanced in reading, writing, and math.

In his groundbreaking book *Built to Last*, Jim Collins writes about the traits that distinguish good companies from great ones. He contends that one fundamental difference between the two is that great companies have a Big Hairy Audacious Goal or a BHAG. These BHAGs are goals that are so lofty that it could take between 25 and 50 years to achieve. They are so lofty that your chance of success is between 10 percent and 25 percent. Even still, it is that loftiness that creates the outcome of greatness.

Today's schools are far too content with goals that are mediocre and reasonable. Educators have been taught to take baby steps toward reasonable outcomes and shy away from plans that exemplify idealism. This may be acceptable for schools where students are consistently on track for success, but it does little to support the extended gains that must take place in order to get our students of poverty caught up. It is for this reason that a BHAG is so important to a school. Instead of having 12 goals as part of a site strategic plan, choose one BHAG that every staff member can strive for and hold each other accountable to on a daily basis.

Belief #2: The academic accomplishment of every student is an obsession.

Think about one of your most challenging students in your class who lives in poverty. Imagine their home and the struggles that take place in their life. Now ask yourself this question: Did their parents grow up in poverty? Did their grandparents grow up in poverty? Chances are they did. If this is the case, what do you think is going to reverse this cycle? The answer, without hesitation, is education.

For your average, middle-class student, the K-12 education system is a marathon, but to the at-risk student of poverty it is a sprint where every second counts. It is our duty to be obsessed with our students' success and to display a sense of urgency in what, when, and how we teach our students each day. We unfortunately do not have the luxury of "winging it" for the students who need us most because the cycle of generational poverty that they are currently a part of is moving rapidly toward claiming another generation. As Super Bowl-winning coach Steve Mariucci once said, "I never wear a watch, because I always know it's NOW and now is when you should do it."

Belief #3: The school can neutralize many challenges that students bring to the classroom.

Let's face it, it's easy to get wrapped up in the injustice that is taking place at many of our public schools. Many students come to school unfed, tardy, and without their homework completed. As a teacher, I battled this issue on a daily basis. Looking back, I'm embarrassed by the amount of time and energy I put into fighting the wrong battles and directing my frustration at the wrong people. When students would enter my class without being fed, I would question why their parents didn't feed them as I told them about the importance of a healthy breakfast each morning. My inward concern for the student was all too often displayed with an outward frustration at them. Looking back, I should have handed them a granola bar and a juice box, told them how happy I was to have them in my class, and begun our day together. While I have since seen the error of my ways, many educators continue to fight a battle that misdirects their frustrations for what might be happening in the home and aims it directly at students. The solution? Decide right now that no matter the challenges that your students bring to the classroom, it is your job to neutralize it in the quickest, most professional, and proactive way possible. If a student is hungry, feed them. If they show up late to school, have them get right to work and then discuss the matter with them at the break. The point is not to ignore these frustrations that we have, but rather to deal with them in a way that gets results. As you think about all of the challenges that students bring to your classroom, many of you may question whether or not your school has the tools to neutralize all of the daily issues that are being transferred from the home environment to the campus. Of course it doesn't! The solution? Take a look at the churches in your area.

Many states draw such a deep line in the sand between faith-based organizations and schools, it separates students and families from great opportunities to be supported. Whether you like it or not, or find it unjust or not, many of our families are struggling with making ends meet for their most basic needs. This creates a level of stress that children are exposed to on a daily basis, that manifests in the issues that we see at school. The best tool for alleviating these issues in a way that allows us to focus on the education of students is family outreach.

However, we as schools lack the resources, knowledge, and dare I say passion to do this. It's not our field of expertise. Because of this, it only makes sense to partner with organizations that do specialize in this kind of outreach: churches. Our plan: If a church wants to arrange 100 Thanksgiving meals for families, we don't care what religion you are; we'll take them. If they want to coordinate a food or clothing drive for our kids, we'll work with them on it. If they want to volunteer to run an after-school program that helps students with homework while reinforcing character, we'll provide the facility for them to do so. We embrace this kind of outreach not because we are believers in the doctrine of any specific church, but rather because we are believers in supporting our students. Don't make it more complicated than it needs to be. Use caring people with a heart for students to fill these "basic needs" gaps that exist on your campus.

Belief #4: Student achievement is the number one topic of conversation.

Most schools have between five and six hours a day to educate their students. All would agree that this is not a lot of time. The rigor that we are asking teachers to expose their students to increases with each year. In fact, it's a daunting task that I would contend no one teacher can live up to within this time frame. The only way to truly transform the lives of our students in the long term is to stop thinking about the short-term environment in our individual classrooms. The work of changing lives must take place year in and year out with a level of unity that many schools just don't show because their conversations are segmented and without a clear purpose. A belief that every staff can practice is to constantly, regardless of grade or subject matter, focus on student achievement. Great staffs talk about this in the hallway, the staff lounge, and the parking lot. It's seen in the quotes scribbled in the staff lounge and the benchmark data posted throughout the school. It is the focus of every staff meeting and collaborative session. In fact, it's the only reason why they meet in the first place. Recently, while visiting a school, I headed to the men's room for a quick bathroom break. Posted at eye level above the men's urinal was a graph with the latest reading scores for each grade level accompanied by this quote, "80 days left, aim high!!" A little much? Maybe, but that's the kind of focus that makes schools successful.

Belief #5: A maverick spirit must lead the way.

If you're reading this book, chances are that you are highly passionate about being a part of a school that wants to be more successful than it is today. There's probably a good chance as well that you have heard your share of discouragement from others that makes you wonder if it's even possible. Take joy in that negativity and use it to your advantage. I have found, and my NEU colleagues would agree, that one of the greatest motivators for our success has been the fact that we love being the underdog. We love proving people wrong. We love showing others what can be done in spite of incredibly difficult demographics. Schools that wish to be highly successful must never be afraid of this kind of maverick spirit. They have to work daily to create systems that are not only highly effective, but worthy of sharing with others. They have to embrace an entrepreneurial drive that loves to ask for forgiveness instead of permission as it takes educated risks that have the potential for great results. This spirit ensures that we are constantly working to break free from the status quo. It is an attitude that, while others may suggest is pompous and arrogant, out of jealousy, when done right creates the most positive work environment that any educator would want to take part in.

Belief #6: There are no excuses for poor effort.

For many students, we are and will forever be the most positive and caring adults in their life. To suggest that the no excuses equates to no compassion would be a drastic mistake. The NEU philosophy by nature is meant to create the most positive and uplifting environment that any student at any level might encounter through their educational career. As I'm sure you'd agree, one of the best forms of compassion is to have high expectations for the effort that our students exhibit. But before we can even begin to set those standards for students, we must first embrace those standards as adults. No excuses begins with adults. We are the professionals. We are the models for good behavior and attitude. From the way that we prepare our lessons, to the care we take in our own appearance, the standard will never be set by our words but instead by our actions. When we have taken great care in setting those standards and living by them, then and only then can we hold our students accountable to do the same.

As you practice each of these six beliefs you will undoubtedly encounter questions as well as frustrations along the way. You will experience times when you want to vent to your colleagues and throw up a surrender flag because of the challenges that many of your students are bringing with them. During those times, please know that this is normal. It's in our nature to be disheartened from time to time, especially in an industry where so much is at stake. As you struggle, remember the difference between reasons and excuses. A reason offers examples for why a student is struggling in the first place. Reasons can be overcome. An excuse is made when defeat is accepted and all hope is lost. When dips in morale arise, don't become jaded and allow your reasons to become excuses. Take the time to remember why you got into this business in the first place.

When I became a sophomore in high school, my former elementary school principal, Kevin Ogden, created a special arrangement with my high school principal to allow me to work yard duty for second- and third-graders at Julian Elementary as part of an elective class. I will never forget my first day with those kids. The instant my foot hit that blacktop, it was the defining moment of my life. I knew right then and there that I wanted to spend the rest of my life working to support elementary school children. Twenty-five years later, the significance of that day has never worn off. I believe that such an experience is not unique to me. In fact, most of the educators whom I have met across the country can easily recall their moment as well. The key, however, to maintaining a passion for our work is not whether or not we can recall such moments, but whether those moments drive us on a daily basis. Because experiences like these represent the times in our lives when we were most passionate about our profession, we have to maintain a personal commitment to recapturing that passion every day. Doing so reminds us of our need to fight the kind of selfishness that sometimes pollutes our profession, and to act as stewards for our students' success. When we do, we foster a culture of universal achievement.

Chapter Five

Theory to Practice

Items for Articulation

- ❏ What was your moment? When did you know that you wanted to be involved in the lives of students?
- ❏ What are the most common reasons why educators become jaded? What actions might ensure that we don't lose sight of the commitments the we once made as new educators entering the profession?

Items for Action

- ❏ As a school, decide on one goal that drives everything that you do. Get it in writing and live by it. If you have several goals, stop thinking of them as "goals" and start thinking of them as steps to help you achieve your ONE GOAL.
- ❏ Break up into small groups during a staff meeting. Make a list of ways that you can practice the six beliefs of a culture of universal achievement on a daily basis.

Chapter Six

Key Concepts

"Candor gets more people in the conversation, and when you get more people in the conversation you get idea rich."

— Jack Welch

1

Collaboration and professionalism go hand in hand.

2

A collaboration commitment selects four to six areas of focus that help teams generate results.

3

Because candor does not come naturally to most, it needs to be taught and practiced through "candid collaboration."

Collaboration

Every year, millions of geese begin to migrate from the upper parts of North America in search of a warmer climate during the winter season. Their instinct brings them to the southernmost parts of the United States and into areas of Mexico. Many find it amazing that this inner compass drives them every year, but to me what is most fascinating is not the fact that they make such a yearly trek but rather how they go about doing so.

On occasion, I have encountered a flock of geese overhead in the common "V" formation that most are familiar with. I never questioned why they flew this way until recently when I wondered why it was that one goose was always the leader. How did he become the leader? Is there an annual geese convention that elects the best flyer among the millions and puts them in charge? In search of answers, I did what all new aspiring ornithologists do: I Googled the geese. What I found were answers that unlocked my mystery of the "V" formation while offering a parallel example of what true collaboration can look like in our schools today. Take a look at the reasons why our feathered friends fly this way and think about the lessons that we can take back to our teams:

- Geese fly in the V formation to cut down on wind resistance. Because each goose flies slightly above and behind the one in front of them, they are able to conserve energy for a long flight.
- Geese take turns at being the leader. The toughest position to fly in as part of the V is the front because there's no one creating a draft for the leader to fly behind.
- Geese honk with encouragement from the back of the V. They understand that as tired as they may be, the one in front of them always has a slightly more challenging job.
- Geese help each other during hard times. When one goose takes a break on land, two others join in the descent because they know that there is strength in numbers.

Don't you wish that our instincts as educators worked the same way when it comes to collaboration? Unfortunately, our lives are far more complex than those of geese. The dynamics of our individual jobs, mixed with the expectations of our personal lives, establish instincts within each of us that all too often send us into isolation. This flawed intuition only leads to us working harder and feeling more discouraged. By the creation of an exceptional system in the area of collaboration, we will not only find ways to work smarter in pursuit of better results, but also to establish greater balance in our own personal lives.

Why Collaborate?

The question isn't why we should collaborate. It's really, why don't we collaborate? Many avoid working with their colleagues because they:

- ❖ believe they can do the job better alone.
- ❖ don't want to deal with building relationships with others whom they do not have much in common with.
- ❖ aren't required by contract to do so.
- ❖ work according to a different schedule.
- ❖ like the freedom of being in charge of their own routine.

These are just a handful of the reasons that educators use for working alone. Just as I did at one time, you may identify with one or more of them, as well. The problem is that each of these examples runs the risk of limiting our results for students and, at the same time, lacks professionalism. When it comes to collaboration, the old saying "*If you want something done right, do it yourself*" does not apply. This is actually one of my favorite sayings. I'll be honest, I often live by it … when it comes to fixing something around the house. But when it comes to educating children and young adults, it's the last thing that we should consider.

When comparing the work that educators do in isolation versus the work that they do when operating effectively as part of an exceptional system, the results of a team are always better. This applies not only to education, but nearly every aspect of business. Take it directly from one of the world's most successful companies, Southwest Airlines. CEO Gary Kelly said, "*Our people are our single greatest strength and most enduring long-term competitive advantage.*" Can you imagine Southwest finding success with Mr. Kelly flying the planes, handling the luggage, and checking in passengers all by himself? It would be impossible and his company's results would be limited. Sure, we often come across educational dynamos who are incredibly talented and find ways to get amazing results. But there is a ceiling for their success that can be removed only when they work with an effective team.

When you have an exceptional system for the way that you collaborate, along with getting better results, you ensure that you are behaving as a professional. With the public's perception of public schools in the tank, this is more important than ever. The number of students enrolled in public charter schools has tripled in the last 10 years. In places like New Orleans Public Schools, more than 70 percent of their students are enrolled in public charter schools. And they are not alone. Places like Washington, D.C. and Detroit have almost 40 percent of their students in such charter schools. Why this migration from the public school sector? Clearly parents have had it with the lack of results that their children are getting, but I think it runs far deeper than that. I believe it also has to do with the fact that we, myself included, have not practiced our craft with adequate professionalism.

In my visits to hundreds of schools over the years, I have decided that it's no coincidence that the most successful ones just so happen to be the most professional ones as well. Let me be clear; there are always exceptions to this rule. I have been on campuses with some of the most amazing professionals you've ever met whose schools are in the highest levels of program improvement. In contrast, I have also been in some of the highest-performing schools on earth where professionalism has been replaced with arrogance and elitism. That said, as an industry, it is time for us to grasp the reins of the future of public education by elevating our own professionalism. We must be professional in our presence and appearance, in our interactions with parents and students, and in our collaborative relationships. As much as the naysayers among us would like to pontificate on the conspiracy theories for why some schools are successful and others aren't, it's really pretty simple. Great schools have talented ***professionals*** who find the very best ways to work together in order to get results. It doesn't need to be more complicated than that. The deciding factor in my opinion always hinges on the systems that these schools do or do not create.

The Collaboration Commitment: An Exceptional System Simplified

If you look at the documents in the appendix, I hope you can see that we're big fans of simplicity. If it were up to me, I'd require that every commitment a staff makes has to fit on the back of a cocktail napkin. The optimist in me must surrender to the realist and make a compromise from a napkin to the front side of a piece of paper. I believe this firmly. If you can't explain your school's system, any system, on one piece of paper, start over. Lengthy declarations are a sign of bureaucracy. Don't believe it? Look no further than our own government. The original U.S. Bill of Rights is just more than 1,400 words long. That's just a little more than the number of words you've read so far in this chapter. Comparably, the Health Care Reform Act of 2011 is 400,000 words in length and greater in size than *War and Peace*. In an age where Twitter allows us to communicate with the world in 140 characters or fewer, I think we can do better.

The average educator today, myself included, doesn't have the patience or desire to read or memorize lengthy documents. They would much rather participate in action-oriented solutions that get the job done in a way that creates greater balance in their professional and personal lives. All of this can be accomplished by creating the second exceptional system on our staircase, a collaboration commitment.

Every staff needs to create collaborative commitments that are dedicated to achieving results through action in a professional manner. These commitments should contain between four to six areas of focus. While it's absolutely acceptable for you to choose areas of focus that you find to be unique to your school, be sure to limit them to no more than six. Here are five areas of focus that make up the Collaboration Commitment for many No Excuses University Schools in our network. The full commitment can be found in the appendix of this book. Because educators like yourself created this system, I hope that you will find the words practical and easy to live by.

Clarity of Purpose: **Team members remain driven by our one goal to ensure that each student is proficient or advanced in reading, writing, and math. They meet with a purpose and devise agendas and timelines to ensure success at every collaborative meeting. They take the time to decide upon meeting topics in advance. After meeting, they follow through with collective agreements as a team.**

The idea of having a clarity of purpose is all about declaring our desire to be productive during our collaborative time. We must always remember that our results become a reality only when we make plans that are action-oriented in nature. In order to do this, every meeting that takes place on your site must have a clear purpose. Sitting around a table, staring at each other, asking "What are we supposed to do?" is a waste of everyone's time.

Respectful of Time: **NEU professionals are action-oriented professionals who value one another's time. They are prompt to staff and team meetings. They make the most of their time by collaborating during the school day with colleagues as they creatively group students in an effort to meet every student's needs.**

As a principal, I never personally got excited when I noticed a multitude of staff cars parked late at night. In fact, I silently wished that my staff would find better ways to manage their time so that they could find balance in their personal lives and hence spend more time with their families. Staff members in every level of education run the risk of burning out as much as any profession out there. The only way that we can be both productive at school and have balance at home is to work closely with our colleagues in a way that is respectful of time.

Time Banking: **Once a week, on our early release day from 2:15 to 3:40, we set aside time for teams to work closely as they design instruction that translates into academic achievement for all. This time is held sacred by all members of the team, and should not be used for personal appointments or individual work time. This time may be used for staff meetings once every other month.**

Many of our schools have worked closely with their district to imbed a minimum day each week. This day allows students to go home early in an effort for staff members to work collaboratively. Such an arrangement is not unique to our schools, but the way that we use the time just might be. As a leader, I discovered early that while I had the ability to capitalize on this "time banking" day and use it strictly for meetings and professional growth, it was more valuable for me to allow grade level teams to plan lessons, talk about assessments, and devise interventions for the week ahead. I won't lie, this took tremendous trust on my part, but in the end it was the best decision I every made. My staff knew that I only had one requirement as they met: ***Work together to get results.*** Year in and year out, they delivered. You must know that this is really a chicken or egg scenario. Is it the leader's job to trust first, or the staff's job to deliver results first? This is a tough call, but here's my take. I believe it's the leaders' job to trust their staff with the understanding that they expect results. When a team lets you down, there's no need to micro-manage or rob the autonomy from everyone on the staff. Instead, place a greater energy in giving clear direction to the teams that are not generating results. The teams that are getting results will work hard to honor your leadership, and the ones that aren't will work hard to get you off their backs. It's a win-win-win for you. The third win being the fact that you get to enjoy watching amazing people do right by kids without having to always be heavy handed. There was nothing I enjoyed more than visiting teams on Wednesday just to pop in, say hello, celebrate their success, and answer any questions that they might have for me. After these 5- to 10-minute visits, teams went back to working on lesson planning that would affect their teaching the very next day.

Professional Growth: **NEU professionals are open to learning new methods, ideas, and strategies that will lead to greater academic success for all. They participate in on-site Thursday Collaboration workshops. They seek ways to learn from one another, and are committed to growing professionally together.**

Because I had committed to allowing "time banking" to be used for teams to work together, I needed to find a way to find other blocks of time for consistent professional growth. As seen in the appendix, Thursday Collaboration was the answer. It is a simple, no cost way to allow your teams to grow professionally together. Here's how it works.

During the last hour of school each Thursday, I and every available support staff member I could find would take every student from two grades out to the playground for a comprehensive P.E. rotation or into the multi-purpose room for an assembly. While we were with the students, their teachers were working together to learn or share ideas about one specific topic. Typically the groups would be K and 1st, 2nd and 3rd, and 4th and 5th grades. From time to time I get questioned about this model by people who say that the weather in their region would never allow them to pull this off. My response: You don't have to do it every month. Do it once, or twice. However many times you do it this year will be more than you did it last year. You have to think about steps like these in a value-added way.

Building Candid Professional Relationships: **No Excuses University staff members are committed to developing strong professional relationships with each other. They praise one another during times of individual, team, and school-wide success. They are honest with one another as they respectfully confront concerns through "Candid Collaboration." They support one**

another during times that are challenging both professionally and personally. They celebrate with one another as friends and colleagues outside of the school community.

While this may be the last area of focus in our exceptional system, it's arguably the most important. When you think about it, we spend more time during the school year with the people we work with than we do with our own families. Our NEU professionals recognize this and wish to make the most of that time. We embrace the challenge of learning the intricacies of each other's personalities. We enjoy celebrating the successes of one another with genuine praise. And we take on the burden of holding one another accountable in spite of any discomfort that it may bring us. This is NOT easy to do. In fact, it's one of the most challenging responsibilities that we have as part of our collaboration commitment. It is so difficult that we actually take the time to teach every staff member the art of candor by what we call *candid collaboration*.

Candid Collaboration

Several years ago I sat with Fran Hjalmarson in my office at Los Peñasquitos Elementary School looking over the most recent state test scores. Fran, our school counselor and author of the book *Differentiated Parent Support*, and I celebrated the tremendous gains that our amazing staff had helped to create for students. As we looked at the data, we realized that many of the difficult conversations we'd had with some of our struggling teachers over the years appeared to be paying off. Within moments, however, like the air being let out of a balloon, we were deflated by the thought of our school's future, for one very important reason. Of all the people on the staff, only Fran and I had the knowledge and training to be highly candid with teachers and classified staff members when they needed to be held accountable. Knowing that neither of us would be at the school for the rest of our careers, we sketched out a game plan on the white board in my office for a concept that we titled Candid Collaboration.

Candid Collaboration was created as a way to train staff members to use candor to handle concerns that might come up between them. Instead of coming to Fran or me to solve their issues, which was typically the case, they would need to go through the steps of candid collaboration on their own first. Doing so would help them to solve problems while building leadership capacity at the same time. As we developed the concept, we devised four levels of candor that we would teach every staff member about during a professional growth day. In addition, we developed scenarios that we would use during role-play sessions so staff members could practice increasing stages of candor throughout the four levels. (Some of these scenarios can be found in the appendix.) These scenarios helped to train our staff to use candor during discussions related to instructional practices and relationships. Take a look at one specific scenario, followed by the four levels of candor that many NEU professionals across the country are currently practicing as part of Candid Collaboration.

Scenario: Assessment Scores Are Due on Friday

Assessment scores are due to Cathy, the data clerk, by Friday. Like everyone else, you have been working diligently to ensure that all of your assessments are turned in on time. While eating lunch in the staff lounge, you overhear the newest teacher at your grade level, Julie, tell another colleague how she plans to "blow off" the due date. This raises obvious concerns to you.

Level One: Supporting

The first step in Candid Collaboration is the most basic level that we can offer to any of our colleagues during a challenging situation: support. What we may see as negativity from our colleagues is actually nothing more than a cry for help that manifests itself through frustration. During this level of Candid Collaboration, it is our job to open the *door to communication*. We want to be sure to *identify the problem* and *seek to understand* all aspects of the issue. When we are candid during level one, we do so in a *one-on-one* environment that *happens when both parties are calm*. When we approach someone in a candid way, we always run the risk of them becoming defensive. Because of this, it is important that we are *genuine* and *respectful of their time*. In our experience, Fran and I have found that the majority of issues that require Candid Collaboration can be resolved during a level one conversation. When you have a moment alone with Julie, your conversation might go something like this:

You: "Julie do you have a minute to chat?"

Julie: "Sure."

You: "I overheard you in the staff lounge regarding assessment scores. It sounds like you're really frustrated. I remember what it was like to be a new teacher and I really identified with that same stress."

Julie: "Yes, I've really kind of had it with timelines. It seems like I just can't get through all of the assessments by Friday. I can only do what I can do, you know?"

You: "I really do identify. How about this: What if I can make some time this week to help you complete the remaining assessments together? We can creatively group our classes, do some assessments after school, or find some other way to divide and conquer over the next four days so that your assessments are turned in on time."

Julie: "You would do that?"

You: "Absolutely. Why don't we meet after school today in your room and map out a plan to begin tomorrow. Sound good?"

Julie: "Thanks so much! See you after school."

Level Two: Accountability

After we have offered support to a colleague, there are occasions where we need to increase the level of candor when we do not get the results that we desire. Situations like these typically occur when staff members don't feel like they can improve on their own or, even worse, don't see a need to make a change in the first place. When moving to level two in Candid Collaboration, it becomes time to *heighten our concerns*. What was seen as supporting our colleague in level one, needs to be seen as holding them accountable in level two. Remember, true collaboration takes place when *accountability is high, but anxiety is low*. Because of this, conversations in level two are still one on one, calm, and professional. They are also *results driven* and *specific* in nature, with very *direct timelines*. Let's take a look at how our conversation with Julie takes a turn when she forgets to show up for her meeting with you after school. While paying a visit to her classroom the next day before school, your conversation might look something like this:

You: "Julie, I know you're busy getting ready for the day, but I wanted to follow up on our plans for yesterday. Do you have a minute?"

Julie: "I do have a minute, but that's it. I'm really busy prepping for the day."

You: "No problem, a minute is all I'll need. I have to be honest and say that I was disappointed that you did not show up for our meeting after school yesterday.

I waited for you in front of your door for about 15 minutes and spent another 15 minutes walking the campus looking for you."

Julie: "I'm so sorry but I had an emergency. I needed to take my cat to the vet. It's a long story."

You: "I'm really sorry about that. I hope your cat gets better. That said, we now have one less day for us to get your assessments done by Friday. Do you still want my help?"

Julie: "Yes, I do. I actually still planned on assessing some kids after school with your help today if you're still available."

You: "Great. Here's what I need you to bring with you. A list of your students who need to be assessed and printed testing protocols. Let's meet in your room at 3:15. That will give us time to take a quick break after school and then get right to work. I am available until 5:00 today. Will that work for you?"

Julie: "Got it. I've written it all down and I'll be here at 3:15."

Level Three: Intervention

Despite our best efforts, sometimes a one-on-one conversation does not command the kind of candor needed in order to convey the seriousness of a situation to someone. When support and accountability do not achieve results, it's time to up the stakes with intervention. Intervention takes place with *two or more people*, typically in a team setting. The most important component of intervention is that it is done in a professional manner that *lists the facts* behind your concerns, as well as the *next steps* that have been brainstormed by your team. Remember, your desire is to help your colleague improve so that they can better help students achieve success, not to make them feel like a loser. In order to do so, it's crucial that interventions are facilitated by a member of the team whose approach is unintimidating yet straightforward at the same time. After you make direct plans with Julie to conduct assessments after school, she once again is a no show. Take a look at how the intervention level of Candid Collaboration during a team meeting is your next best hope for improvement:

You: "I know we have a lot to get to on the agenda, but before we do there's something that we need to address right away. Julie, the team and I don't want to put you on the spot, but we do have concerns related to your assessments not being turned in. As you know, I made two appointments to try to help you, and neither was followed through by you. Because we now have only one more full day to have all of your assessments completed and turned in, the team and I have devised a plan to help you get them completed. In addition, we'd like to discuss how we can avoid this situation in the future. Are you supportive of that?"

Julie: "To be honest, no I'm not. I feel like you are all ganging up on me! I tried to meet with you twice, but you know that my cat has been having issues. Yesterday I got called by the vet again and needed to get her some new medication at the pharmacy, I …"

You: "Julie, I don't want to interrupt you but I do want to stay focused. Are you supportive of us helping you get the assessments done and also making a plan to avoid this issue in the future?"

Julie: "Not really. I think I can do it myself."

You: "Respectfully, let me share some of the following data with you. Cathy, the data clerk, came to me this morning and said that our grade is the only one in the school who has not turned in their scores. With the exception of you, everyone here has already turned in their scores. That means that you are the only teacher in the school that has not turned in your scores. As I said during our first conversation, I think this is because you are overwhelmed like all of us have been as new teachers. Today, however, you have a decision to make. You can either be overwhelmed and take the support that we are offering, or you can be unwilling and deal with the consequences from Principal Collins once he finds out that you have not completed your assessments. It's really up to you."

Level Four: Resourcing

What choice did Julie make? Let's hope that she took the support that was offered to her. While it is rare, there does come a time when all of your best efforts just won't work. The specific issues involved, combined with the personality of the person whom you are trying to be candid with, sometimes cannot create a recipe for success. If this should happen, it's time for you to do two things. First, give yourself credit for exhibiting leadership as you tried to support a colleague. While your outcomes may not have been successful, your steps in Candid Collaboration were by no means a failure. We can learn the most in situations like these. They will surely add to your experience for the next time that you need to practice Candid Collaboration. The second thing you must do is simply send the issue on to someone more experienced and with greater leverage to deal with the situation. This may be the principal, counselor, or another teacher leader. Regardless of who the leader is, he or she will be pleased that you and your colleagues have taken the time to try to handle the situation on your own before it got to him or her. This process is far more productive, as it allows colleagues to handle concerns on their own (which most would agree they would rather have done in the first place), while at the same time cutting down on the involvement that the school leader has to take on.

A *special note to leaders, especially principals, related to Candid Collaboration:* When your staff attempts to handle concerns like these, it builds capacity for true leadership throughout the school. Encourage this! When they exhibit leadership but must send an issue to you, always be sure to follow through in a manner that honors their hard work. The worst possible outcome is to send an issue to a principal, only to have the leader of the school exhibit a lack of candor. Doing so will discourage your staff from practicing Candid Collaboration while having them lose faith in your leadership at the same time.

In the fall of 2011, the No Excuses University endeavor achieved a major milestone by opening our first NEU Academy Prep School in the nation. The Telesis Academy of Science and Math, located in Rowland Heights, California, is a K-8 school dedicated to promoting college readiness for some of the neediest students in the neighborhood. With nearly 90 percent of the students living at or below the poverty line, this academy has become a godsend to parents and a bright light for the Rowland Unified School District. During two days of training the Telesis staff, I shared the analogy of why geese fly in a V formation. Later, the team created five areas of focus that made up their exceptional system for collaboration. While similar to the ones that I have shared, the first area of focus was unique but quite appropriate. In fact, it wasn't an area of focus as much as it was a question that they were committed to asking each other every day: "Are you flying in the V?"

Chapter Six

Theory to Practice

Items for Articulation

- ❑ Are you flying in the V? What is it that holds you, your team, and your school back from creating an exceptional system for collaboration?
- ❑ What are your strengths as a team member? What are your weaknesses?

Items for Action

- ❑ Use the ideas shared in this chapter and select four to six areas of focus that will help to create a collaboration commitment at your site. This process should take no more than a month to have finalized.

Chapter Seven

Key Concepts

"It takes less time to do a thing right than to explain why you did it wrong."

— Henry Wadsworth Longfellow

1

Aligning our standards has to be a daily commitment.

2

Some confuse alignment with pacing.

3

Creating a system that features four groups—skills, assessments, instructional methods, and resources—keeps our work practical.

4

Great results in the area of standards alignment always follow exceptional collaboration.

Standards Alignment

One of the best parts about my job is that I get to travel all around the country and meet thousands of educators with equally as many opinions about a variety of topics. This has no doubt broadened my perspective as I have learned as much from them as I have been able to offer. Such was the case after visiting a school that needed support in the area of standards alignment.

Not long after I began laying out the steps on how to create an exceptional system for standards alignment, a young teacher sheepishly stood up with her hand raised. You could tell that she was trying to say something to help keep me from embarrassing myself. I've had this happen before, only to have someone tell me that my zipper was down or that they couldn't hear me in the back of the room. This was different, though: "Mr. Lopez, I really appreciate you coming here, and I think I speak for the staff when I say that I don't want to offend you, but you need to know that we've already done this."

A little confused, I asked, "You've already done what?"

“We’ve already done planning around standards alignment. This really isn’t new to us.”

Wanting to dig a little deeper, I asked, “When exactly did you do this?”

She responded, “Oh, we did this like … six years ago.”

Trying to be as respectful of her as she was to me, I said, “Standards alignment is not something that you’ve done; it’s something that you do.”

When the standards movement began, many decades ago, there were many commitments that districts and schools made to jump on board. Unfortunately for some, those commitments were more about how to align standards through protocols and flow charts than they were about practical applications that teachers could put into use in their classrooms. In spite of the plethora of information and tools that we now have that can help us better align our standards, not much has changed for our most struggling schools. For those schools, it appears that educators are expected to know what the standards are, which essentially equates to them having the ability to look online on their state department of education website. Rather than beginning with the standards and shaping their lessons around them, teachers begin with what they want to do and then attempt to squeeze in a standard here or there in order to meet the expectations that their schools or districts have put on them. Sure, they write down the standard being taught with every lesson on their whiteboard each day, but is that a result of a conscious effort to let the standards drive their instruction? Don’t get me wrong; I understand why so many teachers today are more likely to embrace this form of standards alignment in their classrooms. The fact is, this is some of the hardest work that we ask our educators to participate in today. I’d even go a step further by saying that, because of the current systems being used to align our standards in schools, it’s also among the most boring.

Let's face it—aligning your teaching to state standards lacks a sense of educational romance, if you will. In fact, it is often described as the trenches of teaching. Belaboring as it may be to some, it is critical for the overall success of a school. Unfortunately, there are those who think that aligning one's standards is simply a matter of opening a textbook and following the pacing guide. If you are among those who think this way, please understand that the greatest joy of a teacher can never be found in the completion of mapping out the standards for any given year. It is found in the journey that allows you to discover new, better strategies to align your work as a grade level or department and hence create better results for your students on a regular basis. If the concept of standards alignment has been a source of frustration for you over the years, suspend that frustration through the rest of this chapter as I attempt to share a simple and practical exceptional system that will give standards their due attention without making it a laborious process.

Why Is Aligning Standards So Critical?

As professionals, we are called to participate in activities that improve our results while learning from our successes and failures. Aligning standards provides an *objective framework* that can guide our path. The beauty of this framework is the ability that it has to allow continuity from one grade level to the next. When we participate in such continuity, our instruction becomes more meaningful and purposeful. When every grade level follows this framework, our instruction can never be in vain. But this can happen only when it is completed with the aid of systematic collaboration. Which is exactly why standards alignment follows collaboration on the exceptional system staircase.

Common Mistakes in Aligning Standards

Two common mistakes are made when schools attempt to align the standards at each grade level. The first is that they confuse standards *alignment* with standards *pacing*. Pacing takes place when we chart the course to ensure that we introduce and give the proper amount of time to grade level standards throughout the school year. Pacing gives us instructional consistency so that every member of our team remains on track to teach the standards. Pacing is what ensures that Mr. Smith is teaching mixed fractions at a time that is relatively similar to his colleague across the hall. The pacing of our standards is absolutely important, but it is much different from the work that we do with standards alignment. In a nutshell, standards alignment is different because it focuses on the who, what, and how of standards. It is not driven by dates or timelines, but instead by the ideas and strategies that we plan to use as we teach students the standards.

Before I go any further, let me give this disclaimer. I don't care what state you live in—chances are that you disagree with some of the expectations that it may have related to standards. I'll be the first to say that I believe wholeheartedly in the instincts of a classroom teacher over someone with little to no experience with instruction. That said, we live in a world of accountability. That accountability is tested according to the standards that your state has chosen. Like it or not, it is what our schools are judged by. This to me is reason enough to embrace the standards. The alternative is to ignore this accountability, risk the probability of getting terrible results, be scrutinized by your community for failing students, and shape a negative image for them about the lack of success. Doing so is an injustice to your students and yourself.

The second common mistake when it comes to standards alignment is that schools rely too much on what it is that they want to teach instead of what it is that the state requires them to teach. If you've been in this profession for some time, chances are that you have seen this in action on one or more occasions. For example, have you ever caught a colleague say something to the effect of, "But I don't want to skip that lesson; I love teaching it" or "Third grade's going on that field trip? We wanted to go there first!" These are dead giveaways for an attitude that is pervasive in some of our most struggling schools, where teachers are driven to do what is most comfortable to them. I can still hear the echoes in the hallways of schools that I've visited:

Owl pellets are a fourth grade science standard? Who cares? Let's do them in second grade!—It's October, so let's all do a unit on bats!—Our school mascot is the bear, so let's be sure that every grade level spends a month on teaching about the variety of bears throughout the world and post some of our favorite sayings like "Have a beary good day!" all over the campus.

The Road Map

If any of this sounds familiar, let's work to simplify the process of aligning standards while at the same time making it highly practical. Reduced to its simplest form, aligning standards can be completed in four steps. First, we want to *identify specific skills* that we are expected to teach. Second, we need to secure a variety of ways that we will use *assessments* along the way. Next, it's necessary for us to brainstorm *instructional methods* that will act as the vehicle for our teaching. Finally, we need to make a list of the *resources* necessary during these instructional practices. These four steps of identifying specific skills, assessments, instructional methods, and resources make up what we refer to as "The Road Map." This process is so practical, it can work with aligning any standard at any level. Let's take a look at each step by using the following fourth grade standard and sub-standard as an example. An example of a full "Road Map" can be found in the appendix.

Students understand the basic features of reading. They select letters, patterns and know how to translate them into spoken language by using phonics, syllabication, and word parts. They apply this knowledge to achieve fluent oral and silent reading.				
Sub-Standard	Specific Skills	Assessments	Instructional Methods	Resources
1.1 Read narrative and expository text aloud with grade-appropriate fluency and accuracy and with appropriate pacing, intonation, and expression.	❖ Fluency ❖ Pacing ❖ Accuracy ❖ Intonation ❖ Expression	❖ Fluency rubrics ❖ Reading inventories	❖ Fluency timings ❖ Introduce college readiness lit circles to students and teach them how to read aloud together. Teach students to share outcomes created while working on their "career templates." ❖ Poem of the week	❖ The 6-Minute Solution by Gail Adams ❖ Lit Circle Templates and kid-friendly PowerPoint that introduces the careers to choose from ❖ Revolting Rhymes by Roald Dahl

Identify Specific Skills

There's a reason why I included the sub-standard in this example. As you can see, standard 1.0 presents a broad commitment to teaching word analysis, fluency, and systematic development, but it is each of the sub-standards that cut to the heart of a standard. This is critical to understand, as too many educators look only at the broad standard. Doing so ignores the details that help to generate progress for individual students.

As we look at sub-standard 1.1, it is clear that the skills we are trying to focus on are that of fluency, pacing, accuracy, intonation, and expression. Identifying the specific skills is no more than framing our sub-standard and simplifying our expectations. It takes what can often be a long narrative and puts it into checklist form. This sets the stage for the steps that follow as we design our standards road map.

Assessments

If the specific skills tell us what we will need to focus on, then the assessments will help us know if we've done our job. Because standards road maps should act as a resource of information for you to go to, the purpose is never to task yourself to death. The key to remember when selecting assessments is to list a variety of assessments that you can use to analyze your progress. You do not have to use all of them just because they are listed.

Instructional Methods

As we make a list of instructional methods, we want to keep these two words at the forefront: *engaging* and *explicit*. Because so many of today's educators are constantly feeling the pressure to get through all of the standards, these two words are often abandoned from their vocabulary. We must not only bring them back into our personal lexicons, but also make them the focal point. Instruction is always best when students are involved in the conversation, partnering together, and active in their learning. It flows so much better when we've defined the goal before the lesson is delivered and given our students explicit expectations before we begin. A perfect example of this is in the College Readiness Literature Circles that were developed at the NEU at Rosemary Kennedy in Riverside, California.

Led by the principal, Jackie Casillas, and her support specialist, Carol Hall, this staff took the concept of literature circles to the next level. As many of you know, literature circles is a method of having a student read books with a group of students who are reading at the same level. After reading together, students then work individually on a different "job" guided by templates given to them by the teacher. NEU at Kennedy staff took those jobs and turned them into "careers." What used to be known as the "word wizard" job is now the career of a "journalist." What was formerly called the "character analyst" is now the "sociologist." Included in this shift, which promotes literacy while also focusing on college readiness, was a kid-friendly PowerPoint that described each career to the class before they even began working in this format. The teachers at the NEU at Kennedy understood that their explicit introduction into this form of engaging reading instruction would be more successful if they took the time to explain the details of this model. Because they did, many of our NEU schools today have been exposed to this engaging and explicit concept.

Resources

Getting the best resources is all about joining forces with those at your grade level or in your department. Without high levels of collaboration, you'll use only what you own. Doing that will ensure that you make very little change along the way, because all you're really fostering is self-dependence. As we discussed in the previous chapter, our collaborative efforts have to be more about students than they are about adults. When we share ideas from one class to another, ALL students benefit from those ideas. For those of you with children of your own, or those who hope to be parents one day, think about this question: *Don't you want your kids to participate in the stellar lessons and engaging units that are taking place in the classrooms next door to them?* Sharing resources as part of developing a standards road map ensures that you get the answer that you want, which surely has to be "yes."

Veteran teachers will admit that all of this is a trial and error process. That's all right! Give yourself the freedom to make mistakes, to look back and say to yourself, "Boy, that lesson didn't turn out too well!" Being successful every time is not the most important thing. Learning from those mistakes and improving your teaching over the years is, though. While generating the ideas for this chapter, I asked Kristie Szentesi, one of the best teachers I have worked with, to show me an example of one of her road maps. When she delivered it to me, it was covered with notes, highlight marks, and sticky notes. It looked as if it had been through battle over the last several years as it was constantly being updated. This is *exactly* what your goal should be as you create road maps of your own.

Where Do You Begin?

After taking in all this information, many schools may find themselves asking the question "Where do we begin?" For this, there are two very acceptable options. As school leaders consider both, remember that while it may be easier for you to ask your entire school to focus on the same standard, each grade level or department may have very different challenges to address. What good does it do you to have all of your teams focus on standards in geometry, when first grade's lowest-performing area is in fluency and third grade's is in literal comprehension? Aligning standards cannot be a process in which the principal assigns one standard and asks the staff to turn it in by the end of the week. Setting reasonable timelines for this process is absolutely fair to do as a leader, but we need to make sure that those timelines are reflective of an attitude to affect our students in a timely manner and not one driven to complete a task by a certain deadline. Allowing individual grade levels to choose starting points based on their needs shows leadership. Asking them all to do the same thing at the same time shows management. The choice is yours.

Starting with the Greatest Need

One path to choose as you align standards is to begin in an area of the curriculum where you display the greatest weakness. Too many schools select subject matter based on what is the easiest to begin with. This makes no sense at all. Why should a school or grade with 80 percent of students performing at levels of proficiency in math choose math to focus on, when only 30 percent are proficient in reading? Let's take it a step further. Not only should you choose your lowest-performing subject matter, but you should also choose the standard within that subject matter where your data show the greatest need for growth.

Imagine you have a big backyard with grass, trees, and flowers throughout. As the seasons come and go, you experience a variety of issues that require your attention, the most common of which are the weeds that take root on the dirt paths throughout the yard. As you consider the areas of need in your yard, you wouldn't first decide to up the watering on the lawn or add more fertilizer to your flowers, would you? You'd do something about the weeds! Of course, focusing on the beautiful portions of your yard is certainly more personally fulfilling, but it does nothing to improve the problematic areas that take away from the overall beauty of your backyard. Furthermore, failing to address the problems in your yard may someday wind up infecting all the other areas that you made successful. Aligning our standards has to be the same way.

Starting with the Greatest Accountability

The other possible route by which to begin your standards alignment journey is the greatest area of accountability. As an educator in California for 15 years, I watched as state standards and levels of accountability changed over the years. This was not unique to California, nor was the way that the state department of education helped weigh the standards. In fact, in many states, standards blueprints are readily available online to educators. These blueprints display the standards, tell you what percentage of the state test is made up of each standard, and give you the number of questions on the test related to that standard. As you sort through these blueprints, within moments you can see that standard 1.5 makes up 3 percent of the test and has only one question, while standard 2.7 makes up 27 percent of the test and has 9 questions. If this is the case, there is absolutely nothing wrong with schools making a list that shows the standards, weighted from highest to lowest. I know what you're thinking right now: "But that's just teaching to the test." No, it's not; it's teaching to the standards! Some standards have been deemed more important than others at any given grade level. Giving more attention to some standards that are more significant mirrors the way we live our own lives.

Think about this for a moment. In life, there are some values that we hold as more important than others. For me, it's more important that my six-year-old knows how to cross the street safely than it is for her to bathe every night. Don't get me wrong; I'm not a fan of dirty kids, but there's no comparing the safety of my daughter with that of her personal cleanliness. Furthermore, holding the value of her personal safety is paramount, as it is a building block to similar values that she will find important in the future. Why is it that some standards are given the greatest attention at one level and little attention at another? It's because they have been chosen as foundational standards that must be mastered in an effort to breed success at the next level. If state standards are reflected on high stakes state assessments and some of those standards are deemed to have more value than others at a particular grade level, there is nothing wrong with gearing your instruction to those very standards.

Two Activities to Get Started

Before you begin the process of creating your exceptional system in standards alignment, I would suggest you introduce the four-step process that I've shared in this chapter by participating in a couple of practical activities. These activities are known as *everyday life standards and speed mapping*.

Directions for Everyday Life Standards: Make a list of activities that we as humans participate in on a daily basis. From driving a car, to feeding our kids, to changing the diaper of a baby, list these ideas individually on a template that includes this everyday life standard. Include a heading for skills, assessments, instructional methods, and resources on the template as well (see below). During a staff meeting, give individual teams a different *life standard* and ask them to creatively map it out within five minutes in a way that would help someone teach the concept to another person. When they are done, have them share as a team. The purpose of this activity is to ease any anxiety that educators might feel about going forward in this process by showing them how we naturally go about aligning standards in the first place. In life, we know when our kids are hungry and what to do. We've created strategies and sought resources for how to change diapers without even thinking about it. After much practice, aligning academic standards can be viewed the same way.

Standards of Life	Specific Skills	Assessments	Instructional Methods	Resources
1.1 Change the diaper of a child with appropriate pacing and accuracy.				

Directions for Speed Mapping: Select a state standard from any subject. Make sure that the standard has at least four sub-standards. Divide your staff into four teams. Assign a different step for each team to work on. One team will focus on skills, another on assessments, the next on instructional methods, and the last on resources. Make sure that each team focuses on only its part. Give each team a blank template with one of the sub-standards written on it (see below). For instance, team one will have sub-standard 3.1, team two will have 3.2, and so on. When you tell them to start, they will have 90 seconds to brainstorm and make a list of suggestions on their template. At the end of 90 seconds, have them rotate to the next team and focus on the next sub-standard. When you have completed four rotations, have each team share its road map. The lesson here is to show what was completed by staff members from a variety of grade levels in a matter of six minutes. What could they accomplish with their own grade level in 60 minutes if they divided and conquered? What would they be able to do in six weeks, or six months together?

California State Fourth Grade Reading Standards

Students read and respond to a wide variety of significant works of children's literature. They distinguish between the structural features of the text and the literary terms or elements (e.g. theme, plot, setting, characters). The selections in "Recommended Literature, Kindergarten Through Grade Twelve" illustrate the quality and complexity of the materials to be read by students.				
Components of the Standard	**Specific Skills**	**Assessments**	**Instructional Methods**	**Resources**
Structural Features of Literature				
3.1 Describe the structural difference of various imaginative forms of literature, including fantasies, fables, myths, legends, and fairy tales.				

The system discussed in this chapter, as well as the activities offered, should encourage a higher level of collaboration among team members. Aligning standards is tough work when done alone. When it is achieved together, however, we are far more likely to be encouraged by the results that we find along the way. And because aligning standards is not *something that you've done* and instead *something that you do*, it must be a lasting commitment that we make year in and year out as a staff.

Chapter Seven

Theory to Practice

Items for Articulation

- ❑ Can you name the standard or sub-standard that is your grade level or department's greatest area of need? If so, how do you know?
- ❑ What have you read in this chapter that validates your current work in the area of standards alignment? What encourages you to make changes?

Items for Action

- ❑ Participate in the life standards and speed mapping activities as a staff.
- ❑ Have each team select the greatest area of need or highest level of accountability related to the standards at its grade level or department. Set a timeline of one month to have a completed road map related to that standard.

Chapter Eight

Key Concepts

"Make no judgments
where you have no compassion."

— Anne McCaffrey

1

Assessment is not about the teacher; it's about the student.

2

Leadership teams play a key role in creating an exceptional system for assessment.

3

Educators at all levels must fight through bureaucracy in an effort to be explicitly practical in the area of assessment.

Chapter Eight

Assessment

It always happens in the middle of the night, doesn't it? Your little one complains of the aches and pains that come with being sick. It's all parents can do to wipe the sleep from their eyes and muster just enough attention to shine a flashlight in the mouth of their child or place a thermometer under their tongue before Dr. Mom finally decides to see the pediatrician first thing in the morning. If I were to give my wife a nickel for every time she took on this duty, let's just say that the royalties from this book would be going straight to her.

On occasion, I've stepped up to the plate to take my girls to the doctor, such as the time we thought our daughter Olivia had strep throat. I suspected that the result was not going to be good, but like most dads I tried to ease her anxiety. As hard as I tried, my words of support fell on deaf ears as Olivia just kept asking me the same question in a million different ways: *Am I going to need a shot, Daddy? Will it hurt? Oh, I hope I don't need a shot! Have you ever had a shot for a sore throat? Why aren't you answering me, Dad? Is it because you know I'm going to need a shot?* To say that I was relieved by the doctor's bedside manner is an understatement. I'll never forget the way he put my girl at ease as soon as she sat on the examining table. His words not only comforted her, but also taught me a thing or two about how children perceive the unknown. Instead of having Olivia open her mouth and jamming a cotton swab down her throat to test for an infection, with calm confidence, he looked Olivia right in the eyes, held up the testing swab, and said, "*Olivia, this is a* cotton swab. *I'm going to gently wipe the back of your throat to test for something called a strep infection. If you have this infection, don't worry; YOU'RE NOT GOING TO GET A SHOT. I'll only need to give you some medicine to drink, and I'll even have the nurse make it taste like bubble gum. Deal?*" Immediately, any anxiety that Olivia had about the test turned to relief before it even began. She shook his hand, wiped her tears away, and opened her mouth as if she were the world's greatest patient.

So what's this have to do with assessment? Today in our schools, teachers are jamming numerous assessments down the throats of our kids without any explanation of what they are measuring or how it will help them achieve success in the long run. In our classrooms, we often call our students to the back of the room so we can meet with them individually. Without showing that bedside demeanor that made all of the difference for my daughter in her doctor's office, and usually without any warning or explanation, we jam that cotton swab down their throats. We ask them to count, make a pattern, or read a story until we gather the information we need to consider this ambush—I mean, assessment—complete. Sure, there's value in knowing where our students stand academically, but we can achieve so much more on behalf of our students if we would just take 30 seconds to create buy-in for the process.

As for me, I was as guilty of this as anyone. During my first year of teaching, I spent 90 percent of my time collecting data and 10 percent using it to the benefit of my kids. By my second year, I had discovered that I could turn that ratio on its head by having one simple conversation with my students before each major assessment. It went something like this:

"Miguel, this is an IRI assessment that helps me know what level you are at as a reader. As you can see, you have a copy and I have a copy. As you read aloud, you'll see me making notes, but don't worry; I'm not interested in giving you a grade for a report card. I simply want to know your strengths as a reader and also ways that I can help you become better. The test will only take about three minutes. When we're done, I'll share your level with you, and we'll make sure to pick out some books that are perfect for you as a reader. Sound good?"

I can only imagine that it took you no more than 20-30 seconds to read the previous paragraph. Whether you are a high school science teacher speaking to your class as a whole, or a kindergarten teacher talking with a student on his first day of school, your conversation with students can be achieved in the same amount of time. With an area of focus like assessment, we are often concerned with the bottom line, so let me say this in the simplest of ways: **Assessment is not about you as a teacher; it is about your students.** All of it! Our reason for assessing students has to be grounded in a commitment to use the information in a way that helps us to generate greater success for them. Clearly, this is not an easy job. But the challenging nature of this task should never give educators license to hand out tests, set the timer, collect the tests, grade the tests, post the scores, and do it all over again, and again, and again. Unfortunately, far too many of our colleagues are doing just that. It's time that we recalibrate our priorities by creating an exceptional system in the area of assessment.

Fighting the Bureaucracy of Assessment

Before we go any further, let's make sure we are all on the same page in regard to the topic of standardized tests. This chapter is not about those tests. State tests are required across the country, and they serve a role for districts and schools as they help to track trends over time. Frustrating as they may be to me, you might be surprised by my lack of enthusiasm to even attempt to complain about them. I've learned to accept them as a tool that is used to promote accountability. If you want to waste your time fighting the system or complaining about them to your colleagues, be my guest, but know this before you continue going down that road: *Schools that use meaningful assessments based on state standards that drive instruction tend to be schools where the state test takes care of itself.* In the previous chapter, we discussed the ways we could teach to the standards and hence give our students a better chance at being successful on state tests. Other than that, there's not a whole lot more you can do. And if there were, don't you think I'd dedicate a whole chapter to it? No, this is not the kind of bureaucracy that I am concerned about. What I'm concerned about is the way that some schools and districts blindly mandate assessments to our teachers in such a way that only encourages them to make the priority about getting assessment data turned in by a deadline. This hinders growth for our kids and prevents our teachers from utilizing a number of other skills that they could be spending their time on instead. No Excuses University schools must operate differently.

Defending Our Assessment Practices

Think about the following questions related to assessment:

1. *Why are you participating in the assessments that you use with students?*

2. *Can you share in explicit detail the value that you find in each assessment?*

3. *Do you participate in assessments that you find no value in for students?*

4. *Are you using an assessment you have no idea how to deliver, but are afraid to ask for help with?*

I think I'd be hard pressed to find anyone reading this book who would argue with the practicality of every question that I have raised. Yet they are exactly the questions that far too few of us are asking of ourselves and our leaders. Why? I contend that it is because we have been victim to a frenzy in public education that has us delivering our tests as a judgment that tracks students instead of as a tool that assists their learning. Sure, every teacher across the country knows the concept of *data-driven instruction*, but I have found it to be used more as a buzzword than anything else. It's not that teachers don't want to use data to drive instruction. It's more that they are not given the proper assessments and time, or held accountable to do so. If we are going to create an exceptional system for assessment, we need to begin by asking the tough questions of ourselves. If your school or district is continuing to use an assessment, even one, without first asking why you are using it, then stop. If you are delivering assessments, even a single one, without first considering how you plan to involve students in the process, STOP!

The litmus test for our assessments must include a deep focus on student involvement because it inevitably leads to student achievement. If we cannot explicitly show how students are engaged in assessments that we deliver, then we cannot sufficiently defend the use of those very assessments.

The Role of a Leadership Team

As we head down the path of creating an exceptional system in the area of assessment, it must be noted that a leadership team on your site has to play a key role in its development. Remember, systems that are created by a leader will stay in place for as long as that person leads the organization. However, exceptional systems that are created by the critical mass of the staff in a highly collaborative way are far more sustainable. This highly collaborative component involves the work of a leadership team.

Most leadership teams are made up of grade level or department representation whose role is to support the site administrator in making plans for the future of the school. This concept of site-based decision making is an excellent one that has been around for many years. Unfortunately, decision making has turned into debating as more and more leadership teams work together. For some reason, many school leadership teams think that their sole responsibility is to represent their grade level or department. This often leads to a never ending back and forth between the leadership team and the grade level that produces all talk and no action. And because true leadership can only be measured by the results that it produces, these teams must find ways to operate differently. While No Excuses University grade and department representatives embrace the act of being the conduit of ideas from their team, they do so knowing also that they have been elected to *make decisions* on behalf of them.

Our leadership teams typically meet once a month. In between those meetings, team leaders are given a topic of conversation to collaborate on. Team leaders then bring those ideas back to the monthly meeting, where they spend their time making decisions about that particular topic. While we often actively debate about topics, we fight any efforts to get caught up in the meaningless back and forth that causes delay in decision making. I recall during one such meeting, after a lengthy debate of whether to participate in a new intervention, one team member asked the group, "How will we know if it is the right fit for our school if all we do is talk about it and never give it a try?" To us, one of the worst things to happen to kids is to have adults constantly talk in a room until they agree on something. Leadership teams may not always agree, but they always take action. And they do so in an effort to focus, not for the good of the grade level or department that members represent, but instead for the school as a whole.

Creating an Exceptional System for Assessment

The Los Peñasquitos Elementary assessment plan in the appendix is an example of an exceptional system at the elementary school level. The components within this system have been refined in the past and will continue to be in the years to come. As you attempt to create a system like this on your own, let me guide you in two specific areas. First, I will share the pattern of conversations that we engaged in as a leadership team in an effort to create this plan for assessment. Second, I will break down the main components of the plan and share the value of each. The Theory to Practice section at the end of this chapter will offer some meaningful next steps that your own leadership team can focus on when it comes time to move up the exceptional system staircase.

Conversations Between the Leadership Team

As I began to lead the discussion around the creation of a site assessment plan, I did so by asking the most practical questions of my teachers: "Which assessments do you value? Which assessments do you not value?" During those conversations, I paid close attention to the reasons why my staff valued or did not value the assessments that they were using. Occasionally, we came across an assessment that nobody liked. Their rationale was well thought out and convincing. Because of this, I said that we would simply not use those particular assessments. They were shocked. One teacher even asked, "How can you do that? Aren't we going to get in trouble with the district?" This was a fair concern on their part, but I said that it was something that I would have to handle as the leader. Fortunately for me, I worked with outstanding leaders at the district level who understood the need for teachers to value the assessments that they used on a daily basis. For years, my teachers were using assessments simply because they were told to by previous site or district administrators. To me, this is a flawed concept, as it takes the responsibility out of the hands of the professionals in charge of using assessments to drive instruction, the teachers.

Now, I'm not trying to cause a rift between your school and your district office. Nor am I trying to cause division between principals and staff members. I'm simply trying to bring the practicality back to our profession. To listen to experts in our field about the value of a particular assessment is crucial, but that expertise must be accompanied by evidence of the practical ways that these assessments are useful for teachers as they work with their students. As I write these words, I can just hear the whispers from the "experts" in the field who are cringing at my suggestion to give our teachers more of a role in this kind of decision making. Truth be told, I could not care less. All I want is what most leaders want, which is for my staff members to get great results for their students. The only way that this is going to happen when it comes to assessment is if we as leaders engage in no-nonsense conversations with our teachers. Once your leadership team is able to decide upon the assessments that are most valued by their colleagues, everything just begins to fall into place. As you engage in those conversations, here are the three requirements that our NEU teams agree upon as we select assessments.

1. *Participating in state-required assessments is non-negotiable.*

2. *You must choose at least two assessments to use in each subject so as to offer multiple measures that provide data to validate your work.*

3. *The team must be driven to choose assessments that can be used from one grade level to another in an effort to track a student's progress over time.*

Making decisions about assessments is never easy. There's no guarantee that the assessments you choose to use will work perfectly for every teacher or student. This alone creates a hindrance for many to even attempt to be courageous in their decision making. But what's the worst that can happen? You find out that the assessments that you use are not all they were cracked up to be? So what? Wouldn't you rather try assessments that teachers value and are willing to stand behind instead of having them go through the motions on mandated assessments?

Components of the Assessment Plan

As seen in the appendix, an exceptional system in the area of assessment can be detailed without being cumbersome. It can remain practical without needing to be micro-managed by a site leader. All of this is because the system was created by the same professionals who are expected to implement it, the teachers. While your exceptional system in the area of assessment may have several components and a variety of different kinds of assessments, I would urge you and your staff to include sections that address the following key elements.

Declaration: Like every exceptional system, if you can't explain it on one page then you need to start over. Declarations related to assessment systems must work the same way. Think about it this way. If visitors from another school were to come to your campus and ask you to summarize how your staff works in the area of assessment, you should be able to give them one page that explains your plan in a way that they could take back to their site to begin similar work.

Assessment Grid: I'm a big fan of the Food Network. I have learned many tips about cooking over the years. One of them is the idea that *if food is pleasing to your eye, it will also be pleasing to your palate*. This relates directly to the way that we organize our exceptional systems. If I were to give you a long list of assessments at each grade level that spanned three pages, you might not get past the first page. You might even think that the assessments you were reading about were too lengthy and lacking connection between the grade levels or departments at your school. However, if I were able to bring these assessments all together on one page in a way that shows when they were given, what the benchmarks were at each stage, and how they related to the preceding and following grade levels, you would feel much more at ease. The task would be far more attainable. The example of our assessment grid in the appendix exemplifies this belief.

Assessment Table of Contents: Having a table of contents that defines each assessment and how it can be used as an assessment that drives instruction for students is done for one reason: to ensure that all staff members know why they give the assessment in the first place. This sounds so simple, but my experience shows that if you ask ten teachers about ten different assessments, you'll get one hundred different opinions. Exceptional systems ensure that staff members are on the same page by asking the right questions, making sure that everyone understands the answers, and taking explicit steps to guarantee that nothing falls between the cracks. As you can see in the appendix, that's exactly what we've done.

Commitment to Involving Students: While the assessment table of contents asks how we "can" involve students in the assessment process, the example in the back of the book shows plans for how we "will" involve them. Assessments that used to be delivered without explanation are accompanied by plans that secure student involvement. This not only supports our partnership with students, but also strengthens the collaborative efforts between our teams.

Standardizing Our Efforts: During my teaching experience, I learned of several colleagues who always seemed to get better results than the rest of us. In fact, not only were their overall results better, but so was the growth that they showed for each student. Were they cheating? No, they were simply delivering their assessments differently than the rest of us. While we would give our first assessments on the first day of school, these high scoring teachers started their assessments two weeks later. This was done in tandem with them giving their next assessments two or even three weeks later than the rest of us. When you added it up, they had an extra month of instruction between assessments. Of course their kids were going to show greater results! This may seem totally ridiculous to you, but you must understand that because there were no systems in place at the school, it was every teacher for him- or herself. It wasn't until we created our systems that we finally sat down and decided on the ways that we would standardize when and how we delivered our assessments to students. Is it easy to do? Yes. Is it done at the majority of schools across the country? Not by a long shot.

Assessment Calendar: Having an assessment calendar as part of your assessment system goes hand in hand with standardizing your efforts. Most schools and districts have calendars like these, which is great. Many, however, don't display them in a practical format, which isn't so great. As you create your assessment calendars, be sure to present them in a crystal-clear format for your staff. Print them on a magnet or on a bookmark that can be placed prominently next to a teacher's work area. Use technology like Outlook, I-Cal, or Dropbox to ensure that assessment dates and protocols are just a click away. It's all about making sure that we're all on the same page.

Remember, the creation of an exceptional system is far different from the implementation of one. Creating one is a start, but the results can be found only when you turn talk, or writing, into action. Once you have created your exceptional system in the area of assessment, you are now in a place where you can speak the same language as a staff. At Los Peñasquitos Elementary School, we had nearly forty different languages represented within our student body. Knowing this, people always asked me, "What's the most common native language spoken at your school?" My answer: "Data." We taught it to our students, parents, and staff. The only reason that we were able to do this was because we have an exceptional system for assessment. Until you have taken this step up the staircase, consider yourself speechless.

Chapter Eight

Theory to Practice

Items for Articulation

- ❑ In what ways have you succeeded/failed to make students your partner in assessment?
- ❑ What assessments do you value, and why? What assessments do you wish you did not have to deliver, and why?
- ❑ How aware are you about the assessments that are being given by your colleagues at other grade levels or departments?

Items for Action

- ❑ As a leadership team, use the assessment plan in the appendix as a guide as you begin to engage in conversations about the components that were discussed in this chapter. As you do, remember to keep students at the forefront of the exceptional system that you create for your school.

Chapter Nine

Key Concepts

"Don't be buffaloed by experts and elites. Experts often possess more data than judgment."

— Colin Powell

1

Data must be easily accessible.

2

Information about students needs to be openly shared.

3

Leaders must offer data that are deliberately arranged.

Data Management

In 1995, I began my first full year of teaching fourth grade. Like all teachers, I spent several days before the school year began getting my classroom ready for the thirty-plus students I would be receiving in the coming week. In the middle of one day, an all-call announcement went off like an alarm throughout the school. The words of the principal were simple: "State testing data has been delivered to your boxes." Because this was my first year, I wasn't given any data, but my observations as an outsider produced opinions that would stay with me forever. This yearly occurrence, which I refer to as Groundhog Day, was one that has affected my opinions about assessments and data collection to this day.

I call this yearly ritual Groundhog Day because of the behavior that took place following the principal's announcement. Once the call was made, the teachers began to scurry out of their rooms and into the staff lounge, where they grabbed a manila envelope containing data from the previous year's state test. Upon receiving their scores, they headed back to their classrooms, locked their doors, and shut their curtains. If the results were acceptable to them, teachers peeked outside their doors and congregated in the hallways with other teachers who had done well on the test. While all of this took place, teachers like me sat at our desks with one thought: "I must be the worst teacher in this whole school." Was I a terrible teacher according to the data? I have no idea, because no one shared their data with me. In turn, no one ever asked me to share my data with them. This event, which caused anxiety on the part of some and elation on the part of others, was the only time we as teachers ever saw data.

As I look back on that experience, I think of all the wasted opportunities to have staff members put their heads together in an effort to learn from each other. I think about the students who slipped through the cracks because of our desire to keep the data to ourselves. And I think of the selfishness on all of our parts that let the fear of judgment keep us from being transparent for the sake of our kids. Thankfully, I also look back with pride as the staff at Los Pen ultimately decided to create an exceptional system for data management that would lead to the great results for students that it now works toward. How did we do it? It started with a 180-degree shift in our thinking. It started with students.

Data on Loan

Every teacher in America has a grade book. Some are found in binders, while others are in high-tech databases. And whether your grade book is lying open on your desk or virtually on your laptop, each one contains a special key that is needed before entry. Each one requires the teacher's permission to view the information.

Educators from kindergarten to high school have been trained to treat data securely and with the highest degree of integrity and confidentiality. In doing so, they guard the data as if it is their personal Fort Knox, never to be seen by anyone outside their choosing. They fail to share the data with their colleagues out of fear of judgment and sometimes even decide to hold back information from students unless specific request protocols have been followed. When they do share scores with students, it is often done with high degrees of judgment and risk of embarrassment by posting scores on the classroom doors. Sure, they never post names next to scores and instead use student IDs … as if that code can't be cracked. Such efforts are ignorant at best and arrogant at worst. Why? Because none of the data belongs to teachers! Every percentage, score, and grade that makes up our abundance of data belongs to students. It is on loan to us *from* them as an unspoken contract of sorts. I contend that these data are given to us for one reason and one reason only: to use as a means of securing greater success for each and every individual student. To keep these data from our colleagues hinders opportunities for us to work together to achieve the very purpose of having data in the first place—to help students.

I'll admit that this concept is not only foreign to many but incredibly scary as well. If you feel great trepidation over the judgment that may come with revealing your data to your teammates, I feel your pain. But put that fear aside for just a moment as I share with you the three pillars of data management that can help you to create an exceptional system in this area.

Three Pillars of Data Management

Many might think that the key to data management is dependent on the quality of database that you have access to on your campus or in your district. While I would never discount the importance of a high-quality database, I can tell you from experience that this is not nearly as important as the belief about how that very database is going to be used by your staff. To create a database without developing a commitment to endorse why the database was created in the first place will leave you in the same place you were in at the start—a bunch of numbers that are stored on a computer or in files throughout the school. To avoid this, schools must come to an understanding that their exceptional system in the area of data management must be based on three pillars. Data must be easily accessible, openly shared, and deliberately arranged.

Spending our time in this chapter discussing which database to purchase or how to create one on your own is futile for two reasons. First, because there are many database tools available to schools in each of the fifty states that offer benefits that are unique to your state or region. To endorse any one of them would be foolish on my part. Second, because I'm the last guy who knows enough about the inner workings of a database to give you credible suggestions on the technology that is best suited for supporting your needs. When Los Peñasquitos Elementary created our first database, we did so by paying a data analyst $25 an hour to fine-tune Microsoft Access in a way that met our specific needs. Today, such thinking is archaic, as the world of technology has evolved dramatically. My point? It doesn't matter which database you use for input as long as the output allows your data to be easily accessible, openly shared, and deliberately arranged.

Easily Accessible

It's one thing to give assessments that offer details about students. It's another to have access to that information in a timely fashion. From online websites like GradeCam.com that display instant feedback on your smartboard to on-site databases that offer detailed information about subgroups throughout your school, all databases must be easily accessible. I have visited too many schools where teachers require the highest level of clearance to access the school's database. Even if the database is open for viewing, if the system is hard to use, it is too much of a deterrent. Your data must be easily accessible.

A few years ago, our school clerk delivered to me one of our regular data reports about our major subgroups. As she did, she warned me of the concerns about the students listed and how our school was on track to miss AYP because of their lack of proficiency. Ten minutes after she left my office, our intervention specialist, Tiffany, came in to tell me that she had already worked with our clerk to pull the detailed data about each student within the subgroup, verified that all of them were involved in an intervention to get them on track, and created a special afterschool group for a small group of students that needed even more time. The only reason that Tiffany was able to achieve this was because she had easy access to the information. Had she waited for permission from each teacher to view the data or been required to follow lengthy bureaucratic protocols, students may have missed out on achieving success in a timely fashion and our school may very well have missed AYP that year.

Openly Shared

Several times a year, No Excuses University staff members come together to look at data as teams. Armed with data sheets like the example found in the appendix, teams discuss the needs of individual students and brainstorm strategies that will help each of them achieve academic proficiency and beyond. Sometimes those strategies are to include students in afterschool interventions, and other times they are to find new and better ways to work with them within the classrooms. On occasion, these conversations, known as "articulation meetings," result in grade levels creating data-driven groupings in which students throughout the grade level are rotated to different teachers in a way that matches the student's needs with the teacher's strengths. All of this comes as a result of educators sharing their data with one another.

While the example given in the appendix has the last names of students and teacher erased for confidentiality purposes, this is not the case during an actual articulation meeting. These meetings begin with an entire grade level or department receiving a copy of every teacher's assessment scores up to that point in the year. These scores, which align with the assessment plan at each site, are an open book that has the potential to provoke judgment and accountability from all in the group. But the funny thing is, that's never the case. In reality, the bark of this concern is far worse than the bite. I've been in dozens of articulation meetings over the years, and not once have I seen anyone look at a colleague's data and then exclaim, "Gosh Pam, you really stink at teaching reading!" No one says that. In fact, it's quite the contrary. Most share things like, "Pam, Demitri is really struggling in number sense. What can we do to help out?" or "Wow, your fluency scores are off the charts. What can you share with the rest of us so that we can follow your lead?"

No doubt, sharing data with your colleagues is an activity that requires a ton of trust. This is exactly why data management is fifth on the exceptional system staircase. If you have created a culture that is highly collaborative and built around standards that are judged using assessments that are valued by the critical mass of the staff, the sharing of data is destined to come naturally. In fact, most educators find it to be a highly enjoyable experience for one big reason: It makes them better teachers.

Deliberately Arranged

I, like many principals, believe that there's nothing I'd rather do than to remove the roadblocks along the way for hard-working educators. One of those roadblocks is data. In short, I'm not a big fan of giving stacks of numbers to teachers with a directive for them to "figure it out." As the articulation sheet demonstrates, I want my teachers to be able to view the most important data in a format that allows us to make sense of it. Whether it is charts or graphs, articulation sheets or spreadsheets, it is our job as leaders to deliberately arrange data for teachers. And while the benefit to them is that they are not being asked to use massive amounts of time sifting through the data, the benefit to us as leaders is that we are able to get our points across in effective ways.

Throughout the year, it was my practice to give a variety of data to teachers that showed how their kids were performing as a whole. Some of that information was found in graphs that illustrated their success compared to the rest of the grade level, while others showed their gains from one year to the next. At the forefront of this practice there was always one very important question that I was trying to ask of my teachers: How are your students showing growth from one year to the next? These conversations around growth were far fairer than conversations that might instead compare teachers with one another based on proficiency. At least I thought so, until I met Bea.

Bea was a second-year teacher who was struggling to find gains for her students. It wasn't that she didn't have the skills to be successful; it was that she didn't have the passion to be. In addition, she often stuck her head in the sand and refused to believe that her students were struggling more than anyone else's. For months, I had been discussing the lack of gains in her class only to have her turn the conversation around and accuse me of comparing her proficiency levels to those of other teachers at her grade level and throughout the school. She used classic lines like, "I have the hardest class in the whole grade" and "My kids are doing great in spite of their unique challenges." Finally, I shared the deliberately arranged graph found on the next page with her. Within a minute, Bea was able to see that when the students entered her classroom, 73 percent were proficient in English Language Arts and 93 percent were proficient in Math. When they left her class at the end of the year, only 60 percent were proficient in both ELA and Math. Her silence said it all. It was a breakthrough for Bea, as she immediately began to shift her teaching practices and ask for support from her colleagues. All of these efforts on my part were never intended to judge Bea or find ways to get rid of her as a teacher. They were done to help students achieve success. These deliberately arranged data were able to convey my concerns to her in a way that I had not been able to do through my words alone.

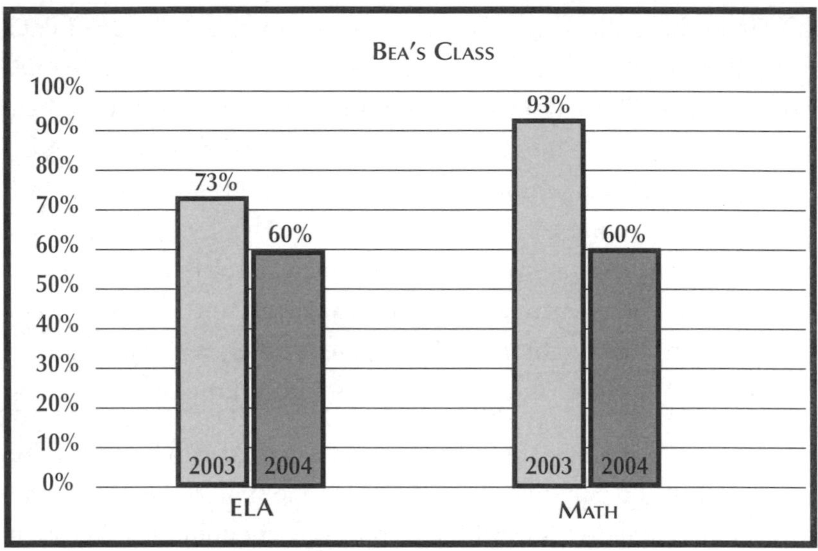

As you create an exceptional system for data management in a way that is easily accessible, openly shared, and deliberately arranged, never underestimate a student's ability to understand data as well. All too often, especially at the elementary school level, we cut our students out of the data equation because we assume that it is far too hard for them to comprehend. My experience shows that we need to do the exact opposite. Every single student at Los Pen, as well as at many No Excuses University schools across the country, creates individual goals based on very specific data. I never truly understood the value of this until I met Emerson.

Emerson was a third-grade student whose native language was Tagalog. I watched this spunky young student skipping through the hallways one day on his way to recess. Even though he had a huge smile on his face, I wondered if there was a special reason for his spirited attitude that day.

I stopped him and asked, "Hi Emerson, how are you doing today?"

Immediately he responded with "Great!" and tried to be on his way.

Not content with his response, I said, "Wait a minute. How do you know you're doing great?"

He paused for a moment, looked up at me, and said, "I know I'm doing great because I just got a 198 on my MAP score. And do you know what's so great about that, Mr. Lopez?"

"No," I said.

Emerson shouted back with excitement, "What's so great about that is that I made the most growth in my goal area, which is in literal comprehension. If I keep it up, I will be past grade level and I'll be ready to make a new goal."

So pleased with him, I gave Emerson a high five and sent him on his way. After he left, I beamed with pride for Emerson and also for his outstanding teacher who understood the value of creating a student-teacher partnership focused on a common language of data. I am convinced that even for the youngest students we serve, stories like these do not have to be unique.

Chapter Nine

Theory to Practice

Items for Articulation

- ❑ What are the common reasons why staff members keep their data private from each other? In what ways might you break down these barriers?
- ❑ How easily accessible, openly shared, and deliberately arranged are your data today?
- ❑ What needs to change in order to make your system for data management exceptional?

Items for Action

- ❑ Devise a calendar to engage in articulation meetings at least three times a year. These meetings should take place between the principal, grade level or department, and any support staff who engage in daily instruction with the students at that level.

Chapter Ten

Key Concepts

"Those who are in a position of strength have a responsibility to protect the weak."

— Thomas Cushman

1

True intervention is to take action in order to improve a situation.

2

Schools should create interventions that take place both in and out of the classroom environment.

3

Not all interventions cost money. Most come as a result of greater collaboration and wiser use of time.

Interventions

A few years back, I took my family on a trip to Portland. (Driving from San Diego to the Pacific Northwest with three small children is an adventure that could take up a whole chapter!) As we drove along the Oregon coast, I noticed a series of logging trucks driving in the opposite direction with enormous loads of perfectly cut trees. After seemingly hundreds of trucks passed by, I thought to myself, "How do they cut down those huge trees so perfectly?" During our next stop for gas, I was so intrigued that I went up to an elderly gentleman who was a local resident in the area. I asked him, "How do they cut down those trees so perfectly and make the most of the wood?" As it turns out, he had worked in the industry for a number of years, and by the lengthy answer that I received, I could tell that he loved to talk about the process. He told me, "First we used an ax and a two-man saw. After that, the chainsaw came along and made life a lot easier for us." He went on. "While they still use a chainsaw, there's now a machine that makes everything as easy as can be. This 'tree-tractor' has a jaw that clamps to the trunk of the tree. As it clamps, it takes a measurement of the circumference of the tree and sends it to a computer inside the tractor where the operator sits. This circumference measurement tells the machine the approximate height of the tree and a chainsaw that is attached to the clamp cuts down the tree and systematically slices it into sections that maximize board length." I was amazed. "All because of one measurement?" "That's right," he said. "All because of one measurement."

I have found a direct correlation between this method of logging and a school's desire to provide data-driven interventions. Good schools are able to take interventions and analyze their effectiveness through the use of data. Great schools, however, are able to take data and translate them directly into the creation of appropriate interventions. For example, just as the tree-cutting machine took one measurement and cut the tree in a way that maximized board length, educators can take a fluency score or math assessment and plug students into appropriate interventions.

At Los Pen, if a student received a fluency score of 80, he or she might be directed to work in our Read Naturally Lab. If a math assessment identified a weakness in problem solving for a student, teams might offer support through six clearly identified problem-solving strategies. The best schools will look at data and say, "If these data—then this intervention." As challenging as this is, and it is, we are living in an educational environment that enables us to make such choices because of our access to exceptional assessments and the interventions that align with them.

What Exactly Is an Intervention?

The term "intervention" has many definitions. Addicts encounter interventions when loved ones strategically band together as they seek to help them out of the addictions that hinder their social, emotional, and physical health. Governments intervene during times of global crisis when smaller countries are invaded or natural disasters affect the less fortunate. Health departments show examples of interventions when deploying methods to stop outbreaks of infection and disease. While each example is unique to a very specific situation, they all share a definition of intervention that relates to us as schools. True intervention is to take action in order to improve a situation. Because of this, we can have interventions inside and outside the classroom, interventions that cost tons of money or interventions that are supported by volunteers, interventions that take place during the school day or after school is out. As long as we seek to improve academic success, especially that of our most needy students, these are all worthwhile interventions. That said, if we go about our work the wrong way, the interventions that we employ to help our students can become another unproductive misuse of their time.

Time Is Better Than Money

There's a perception that the best interventions are ones that can be bought. Sure, if given the chance to solve a problem we would all much rather be able to pay for our success than change our schedules, shift our teams around, or utilize our current resources better. Unfortunately, that's just not the world that we are living in today, nor should it be. The entire premise of our six exceptional systems is based on the idea that money is not what fixes schools; people do. The time that each of us invests in being creative and displaying an entrepreneurial spirit has more capital than you can possibly imagine. And while it is true that some of our interventions do require financial investments, it is important that we first grasp the fact that our greatest interventions are often the ones that come as a result of the way we utilize our time intentionally.

The Double Dip

On far too many campuses, the word intervention means one of two things: First, it means to "fix this kid." Second, it is code for "take this student out of my class and let someone else fix them." When classroom teachers send students out of their classrooms to be supported by aides or other specialists as the first and only line of defense for a student's academic troubles, they shirk their greatest responsibility. Of course, there are always exceptions for this rule when we are working with non-English speakers or students with severe special needs that are best supported by an expert. That aside, it is senseless when our most highly trained educators farm out their most at-risk students for someone else to "fix." Real interventions occur when we offer ***extra*** support, both in and out of the classroom. This applies not just to students who are struggling to meet grade level standards, but to all students who are in need of other approaches in order to reach their

	Before School	During School	After School
Money			
Time			
Volunteer Partnerships			

next level of success. Some refer to this time as a "double dip." I like this idea of "double dipping" because it continually sends the message that the first line of intervention is always within the classroom by the classroom teacher.

Before we go any further, take a moment to brainstorm the current interventions that you have at your site. Which ones are a result of money? Which ones take place because of how you've shifted the way you use your time? Which ones are the result of resourcing volunteers? Finally, which ones take place in the most important place of all, your classroom, and which ones take place outside of your room?

As you can imagine, an exceptional system in the area of interventions is going to look a lot different from one campus to the next. This chapter is not designed to give you the "perfect fix." To do so would actually be falling into the trap of seeking programs as your solution instead of focusing on the creation of an exceptional system. What it is designed to do is to jumpstart your thinking about how to create appropriate interventions at your site that address both academic and behavior concerns in a way that helps you to get better results as a school. As you read through these examples, know that they are constantly being refined in a way to use data better to measure their success.

Interventions in the Classroom

Student Goals: One of the most effective interventions that takes place within the classroom is the creation of student goals. Each goal uses data from a variety of assessments to home in on the greatest need for a student. Every student in many of the schools throughout our network has one student goal that has been created in collaboration between the student and the classroom teacher. As part of the goal, the teacher creates at least three strategies to work on with the student in order to help the student achieve the goal.

When the goal has been achieved, a new goal is created. This kind of intervention guarantees differentiation in our instruction, as it gives extra attention that often turns a student's greatest weakness into his or her greatest strength.

Literacy Support: We have found a variety of ways to make use of the adults on campus in an effort to engage in extra literacy support for our most at-risk students. From utilizing half-day kindergarten teachers who go into the classroom during the second half of their day to work with small groups in first, second, or third grade, to hiring a literacy support teacher with Title I money, extra time means extra learning for students. Often, this extra support comes as a result of grade levels working together to conduct unique rotations that are beneficial for all involved. For example, instead of having every teacher teach every content area subject, a fourth grade team might have one teacher teach science, one teacher social studies, one art, and the last one an extra literacy group. The key to this intervention is to make the science, social studies, and art classes slightly larger, which allows the literacy group to be much smaller and more manageable. Not only is this great for students, but teachers love it as well, as it allows them to focus on their passions and strengths.

Class Lessons by Counselors: In Fran Hjalmarson's book *Differentiated Parent Support*, she discusses our need to be proactive in our approach to behavior. Instead of administrators spending 90 percent of their time disciplining 10 percent of the students in their office, they should spend 90 percent of their time supporting 90 percent of the students proactively in classrooms.

One of the best interventions that supports appropriate behavior is conducting class lessons. These lessons can be led by a counselor or teacher, teaching explicit ways to address issues from bullying to cheating. When class lessons are conducted on a regular basis beginning in kindergarten, the long-term results are nothing short of miraculous.

NEU Prep: Not to be confused with the class lessons that are taught by counselors, NEU Prep are the class meetings that take place during the first fifteen minutes of school in every single classroom. Instead of students rambunctiously entering the classroom, sifting through their backpacks to grab their homework, and shuffling through their desks to start the day, they simply take a seat on the carpet (primary grades) or at their desks and begin their class meeting. NEU Prep is designed to do a few things. First, we want to begin with clarity and structure as we share our agenda for the day. Second, we want to offer a mini-lesson that reinforces appropriate behaviors both in and out of the classroom through a "topic for the day." Finally, we want to allow time for our students to communicate with one another about the day's topic to reinforce their understanding while at the same time developing their relationship skills. Like everything that we have already discussed, the key to the success of an NEU Prep meeting is that they are conducted in very explicit ways. For example, they are always done in the morning so as to set the tone for the day ahead. Topics are decided on by teams and done according to a schedule in an effort to ensure that every student at the grade level is getting the same message. In fact, during the first 20 days of school, every single classroom throughout the school has the same exact topic. Finally, because we know how important consistency is, NEU Prep takes place every day in every grade. To do otherwise would assume that one lesson at one grade will make a lasting difference. Quite the contrary; we need to continually reinforce the message over time.

Unified Management Plans: Before becoming No Excuses Universities, many of our schools had a ton of rules and management plans. They had different rules for the hallway, gym, classroom, office, playground, and lunch area. With so many rules, our students realized that they had a million different ways to get in trouble! Knowing it is important to simplify our work in order to foster success, No Excuses Universities select six or fewer character traits we believe build a Bridge to College. While every school values positive behavior and character in students, the traits that are most important to a school community may differ from one site to the next. The No Excuses University's Bridge to College™ Plan for Character Development is composed of twenty traits. Some, such as kindness, are beginning traits that should be taught at a very young age, while others such as candor may be more suited for secondary students honing their skills for a future in the workforce. Our intent is not to overwhelm schools with too many character traits. Instead, we want to provide our schools with a menu of traits to choose from and a variety of strategies and ideas to support the implementation of each one they select from our Bridge to College. Schools that join our network are expected to:

1. *Select six or fewer character traits for their campus from the* Bridge to College™ Plan for Character Development *that can both act as the rules of their school and also foster positive character in students.*

2. *Find ways to bring their character traits to life in a way that is worthy of sharing with other NEU schools across the nation.*

The No Excuses University provides a framework of Six Exceptional Systems. Each NEU School is responsible for developing their systems as unique solutions to important challenges on their campus. The same is true for each school's Bridge to College™ plan. The No Excuses University provides the schools in the NEU Network with its Bridge to College™ plan utilizing twenty character traits. These are the building blocks each NEU School utilizes to build their own personalized Bridge to College™ plan based on the unique needs of their school community. Featuring the character traits a school selects, each school is empowered to create a personalized character education program and Unified Management Plan. Each school's Bridge to College™ plan is based on a system of behavior management that teaches instead of a discipline policy that punishes.

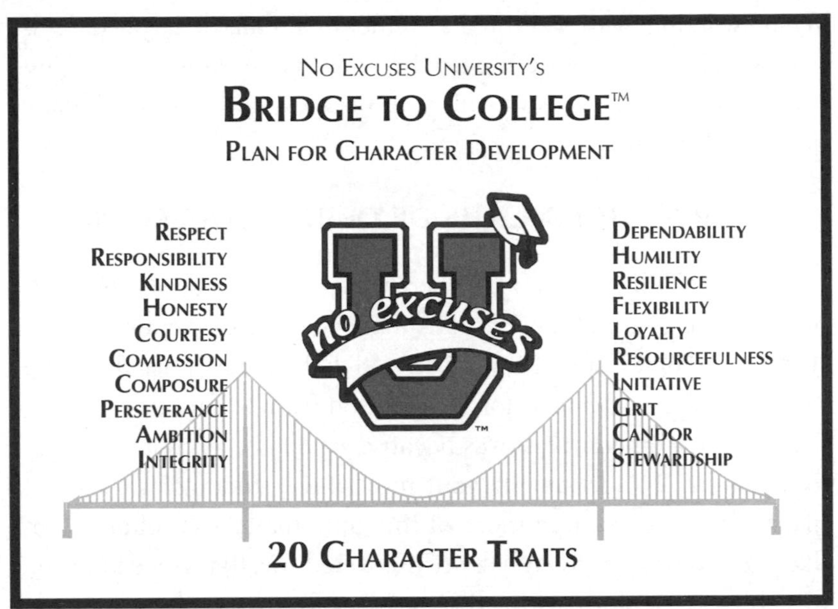

Are there times for punishment and consequences? Absolutely! But only when they are a part of a broader plan to teach appropriate behavior that results in better choices being made by students in the future. President John Adams said, "There are two educations. One should teach us how to make a living, and the other should teach us how to live." The work we do with our Six Exceptional Systems and Bridge to College™ Plan for Character Development is consistent with President Adams' vision. We prepare our students to make a living and to live. In the end it is our hope that through such teaching we are able to foster the growth of the next greatest generation of Americans who make our communities a better place to live.

Volunteer Interventions: Sometimes the best intervention is to have more hands on deck. From retired adults who want to give back to the community by mentoring students at all levels, to high school students who have electives designed to assist younger students in classes, volunteering can be a huge support. In the end, volunteering does one very important thing. It raises the adult to student ratio.

When working with volunteers, remember that their purpose is never to take your place as the teacher; it is to free you up so that you can find more time to work with your neediest students individually or in small groups.

Interventions Outside of the Classroom

Booster Clubs: Our schools used to spend hundreds of thousands of dollars for generic interventions that extended the school day for students. All of this spending only to find that we were not getting the results that we had hoped for. The reason wasn't that our spending didn't make a difference; it was because we had no exceptional plan for our work. To accumulate your most at-risk students in a subject like math and give them more of the same math instruction is not likely to promote gains. What we discovered was that any extra time that we gave to students needed to be accompanied by a detailed prescription based on their needs. Booster clubs take place before or after school and are specific to the needs of our students. Instead of sending failing math students to an afterschool "Tutoring Club," we sent our students with needs in problem solving to a four-week booster club. Instead of extending the day for more reading, we send our students who are struggling with literal comprehension to a three-week booster club. Far too often, we assume that students who are failing in any particular subject are failing at every aspect of that subject. When we dig deep, we realize that this is rarely the case. Students who are failing in math may still be excelling in fractions or geometry. I encourage you to fine-tune your extended day intervention efforts in a way that prescribes a specific strategy for a specific weakness.

Community Supports: During tough economic times, schools are scrambling to find extra support wherever they can. Many elementary schools, in particular, lack specialists in art, music, P.E., and science, leaving all of the responsibilities to the classroom teacher. Most teachers without such "specials" have grown accustomed to this way of teaching and in doing so have become oblivious to the fact that there just has got to be a better way. That better way is sometimes right outside our own front door. I have found that many businesses, both large and small, are consistently looking to be a part of adding value to our school system. From high-tech organizations that send employees to do weekly lessons in science, to fitness centers that offer trainers to do the same in physical education, the expertise of these professionals can be a tremendous support. Schools must sell partnerships like these as an avenue for these businesses to help the school while at the same time creating clients or employees for their companies in the future. I have found one thing for sure: Businesses will never help if you never ask.

Grade Level Rotations: Why is it that teachers feel this responsibility to be an expert in every component of the curriculum? I would contend that it's because we have fostered a system that hinders efforts to change schedules, share students, and move from one classroom to the next. The typical elementary school teacher feels a responsibility to teach reading, writing, math, social studies, science, art, music, P.E., listening, and speaking. (Depending on the state that you are in, I'm sure I forgot one or two subjects.) While I am a strong proponent of every teacher at every level being highly skilled in teaching and being responsible for student success in all components of literacy, I am also a believer in working smarter. Many NEU schools participate in rotations that capitalize on the strengths of the team members at each grade level, as was shared in the "literacy support" section. Other rotations involve creatively grouping students at a grade for one subject, like spelling. This allows a teacher to focus on one or two specific levels of spelling rather than eight or nine. This kind of thinking can turn an amateur into a specialist.

Learning Labs: Creativity and engagement comes in many forms. Sometimes the best way to engage our struggling students is to create learning labs that focus on one area of the curriculum in a structured and exceptional manner. Labs that allow students to use technology or other academic programs with the guidance of a skilled professional can establish tremendous results. There is currently an abundance of resources that can be found throughout the web. A great source for ideas is the Institution of Education Sciences website. This "What Works Clearinghouse" may be the flint to spark ideas for you and your staff the same way it has for many NEU Schools. Visit www.ies.ed.gov/ncee/wwc.

Mentoring: Half of our students come from broken homes. The absence of a father or mother can be tragic for both young children in need of attention as well as adolescents in need of guidance. The best schools in our NEU Network recognize this fact and have created a coalition of community members, business leaders, and parents to offer the kind of mentoring support that has the ability to affect a student's life well beyond his or her K-12 years. And while every mentoring model is different from school to school, there are two standards that must be upheld no matter your location. The first is to screen every potential mentor and ensure that mentoring takes

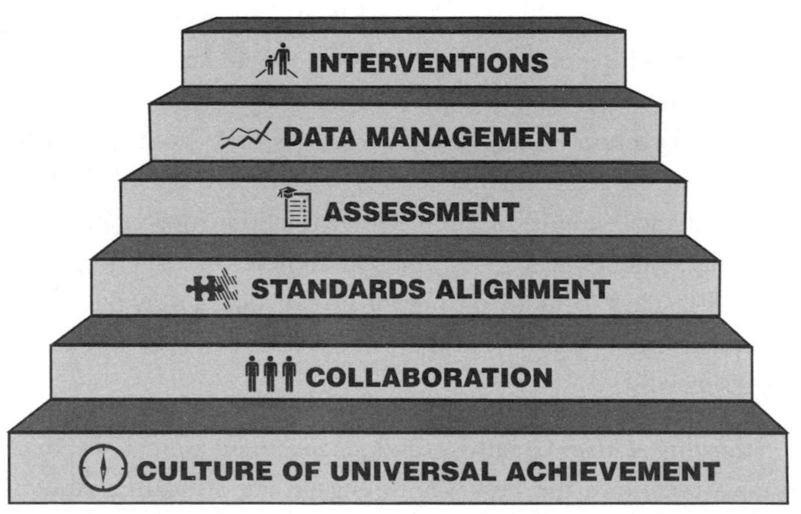

Exceptional Systems Staircase

place on campus and under the supervision of other staff members. This both guarantees the safety of your students and protects the integrity of your mentors. Second, every mentor is matched up with a student in such a way that capitalizes on his or her own personal gifts as a person and in turn develops a positive connection with the student. As many mentors will tell you, their time with students has changed not only the life of the students, but theirs as well.

These examples represent thinking from staff members who have sought to be creative in the way they address the needs of their students. None of these interventions would be successful if they did not build on the previous exceptional systems on the staircase. When you operate with a culture that assumes responsibility, collaborate in a way that embraces that charge together, align your work to standards, assess those standards, and measure your success by discussing real data, then and only then will true interventions be created. To take a less systematic approach in creating interventions may create some results in the short term, but it will never develop the kind of sustainable success that will help to get our students on the path to college from an early age.

Chapter Ten

Theory to Practice

Items for Articulation

- ❑ What is your school's definition of the word "intervention"?
- ❑ Make a list of interventions currently taking place both inside and outside of the classroom.
- ❑ Which interventions are the result of money, time, and volunteers?

Items for Action

- ❑ After brainstorming about the interventions that are taking place on your campus, where do you find gaps? Work as a school to create an intervention model that is exceptional by filling in those gaps.

Chapter Eleven

Key Concepts

"We must accept finite disappointment, but never lose infinite hope."

— Martin Luther King, Jr.

1

Unjust assumptions rob students of hope and silence the call of an educator to create results in areas void of success.

2

Beware of educators who subscribe to a "perfection before participation" attitude.

3

When it comes to school transformation, rather than seek immediate solutions, we must embrace a "value-added" philosophy.

4

Because we cannot predict the future for a five-year-old, we have no choice but to prepare ALL students for a life that includes college.

What's the Alternative?

Questions are not typically common during a keynote address, but the woman in the audience just couldn't hold back. While speaking in Chicago about the importance of promoting college readiness in elementary school, I must have said something that touched a nerve. Heedless of the results that I shared and examples of how our college readiness focus is changing the lives of students, she was compelled to speak up. So she yelled from the back of the room, "Aren't you disenfranchising our kids?"

"Excuse me?" I asked.

She continued, "Many students without U.S. citizenship will finish high school just to find out that they are not allowed to attend public universities. Poor students will do the same and realize that they don't have the funds to go to college. What about them?"

It was quiet. I was stumped. After about thirty seconds of listening to a still room, I looked past the bright stage lights and offered the only words that I could think of: "What's the alternative?"

For years, most of us have been guilty of making unjust assumptions about the students who walk through the doors of our classrooms. Children who live in generational poverty are seen as perfect candidates for low-skilled work in the future. Non-English-speaking students are assumed to have very little chance of finding professions that may some day provide financial and social stability for their future families. And minority students are often given the automatic burden that their best will never be good enough and therefore are taught by many to accept their place in society. But what is worse than all of these labels is the fact that these assumptions are branded on children at the age of four or five as they enter kindergarten. This unspoken and all too common belief, by even some of our best educators, is exactly why we must take bold risks to do things differently. People who think like this audience member are reluctant to take such risks because:

They don't understand the true meaning of "college readiness": College readiness is not the belief that every student will go to college. College readiness is the idea that every student deserves the opportunity to be educated in a way that prepares him or her for college if he or she chooses to attend.

They subscribe to the theory of "perfection before participation": Many educators have been taught that thinking outside the box is a practice that is not acceptable. In addition, many watch school reforms come and go and therefore decide to dig their heels into mediocrity. No matter the case, they fall into what I call the perfection before participation trap. This trap is one that encourages educators to take part only in educational endeavors that are comprehensively perfect in every way. When a program or model is not perfect in their eyes, they eagerly find a flaw and refuse to participate. In the end, their lack of participation is not based on reflective evaluation, but rather convenient excuse making.

They don't embrace a "value-added" philosophy: Recently, I was at a school in Arizona conducting a workshop on creating individual academic goals for students. As I shared several practical strategies with this middle school staff, one teacher shouted out, "Are you crazy? You're in elementary school where you only have 30 kids in each class. We have 125 students to teach every day. Do you really expect us to make individual goals for each of them?"

After trying to validate his concerns, I asked him, "If you can't create goals with all of your students, do you think that you could do so with half of them?"

He laughed and simply said, "No."

I went on. "If I gave you a month, could you make them for 40 to 50 students?"

Again he shrugged off my suggestion and gave me a very solid "No!"

I asked again, "If I gave you a week, do you think you could personalize goals for two or three students?"

He smiled and said, "Of course I could do that."

I finally and firmly stated, "Then that's two or three students that have goals next week that didn't have them this week."

This is a perfect example of someone not knowing what it means to think in a "value-added" way. Too many educators subscribe to an "all or nothing" mentality. Changing the overall results of your school is not done with one sweeping initiative; it is done by finding lots of little ways to add value to the educational lives of individual students. This same idea applies when it comes to promoting college readiness. No matter the long-term outcome, a student who is taught with a college-readiness focus is better equipped academically than one who has not been given that same preparation.

They behave like fortunetellers: The thought that the promotion of "college readiness for all" would disenfranchise students is the epitome of a very misguided assumption. While people rarely say it out loud, they often make assumptions clearly indicating that it would be better not to offer false hope to children by talking about a future that includes college. By doing so, we behave like unsolicited fortunetellers. Think about it for a moment. Should educators be expected to ignore the fact that laws can change, citizenship can be attained, and financial situations have the potential to improve over the course of the 13 years that a student is in school? Furthermore, should we be expected to tell these same students the idea that higher education is a concept that exclusively exists within our country? This kind of thinking is absolutely absurd. Because of this, we should no longer attempt to predict the future of five-year-olds based on the color of their skin, their socioeconomic levels, or their native languages. And because we lack the ability to truly predict the future, we have no choice but to believe in every student's potential to attend an institute of higher education.

As I reflect back to that keynote speech in Chicago, I realize that the woman in the audience, and others who think like her, would have loved for me to offer the perfect solution for getting students out of poverty and into college. Or perhaps she'd be glad if I had no answers at all, for then she could continue to make herself feel better about not meeting the needs of her more challenging students. But the fact is that the business of promoting college readiness is not a perfect science, especially when you are starting in kindergarten. And while some may see it as a risky endeavor, we must decide to ignore the people in the audience who seek only perfect solutions to very challenging problems. True, these bold practices may not remove all of the roadblocks on the path to college for our most needy children, but there's no evidence that would suggest that such measures would hinder their academic potential, either. In fact, as you will read, the data suggest quite the contrary.

Chapter Eleven

Theory to Practice

Items for Articulation

- ❑ What are the challenges that some students face in their pursuit of a college education?

Items for Action

- ❑ If your school stood before a jury, what evidence would they have to convict you of displaying confidence in every student's potential to graduate from college? As a team, seek tangible evidence to present at an upcoming staff meeting. During this time, share your team's view of the strengths and challenges that your school has when it comes to believing in all students.

Chapter Twelve

Key Concepts

"If you think education is expensive, try ignorance!"

— Bok's Law

1

The value of a college education is displayed in abundance in the areas of *personal prosperity and societal wealth.*

2

The level to which a person is educated either drastically increases or decreases his or her financial, physical, and emotional wellness.

3

Single mothers without a high school education are five times more likely to live in poverty than those with a bachelor's degree.

4

There are three times as many Black and Hispanic males in prison cells as there are in college dormitories.

Chapter Twelve

A Rationale for Readiness

Isn't it amazing how one statistic, one injustice, or one experience in the lives of everyday people is often enough to trigger the human spirit to produce remarkable results? Such was the case with two very inspiring young men. Darius Weems was a 15-year-old boy suffering from Duchenne Muscular Dystrophy (DMD). As the number one genetic killer of children, this disease robs an individual of physical tools and prevents many from living to see their early 20s. Logan Smalley was a college student with a passion for supporting children with special needs and an artistic touch for filmmaking. Darius was black. Logan was white. Darius was a high school student who had never traveled outside the city limits of Athens. Logan had been accepted into Harvard grad school and was about to experience a journey well beyond the Georgia borders. This unlikely pair made a series of decisions that have touched the lives of tens of thousands of people around the globe and raised millions for DMD research in the process.

As a college student, Logan Smalley volunteered at Project

Reach, a summer camp for children with disabilities. One of the attendees at the center was Darius's older brother Mario. Before Mario, a Duchenne's sufferer as well, passed away at the age of 19, he asked Logan to "watch after my little brother." The pain of watching his friend die at such a young age did not trigger in Logan depression and hopelessness the way that it does in so many others. Rather, it spurred on action. In 2004, Logan and ten of his friends set out to take Darius on a 7,000-mile road trip and film a documentary at the same time in order to raise funds for DMD research. What began as a pipedream for a dozen college-aged kids has become one of the most award-winning documentaries in recent history. The film, *Darius Goes West*, explicitly recognizes the odds that are stacked against sufferers of Duchenne's, yet chooses to defy the idea that nothing can be done about it. In 2007, this inspirational team set a goal to sell one million DVDs in one year. Some saw such a feat as completely irrational and unlikely at best. However, Logan, Darius, and their friends understood two important facts that necessitated this great sense of urgency. First, Duchenne's was a non-curable disease that was 100 percent fatal. Second, every day and every dollar counted.

The ability for individuals to use the data before them to find unique solutions is unfortunately a very precious commodity in the world of public education. The tremendous progress that the *Darius Goes West* team has made in light of limited resources is an example that should offer perspective for what our struggles are as educators. If poverty is the illness and college is the cure, then our behavior should match that of Logan and Darius. Today, we have data about the value of college that are more than enough to generate a substantial sense of urgency for teachers and develop a cure for students at the same time.

I have worked diligently to compile an abundance of data about the value of earning a college degree. The results that I have found are overwhelming. A life accompanied by a college degree is one that is richer in ways that go well beyond finances. The potential that awaits our society when one college grad becomes a thousand and thousands become millions is staggering. I have arranged these outcomes into two specific categories: ***personal prosperity*** and ***societal wealth***. Both categories display the effect that a college education has on the life of an individual as well as those who live within our communities.

Because this book, and especially this chapter, was written with the practitioner in mind, I have created *data boxes* that clearly display the statistical facts about the value of a higher education. The sources of each data box have come from some of the best researchers and research studies in the field. Educators like Dr. Sandy Baum, Jennifer Ma, and Kathleen Payea who wrote the study "Education Pays" on behalf of the College Board, offer insight on statistical predictors that are inspiring change in educators who learn about their research. Research studies such as "The Big Payoff," a report produced by the Commerce Department's Census Bureau and authored by Jennifer Cheeseman-Day and Eric Newburger, spotlight earnings estimates for those who stand to gain the most in the future—college grads.

The work of these authors, as well as others noted throughout this chapter, share common data that provide a strong rationale for the charge to promote college readiness at an early age. From the significant gap that exists among minority groups to the benefits, or lack thereof, that a college education has on our citizens, the information from each of these sources should generate pause for all of us. As you read, I encourage you to make your own judgments and actively take notes on how you can apply the data to future educational decisions that are made for the students in your classroom, school, and district. Above all else, I encourage you to become the research. In the end, the true value of this chapter will not be found in the *knowledge* that you gain by reading the research, but by the *action* that you take after doing so.

Personal Prosperity

In the 2010 College Board study "Education Pays," Sandra Baum and Jennifer Ma calculate that the gap between the lifetime earnings of a high school graduate and that of a college-educated individual widens dynamically over the course of a lifetime. "The longer college graduates remain in the workforce, the greater the payoff to their investment in higher education" (Baum & Ma, 2007, p.11). The study projects that an individual with a bachelor's degree earns 66 percent more over a lifetime than a high school graduate, while a person with a master's degree earns a whopping 97 percent more than that same high school grad. Individuals with some college or associate's degrees earn between 13 and 24 percent more than those with high school diplomas.

Yearly Earning By Education Level

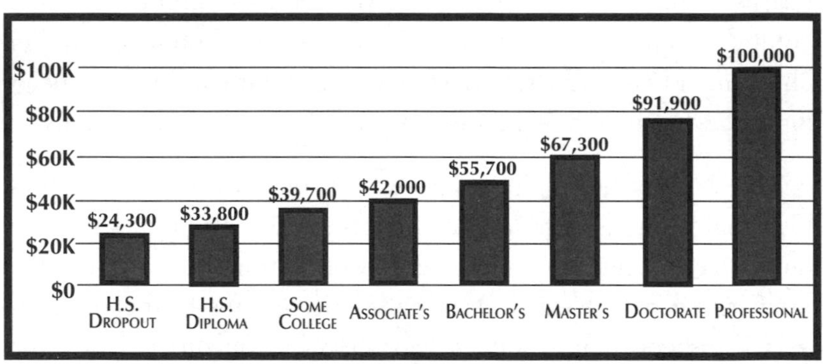

The median earnings before taxes for 25-year-olds and older indicates a 61 percent difference between the value of a high school diploma and a bachelor's degree.

Sources: 2006 Census Bureau; "Education Pays," 2010. Copyright © 2010, The College Board www.collegeboard.com. Reproduced with permission.

The earliest an individual can retire and collect Social Security is at the age of 62. A 25-year-old who works until he or she is 62 has a career longevity of 37 years. This means that in today's dollars an individual with a bachelor's degree would earn nearly $800,000 more in gross income in a lifetime than someone with a high school diploma (Baum, Ma, & Payea, 2010, Fig 1.2). The earnings potential of college grads becomes exponentially greater as their careers progress.

For decades, our society has blindly pitched to students an outline of education that begins in kindergarten and ends with a high school diploma. In 1970, approximately 37 percent of 18- to 19-year-olds attended college after graduating from high school (Baum, Ma, & Payea 2010). In 2007, the U.S. Department of Labor indicated that more than 67 percent, some 2 million high school graduates, were enrolled in college after graduation (Bureau of Labor Statistics, 2007). With high school dropouts generating an average income below the federal poverty level of $27,010 for a family of five (U.S. Health and Human Services, 2012), and high school graduates earning just above that, the game of life is now mandating that a college education is your ticket to personal prosperity. One can only imagine what these numbers will become when today's kindergarteners become tomorrow's high school grads. Because college has become so crucial to a person's financial and social stability, the promotion of college must start the moment students begin their educational career.

> ***Seventy percent of individuals with college degrees work in jobs that offer pension plans. This is 15 percent higher than that of high school graduates and 40 percent higher than high school dropouts.***

Sources: 2006 Census Bureau;"Education Pays," 2010. Copyright © 2010, The College Board www.collegeboard.com. Reproduced with permission.

The National Longitudinal Survey of Youth reported that workers changed jobs an average of ten times between the ages of 18 and 42 (Bureau of Labor Statistics, 2006). With shifts like these, the differences between *jobs* and *careers* are becoming more defined. Many of us have experienced jobs that allowed us to pay only for the basic necessities of life. I, along with so many of you, held numerous jobs throughout my days in college. From taking on serving duties with a catering company to working as a bellman at a hotel, my jobs enabled me to pay my share of the rent, fill up my gas tank, and buy food on a regular basis. Sometimes, there was just enough left over to use in a disposable fashion, but it seemed there was never enough to save for bigger and better things. As I entered the workforce as an educator, however, my monthly income from my career allowed me opportunities that my jobs never did. From being a participant in a 401K program, to the ability to purchase a new car, to a newfound opportunity to qualify for a home loan, my options became far more plentiful in a relatively short amount of time.

As we preach a life of higher education to our students, we must remember that the benefits of a college education are found not only in a greater yearly salary, but also in our ability to participate in the vast array of benefits that a career can provide. The prospect of participation in a retirement/pension plan is a benefit that maximizes long-term financial stability to our families while minimizing undue fiscal burdens on society.

> ***Highly educated individuals have a life expectancy averaging seven years longer than those who have completed a high school diploma or less.***

Source: *The Gap Gets Bigger: 2009*

In March 2008, *Health Affairs* published a study entitled "The Gap Gets Bigger: Changes in Mortality and Life Expectancy, By Education" (Meara, Richards, & Cutler, 2008). The study examined both white and black men and women and offered two classifications. The first, "highly educated," was made up of individuals with some college experience. The second group was made up of the "low educated," individuals with a high school diploma or less. The authors found that highly educated individuals not only lived an average of 7 years longer than their counterparts, but also displayed a rise in life expectancy of 2.2 years between 1988 and 2000. While the life expectancy of highly educated individuals was rising, the life expectancy of low-educated adults dropped an average of 2 years in that same time span. Few would suggest that the act of sitting in a college classroom will add days to your life (many in fact would argue against such a notion); however, studies such as these offer insight into a variety of avenues by which highly educated adults can find access for greater longevity. First and foremost on that list of longevity tools is access to better health care. *The Journal of the National Cancer Institute* published a study by Dr. Ahmedin Jemal showing a decline in deaths from the four most common cancers. Within that decline, the study showed that those with 16 or more years of education benefited while those with high school diplomas or less did not. In fact, in some cases, less educated people experienced an increase in diagnoses of specific types of cancers. "Less educated people have more risk factors for cancer like smoking and obesity," said Jemal. "They receive less medical services for prevention, early detection and treatment" (Reinberg, 2008). Jemal, echoing the "Education Pays" study, noted a significant gap between college-educated adults and high school graduates when it came to both exercise habits and smoking rates. Sixty-one percent of college-educated adults between the ages of 25 and 34 exercised "vigorously," while only 31 percent of high school graduates did the same. By the time college graduates turned 65, they continued to out-exercise their high school counterparts by a margin of 24 percent.

These exercise statistics, coupled with a disparity in smoking rates (9 percent of college-educated adults smoke compared to 26 percent of high school graduates), provide clear evidence of the gap in health habits based on educational levels.

No matter how you interpret these statistics, a crystal-clear argument has been made that the greater your educational background, the better access you have to quality health care. This is not to say that it is fair nor does it suggest that quality health care is more deserved by those with higher levels of education. It simply describes a reality that exists in our society. Such information must be shared with our students as yet another reminder of the doors that are opened for those who have earned college degrees.

2009 Volunteer Rates

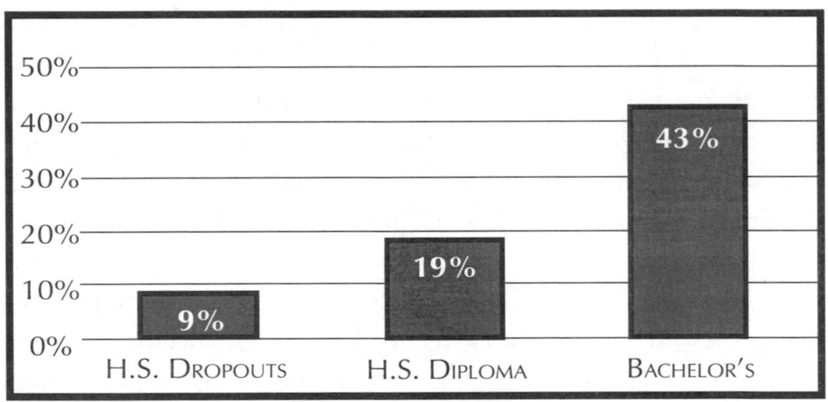

Volunteerism among college graduates is double that of high school graduates.

Source: Bureau of Labor Statistics, 2009

The significance of volunteerism cannot be overestimated. Anyone who has ever given of their time to those who are less fortunate can share about the intrinsic rewards that are gained through such participation. Unfortunately, studies show that most people do not have the time to volunteer. In fact, just more than 25 percent of all adults volunteer one hour a week. This statistic is dwarfed by the number of college graduates who volunteer on a regular basis. So, why is volunteerism so important? Let me offer two reasons.

First and foremost, the opportunity to volunteer is oftentimes determined by our ability to find flexibility in our schedules. Think about all of the parents in your classrooms and in your schools. Think about the ones who work in your classroom or attend field trips on a regular basis. I would wager that the majority of those who do are either in careers that offer flexibility in their schedules or parents with an income that allows one adult to stay home. I would contend from personal experience that parents who work in 9-to-5 minimum-wage jobs have far fewer opportunities to volunteer at school during the week or even in the community over the weekend. With that same experience, I could name dozens upon dozens of those same parents who wish that they could volunteer in order to spend more quality time with their children as well as to give back to the community. Their lack of participation has little to do with their drive to help others and everything to do with their ability to find flexibility in their schedules.

In addition to the joy that one finds in supporting others, volunteerism saves non-profit organizations billions of dollars annually. In 2007, the Financial Accounting Standards Board (FASB) set the average value of a single hour of volunteering at $19.51 per hour. This figure is up 74 cents from the year before and varies from state to state (Lowest: Montana, $13.51; highest: D.C., $30.10). Think about all of the hours that you personally volunteer in your community. Tally up all of the hours that adults volunteer within your school. You do the math. The value that volunteerism has for our society is tremendous. As the data show, the best way to raise volunteer numbers over time is to produce a college-educated workforce with a sense of stewardship for their community. Educators across our country do a wonderful job of teaching such stewardship through the development of character traits as we do with our Bridge to College™ Plan for Character Development. As we teach traits aligned with volunteerism, such as citizenship and responsibility, we should remember to do so under the umbrella of a strong college-readiness message.

Societal Wealth

In 2008, the approximately 145 million employed and 9 million unemployed made the American workforce a total of 154 million people and the average unemployment rate 5.8 percent (Bureau of Labor Statistics, 2009b). As you take a detailed look at the number of Americans who work compared to those who do not, the rationale for college readiness becomes incredibly vivid. The statistics show that roughly 62.7 percent of the workforce is made up of individuals with at least some college. In fact, college graduates have the largest share of the job market, making up 35 percent of the workforce, some 44.5 million jobs. With high school graduates making up approximately 28.5 percent of the American workforce, and high school dropouts following far behind as a collective 8.6 percent, it becomes clear that the benefits of a college education are found not only in a lower unemployment rate, but also in a higher employment ratio (Bureau of Labor Statistics, 2009b).

2011 Unemployment Rate
(25 years or older)

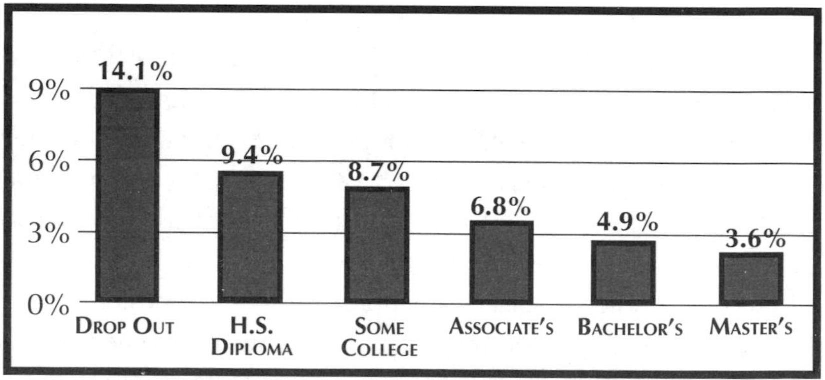

Unemployment rates are three times higher for high school dropouts than for college graduates.

Source: Bureau of Labor Statistics, 2011

Such data fly in the face of those who would suggest "the world needs ditch diggers too!" when in fact the world undoubtedly is seeking to hire well-educated adults. With an overwhelming number of college graduates holding the vast majority of high-paying jobs, the writing is on the wall for our students today. That writing could not be more legible for people of color, especially black students within our school system. While unemployment rates remain within the national average for whites, Asians, and Hispanics, black individuals 25 and older have a significantly higher rate than all other groups. The unemployment rate for blacks is 21.3 percent for those without a high school diploma and 14 percent for those who have graduated from high school. These numbers are almost twice as high as for whites and Hispanics and nearly three times higher than that of Asians. However, with only 7.3 percent of ***college-educated*** blacks filing for unemployment benefits, this gap in employment becomes drastically reduced and far more equitable when compared to other subgroups (Baum, Ma, & Payea, 2010).

These numbers have prompted many within the black community to create change with a sense of urgency that focuses on college readiness for some of the youngest children in the poorest neighborhoods. No example displays this kind of shift better than that of Geoffrey Canada and the Harlem Children's Zone.

As a child of poverty, Mr. Canada grew up in the South Bronx of New York. A graduate from the Harvard School of Education, he has maintained a steadfast commitment to improving the Harlem community for more than two decades. The Harlem Children's Zone he founded supports children and families within a 100-block area with services that help move children from a life of poverty to one of prosperity. With the Children's Defense Fund (CDF) revealing that there are nearly 1 million black children living in extreme poverty, and a reported high school dropout rate of 48 percent among blacks, the challenges that were evident within the Harlem community required drastic measures. As a guest on the Oprah Winfrey show in 2007,

Geoffrey Canada offered a passionate appeal for dynamic change. "Here's the problem we have in this country. We're losing kids by the tens of thousands and we are saving them by the twenties and thirties. It just doesn't add up. We have got to save these kids by the thousands."

UNEMPLOYMENT BY ETHNICITY

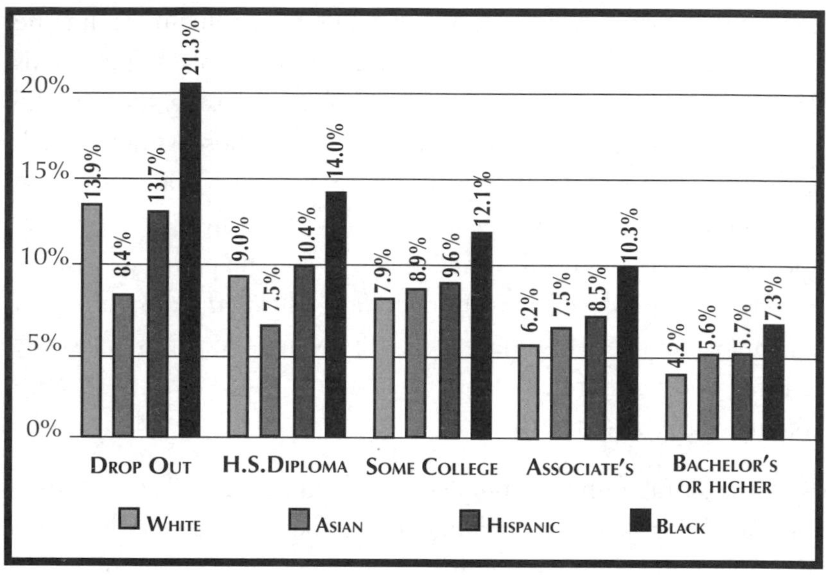

Data provided by U.S.Department of Labor, 2007; "Education Pays," 2010. Copyright © 2010, The College Board, www.collegeboard.com. Reproduced with permission.

Canada expanded on his plan to save kids. "We've got to get these kids through college. With globalization, there is nothing you can do in America with a high school diploma. These kids have got to graduate from college!"

With education at the core of the Harlem Children's Zone plan to change a community, thousands of black students are escaping the grasp of unemployment, crime, and poverty as they become college educated. Geoffrey Canada's dedication to change, as a result of the response to the negative trends within his community, provides a model for each of us to follow.

PERCENTAGE OF ADULTS LIVING IN HOUSEHOLDS OF POVERTY
(25 YEARS OR OLDER)

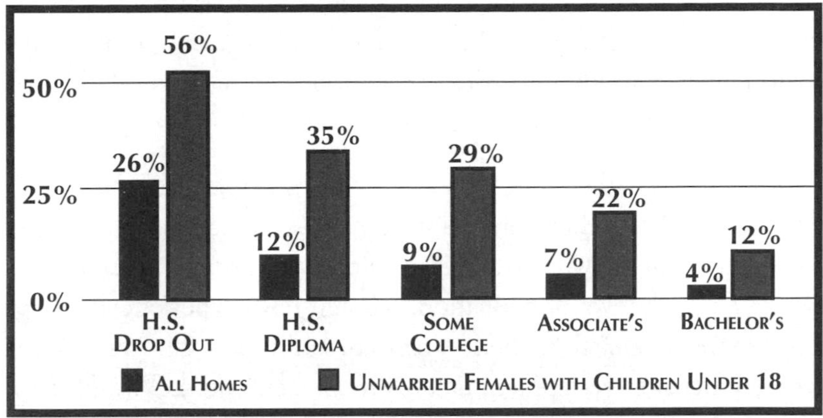

Single mothers who have dropped out of high school are nearly five times as likely to live in poverty as those with a bachelor's degree.

Source: "Education Pays," 2010. Copyright © 2010, The College Board, www.collegeboard.com. Reproduced with permission.

Our students live in a world where a lack of high-paying jobs for those without college degrees will create greater financial hardships for them as individuals, and substantial burdens for all of us as a society. However, the data suggest an even greater importance for a college education when it comes to the young girls of today. As a father of four daughters, these numbers hit close to home.

To think that a single mother without a high school diploma has a 50/50 chance of living in poverty is not only worrisome; it is alarming. The number of children and single mothers who live in poverty doesn't even begin to compare with the rest of society until a college degree is obtained. If we were to view poverty as a disease, this would be a virus of epidemic proportions.

Experts offer many valid reasons for these statistics that range from the absence of fathers in the home to the need to curb teenage pregnancy. The breakdown of a parent's responsibility to his or her children is certainly one reason that has the potential to devastate the overall success of a family. Still, the greatest prescription for this problem is not necessarily to find ways to develop greater responsibility in fathers, although that doesn't hurt, but more so to establish a greater percentage of college-educated women in our society.

In "Women in the Workforce," an article by Peter Rupert and Cara Stepanczuk, the authors cite many gains in the area of employment for women that are worthy of being celebrated. From an increase in pay to a rise in level of education, women have experienced sharp improvement related to their careers over the past 25 years. With women making up approximately 48 percent of the workforce, however, the greatest change needed is to generate high-paying jobs for females, especially those who are single parents. The data suggest that the best way to both exit women from a life of poverty and break the cycle that perpetuates itself for generations is to increase the number of women with college degrees. This becomes increasingly important for minority women, especially black women.

Based on 2006 U.S. Census data, authors Dr. Sandy Baum, Jennifer Ma, and Kathleen Payea state in "Education Pays," "Median earning for Black female bachelor's degree recipients between ages 25-34 were 70 percent higher than median earnings for Black female high school graduates. For Hispanic women, the earnings premium was 57 percent, and for White women it was 49 percent." These numbers suggest that the only escape from poverty for a single Black mother is via some type of post-secondary education. Because of this, our college readiness efforts must be drastically stepped up for all people of color, especially women. Such efforts cannot be expected to begin in high school; they must start in kindergarten.

The burdens of poverty not only shape a challenging existence for our children, but also stifle greater financial prosperity for our society. As you will see, the costs of Medicaid, school lunches, and the Supplemental Nutritional Assistance Program (formerly referred to as food stamps) leave the American taxpayer with monthly bills in the billions. As I share these data, do not mistake my desire for a life of personal financial responsibility for all as denying our call as a society to help those gripped by poverty. Let me be very clear,

PERCENTAGE OF ADULTS LIVING IN HOUSEHOLDS PARTICIPATING IN PUBLIC ASSISTANCE PROGRAMS
(25 YEARS OR OLDER)

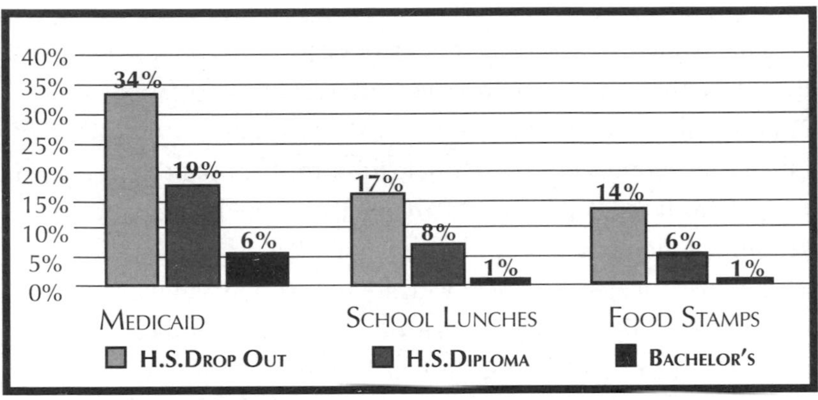

College graduates are three times less likely to participate in Medicaid, eight times less likely to have children participating in free school lunches, and six times less likely to participate in food stamps programs than high school graduates are.

Sources: U.S. Census Bureau; "Education Pays," 2010. Copyright © 2010, The College Board, www.collegeboard.com. Reproduced with permission.

I believe that it is our duty to support those less fortunate, especially the children in our society who have little say in the matter. However, as we lend that support, there must be a plan to reduce an individual's long-term dependence on government aid. I believe that a systematic college-readiness endeavor, like the No Excuses University, has the potential to ensure that more children living in poverty will become college educated. As they do, a generational cycle of poverty will become broken and in turn more tax savings and revenue will be created by an increased workforce. As more dollars are saved in a reduction of welfare programs, more money can be invested in education, which will create a more positive generational cycle of success. I'll admit that such thinking may be seen as nothing more than a "pie in the sky" theory to some. True, the complexities of changing a society of more than 300 million people are so massive that it is hard to find simple solutions within the pages of one book, but indulge me if you will as we move from the millions to one individual child at a time.

The United States Department of Agriculture (USDA) reports that more than 46 million people participated in the Supplemental Nutritional Assistance Program (SNAP) at a cost of more than $6 billion per month in 2011. Participation in this program has grown tenfold from what it was in 1970, 4.3 million participants. Such statistics go hand in hand with the widening gap between those who are highly educated and those who are not. When will it end? When will we as a country decide that our so-called "solutions" are not reversing this negative trend? Albert Einstein's famous definition of insanity as "doing the same thing over and over again and expecting different results" could not be more appropriate.

Medicaid, not to be confused with Medicare, is a health care program that is run by each individual state based on a list of federal guidelines. The federal and state government split the cost of health care subsidies for individuals who qualify. In 2005, almost 53 million people participated (Vock, 2006). Children make up nearly half of all individuals participating in the program, with low-income working parents, disabled Americans, and the elderly making up the rest. With the rising cost of health care for all Americans, the $330 billion-plus spent in 2005 on Medicaid is guaranteed to go up. Because the vast majority of this program serves the interests of children, it's hard to make an argument against such support. I'll be the first to say that my ability to understand the intricate nature of the politics of health care in a way that can truly promote meaningful change is like my six-month-old being able to play Mozart on the piano. Even so, it's hard to deny the data behind the significantly lower numbers of college-educated individuals who participate in this aid compared to the high school graduates who do.

Finally, when it comes to public assistance programs, the support of free or reduced breakfast and lunch for students is one that is among our noblest as a society. Regardless of your opinions of the parents who raise these children, it is our moral obligation to feed our students while they are in our care. In addition, we must never use their lack of nutrition as an excuse for poor results in school. How many times have you heard someone say, "How can we expect that kid to learn when his mother won't even feed him a good breakfast?" Decades ago, venting frustration over this may have been acceptable, but today we know better.

In 2007, the per-student funding for school lunches was $238 a year (Baum & Ma, 2007). With the more than 30 million children participating in the National School Lunch Program comes a price tag of $8.7 billion a year (USDA, 2008). Increasing from $3.7 billion in 1990 to $6.1 billion in 2000, the cost of this program is rising at a rate that is beyond the average annual U.S. inflation rate of 3 percent. Much like the issue of health care, a quick fix does not appear to be in the cards. Rather, a long-term approach to break the cycle of poverty through a college education is the more realistic solution.

As stated in a report by the Alliance for Excellent Education, "Crime Doesn't Pay—Diplomas Do," from the costs associated with loss of wages on the part of victims to the skyrocketing cost of incarcerating criminals, crime has become our country's greatest burden on society.

> ***Seventy-five percent of state prison inmates, sixty-nine percent of jail inmates, and fifty-nine percent of federal prison inmates are high school dropouts.***

Source: Alliance for Excellent Education, 2006

According to a 2008 Pew Center of States Study, there were a total of 2,319,258 adults held in American prisons or jails at the beginning of 2008. This amounts to more than 1 percent of our adult population or one for every 99.1 adults in America. Within that population, men are 13 times more likely to be incarcerated than women. In addition, black males make up the largest percentage of the prison population, with one in every nine black men in America between the ages of 20 to 34 behind bars. In 2007, the U.S. Census Bureau reported that there are more than three times as many black men living in prison cells than in college dormitories. This should spur any educator, or human being for that matter, on to action at the thought of the Titanic-like journey that awaits a newborn black baby boy the moment he is born.

The cost of managing our country's prison population, which happens to be the largest in the world, is astronomical. States spent more than $49 billion on prison in 2008, a massive $11 billion more than was spent in 1988. While the costs vary from state to state, this makes for an expense of nearly $58 a day per inmate. Such a cost has become so burdensome on states that drastic measures are being taken to prevent overcrowding facilities that are often millions over budget. In 2009, federal judges in California ordered that the state begin to make plans to release some 57,000 prisoners, more than one third of the state's prison population, back into society over a three-year period (Henderson, 2009). Shortsighted measures like these may reduce the cost of running prison facilities, but they do nothing to reduce crime and keep our citizens safe. The best answer is a long-term approach to promoting higher education at a young age.

Studies conducted in 2004 indicated that a simple 5 percent increase in the number of male high school graduates would lead to an annual crime-related savings of more than $5 billion (Alliance for Excellent Education, 2006). In addition, an additional $2.8 billion in earnings from productive adults would enter the economy. Such earnings would dramatically increase if these same adults went on to earn college degrees, while at the same time making our society safer and breaking generational cycles of crime that exist within impoverished areas of our communities.

Unemployment, poverty, and crime make for a triple threat to societal wealth in America. While all pose separate but equally challenging problems, the tie that binds them is education. Or, more accurately, a lack thereof. Through these data, we find that the level to which a person is educated either drastically increases or decreases his or her financial, physical, and emotional wellness. Whether you accept or dispute this information is up to you. However, to deny the fact that millions of American families are struggling unnecessarily because of a lack of education is like an ostrich poking its head into the sand. This struggle has become pervasive throughout our society and generational among families.

Our acceptance of such a reality is the first step that enables us to move from knowing to doing. It's time for educators to make decisions shaped around these data. It's time to leave procrastination to the status quo and develop meaningful, results-oriented changes in our classrooms that affect student learning today. It's time to elevate our professionalism and embrace our share of responsibility for the academic achievement of all students, no matter their circumstances. It's time to spread our passion to our colleagues for what is the noblest profession on earth, and to do so in the same manner we did when we first became educators. It's time for action.

Chapter Twelve

Theory to Practice

Items for Articulation

- ❑ Of the statistics referenced, which ones cause you to be concerned and/or take action?
- ❑ How might you use these data with your colleagues in order to promote change?

Items for Action

- ❑ With your team, translate these data into kid-friendly terms to generate a better understanding of the value of a college education. Do the same for parents. Some examples of this might be to:

1. Create a game show in classrooms or during an assembly to bring these statistics to life.
2. Develop a PowerPoint that includes these statistics alongside inspirational stories about famous college graduates.
3. Create posters to place around the school displaying data about the value of a college education as well as information related to what it takes to enter a certain profession.

Chapter Thirteen

Key Concepts

"I will take a verb over a noun any day."

— William P. Young

1

The dynamic change that is taking place within successful No Excuses Universities is happening not because of theory, but because of practice.

2

There is no such thing as "college readiness" at the high-school level; that's called "college prep."

3

College readiness is the belief that all students should be taught in a way that prepares them for college if they choose to attend.

4

Talk is not cheap; it's actually very expensive. Because of this, it is crucial that schools operate with an action-oriented attitude toward continuous improvement.

Chapter Thirteen

Time for Action

I don't know about you, but there have been times when I have noticed that my walk was not in sync with my talk. In fact, there were even periods when my beliefs about what was important professionally were distant from my ability to practically apply those truths to my work in the classroom or the principal's office. When personal reflection was not enough to align these two paths, I always made it a point to seek the support of others. Sometimes friends and colleagues would spotlight these shortcomings to me in an effort to help re-calibrate my inner professional compass. But on other occasions, I found clarity simply by observing the wisdom of those with far greater experience than my own.

On a chilly December evening in 1995, the Malden Mills textile factory tragically burnt to the ground. This company, specializing in the production of Polartec® fleece, was one of the largest employers in the relatively small community of Lawrence, Massachusetts. Owned and operated since the time of its inception by Aaron Feuerstein and his family, Malden Mills and the lives of its 3,000 employees were turned upside down overnight. Within days, every worker was summoned to a company meeting assumed to be a mere formality before the announcement of layoff notices. Packed into an auditorium, the employees burst into tears as Mr. Feuerstein shared his unexpected plan for the company. Rather than collect the more than $300 million in insurance money, Mr. Feuerstein decided to invest every penny to rebuild the factory. As if that were not enough, this modern-day hero paid the salaries of every employee for months as the mill was reconstructed. During an interview conducted by Morley Safer on the television program *60 minutes*, I watched as Aaron Feuerstein was asked why he chose to spend the money rather than retire a very wealthy man. His response, "And what would I do? Eat more? Buy another suit? Retire and die? No, that did not go into my mind. That was not an option, not for a second." He didn't base his decision on money, he said. "I did it because it was the right thing to do." (CBS *60 Minutes*, 2002).

The idea of knowing what is right, the *theory*, is very different from doing what is right, the *practice*. Just as Aaron Feuerstein modeled to his employees servant leadership that was grounded in action, today's educators must also act with similar behavior on behalf of their students. *To understand* the difference between the theoretical and the practical is not enough. Our students will realize their greatest potential only when we are focused on the *action* associated with turning theory into practice.

There's no doubt that the data referenced thus far are incredibly compelling to anyone with a passion for promoting change in the lives of students. However, it's still just data. It's just numbers. As Homer Simpson once said, "Oh, people can come up with statistics to prove anything. Fourteen percent of people know that." Surprisingly, Homer's cartoonish remark has some validity to the discussion that is taking place between you as the reader and me as the author. These statistics were not written on paper so that they could be stored up for the reader to recall during conversations at happy hour or as answers to random trivia dialogues during morning commutes. The purpose of these data is to spur on action. It's a simple concept, but one that escapes thousands upon thousands of educators who participate in professional development workshops or yearly book clubs. (If you are reading this as part of your yearly book club, then forgive my last comment.) The dynamic change that is taking place within successful No Excuses Universities is happening not because of theory but instead because of practice.

Albert Einstein once said, "The world is a dangerous place, not because of those who do evil, but because of those who look on and do nothing." Such is true when it comes to our world of education. We are living in a monumental time in which educators have greater access than ever to strategies and ideas that are proven to make a difference in the educational and social lives of students. Research proves many of these ideas and yet we seem to be stagnant as an industry. Public education in particular has become the finest scapegoat that exists when one wishes to cast blame for society's ills. Truth be told, in many ways it's been our own fault. But unlike those who seek to throw stones at enormous issues such as a lack of funding, massive educational bureaucracies, labor unions, etc., I believe the problem is far less complicated. Our problem is that we wait too long to act.

At the beginning of Los Pen's college-readiness initiative, we found no examples of similar work taking place at the elementary school level. In fact, we were told by many both inside our district and beyond that "college readiness is a high school matter." Some of our nation's largest college-support endeavors only begin promoting college readiness at the junior high school level. This in my opinion is not a knock against the fine work that is taking place within those organizations, but more so a representation of a lack of initiative on the parts of elementary school educators. For years, elementary educators have allowed a top-down approach in regard to meaningful school reform. While high schools and junior high schools introduce students to an increasingly rigorous curriculum, elementary staff members have been seen by many as the "nurturers" whose first job is to teach students the "love of learning." What a crock! Most elementary school teachers would agree that this depiction of K-6 work could not be further from reality. In fact, most educators from all levels recognize that one of the hardest things to do within our field is to teach a five, six, or seven-year-old how to read. Unfortunately, as confident as we are in the importance of our role, we act with a meekness that marginalizes our credibility and stifles our influence. Knowing this, how must educators, especially those at the elementary level, take their place at the table of reform in order to create massive change? The answer quite simply is to ***act***.

Elementary educators must never underestimate the power that they have in changing the life of a child. Furthermore, they must never assume that it is too early to begin making that change. But change cannot take place without the action of a practitioner. Sure, in our hearts and even in our words we profess the belief in our ability to change lives, especially when speaking to parents or community members. But how many times have you known someone to act contrary to this belief on your own campus? Go ahead; think of the name of a teacher, administrator, or classified employee at your school who "talks the talk" in public but lacks the deeds that reinforce such a belief within the classroom. Talk without action and theory without practice is a killer for change and hence impedes the progress that is so desperately required to offer hope to a student in need. When we look at the data and are convinced that our cause is just (and it is), and we believe that our purpose is clear (and it is), then our job is to move forward with a tenacious spirit that is reflective of the importance of our mission. That mission, which is one that is all encompassing for transforming both a school's culture and a student's life, is that of college readiness. Whether you are a kindergarten teacher in the inner city of Los Angeles or an eighth-grade mathematics instructor in a suburb outside of Chicago, it's time to take your seat at the table. If you agree that education is the best way to a successful life, and for our most at-risk students is the only realistic means to escape the grip of poverty, then it's time for action. The first course of action is deciding upon a clear understanding and definition of the term ***college readiness***.

What is College Readiness?

If we can trace the root of our downfall, which is seen so clearly in the data provided thus far, why is it that we continue to have an abundance of public schools failing in our country? Many would lead you to believe that the answer to this question is so complex that it would take decades for Ivy League scholars to determine. It is my contention, however, that the answer comes down to a lack of focus from the time children step foot as kindergarteners, and sometimes even earlier, in our schools.

Everywhere you go, you will find a plethora of schools that are thematic in nature. Many schools are "tech" schools that focus their attention on exposing their students to the latest technology that exists. Other schools plant their flag on the subject of writing, making sure that everything done in the school has some kind of a writing focus. Still others align themselves directly with a series of programs with the hope that mandated unity will create long-term literacy results for their students. While these schools have their fair share of benefits and often find ways to produce immediate academic results for students, they fail to reinforce what I believe to be the most important long-term theme needed by children today, that of college readiness.

In my work with schools across the country, I spend much of my time battling a misperception held by some of our most talented educators. From teachers, to principals, to superintendents and other high-ranking district officials, I continually hear talk about the importance of promoting college readiness in high school. This discussion, and the numerous goals presented around this idea, is as fundamentally flawed as anything that exists today in public education. The idea that college readiness begins in high school is as senseless as the idea that parenting begins when children become teenagers. In fact, I would suggest that there is no such thing as "college readiness" at high school; rather, there is only "college prep." To the outside observer, these may appear to be synonymous; however, I assure you that they are both quite different.

College prep concepts can be found in many schools, typically beginning in sixth grade and moving up through high school. Schools offer college prep classes in an effort to expose students to more challenging courses that present an academic rigor parallel to that which they may find at the university level. And while this concept is an excellent one for students who are determined to pursue a college degree someday, it does nothing for students who may lack the fundamental understanding of the benefits of higher education. In addition, because participation in these courses is often an expectation of those living in upper- to middle-class households, students of poverty are all too often left out of the mix because they don't receive the same encouragement to enroll in such classes from their parents. Because of this, they are solely dependent on what we as educators promote to them in our individual schools. Though many educators would dispute the fact, our track record on endorsing the possibility of college for every child is one that is not supported by the data mentioned thus far. Let's take a look at a typical scenario.

Arturo and his family moved to the United States from Mexico when he was four years old. Immediately he was enrolled in school, where he began to learn English at an early age. His skills in reading and math became average as he left elementary school and attended junior high. Arturo's parents were proud of his progress and found themselves dependent on his grasp of the English language as they themselves had failed to learn how to read, write, or speak English with any kind of fluency. As he entered high school, Arturo had become the only member of his family to be educated beyond the eighth grade. In sitting down with his school counselor, he was presented with two options. The first was to participate in college prep classes that would not only expose him to a challenging curriculum, but also bring the possibility in some cases of earning college credit. The second option was to participate in the high school diploma track that would prove successful as long as he received a "D" or better in every course. Arturo thought about the challenge of the college prep courses and understood that while his grades were average, these courses sounded just too challenging. In addition, he believed that college was a place where "rich kids" went, and because he lived in very humble circumstances, he thought his chances were slim. It didn't take long for Arturo to decide on the diploma track. After four years, with great praise from his teaches and incredible pride on the part of his parents, Arturo graduated from high school. He soon found that the diploma he had earned was not exactly a key to long-term financial stability. Over the years, he worked several different jobs in order to make ends meet. Before he knew it, Arturo had a family of his own. In spite of his hard work in high school and the diploma that he proudly hung in a frame on his wall, the cycle was about to continue all over again with his own children.

Stories like these are all too common when we operate with a flawed understanding and belief that college prep is actually college readiness. College readiness begins the moment students step foot in an elementary school. No Excuses Universities live by the true definition of college readiness:

"College readiness is not the idea that every student will go to college. It is the idea that every student deserves the opportunity to be prepared to enroll in college if they so choose to attend. Furthermore, beginning in elementary school, it is the responsibility of educators to make this concept come to life for each student regardless of their academic or social background."

With this definition, it's now time to learn the details that will help you create a college readiness revolution of your own. As you read, you will discover practical strategies and ideas that can be implemented immediately at your school site or throughout your district. I urge you to go forward with an action-oriented passion that seeks not to make changes for students one, two, or three years from now, but for the children in your classrooms today. As Super Bowl champion coach Steve Mariucci once said, "I never wear a watch, because I always know it's NOW!" With that spirit, let's get started.

Chapter Thirteen

Theory to Practice

Items for Articulation

- ❑ How effective are your team and staff meetings? Do the conversations that take place at these meetings spur individuals on to action?
- ❑ Think of the behaviors that make for a productive or unproductive meeting. Which behaviors should be reinforced to create success? Which behaviors should be reduced to stifle negativity?

Items for Action

- ❑ As a school, find consensus to create your definition of the term "college readiness." After doing so, display this definition in prominent areas of the school in order to ensure understanding by all stakeholders.

Chapter Fourteen

Key Concepts

"People often say that motivation doesn't last. Well, neither does bathing—that's why we recommend it daily."

— Zig Ziglar

1

"Powerful symbolism" is used to market a college readiness message through flags, signage, spirit wear, and school-wide incentive programs.

2

When done right, marketing can make a school's purpose come to life.

3

No Excuses University schools partner with universities throughout the world in an effort to bring the reality of college to life for students.

4

As part of a comprehensive effort to introduce students to college, elementary schools focus on four-year universities, middle schools introduce the concept of community colleges, and trade schools are brought into the mix in high school.

Marketing the Message

Sometimes the mother of invention communicates in very unconventional ways. For Bill Bowerman, that could not have been truer. In the early 1970s, this very successful University of Oregon track coach was in search of innovative methods to make his athletes faster. One day while working in his garage, he concocted a liquid urethane solution and poured it into his wife's waffle iron. What resulted was an interlocking square pattern that was perfect for the bottom of an athletic shoe. This creative idea that began in one man's workshop has become the most recognizable athletic shoe and apparel company in the world. Named for the Greek goddess of victory, Nike is one of America's greatest success stories. Its swoosh logo has become as recognizable as the McDonald's golden arches and Disneyland's Mickey Mouse. As equally impressive as the genesis of NIKE, Inc. is the way in which this company markets its message. From the moment Nike employees are hired, they begin to learn about the history of the organization. Described as "internal branding" in the January 2000 issue of Fast Company Magazine, the Nike storytelling process teaches all new hires the importance of knowing their roots as well as the value of consistently living by their mission. What others see simply as a little white "swoosh," Nike employees see as an icon that was once sold out of the back of a car by co-founder Phil Knight. The words "Just Do It®" may act as an unforgettable catch phrase that prompts you and me to exercise more, but to the 30,000-plus members of Nike, it represents a call to outside-the-box thinking. While Nike understands the importance of spending millions on marketing their product to those outside their headquarters, they know that such spending becomes futile if they do not take the time to cultivate believers within.

The same holds true for today's schools. Many administrators are constantly in search of the right school reform book that will change the culture and solve the ills that have existed within their schools for years. As an author of such a book, I certainly would not knock the value of this pursuit. In tandem with the right guide, I recommend using techniques successful in the world of marketing. It has been my experience that the latter is rarely pursued. Unfortunately, this has resulted in short-lived success for many outstanding school initiatives. This was a lesson learned early on by my staff and me as we created the No Excuses University.

Why Is Marketing So Important?

The Super Bowl is played every year in order to crown the champion team of the NFL. The games are often exciting, the competitors some of the world's best athletes. All this and what do we watch? The commercials. In 2008, the Fox Network reportedly received $2.7 million for each 30-second commercial aired during the Super Bowl. This astonishing figure pales in comparison to the yearly amount spent on marketing food to children. In 2008, the Federal Trade Commission reported that $1.6 billion was spent on marketing food and drinks to children 17 and under. Whether a one-day event or a consistent year-long campaign, marketing like this has resulted in millions attending movies, buying cereal, or purchasing electronics that collectively generate trillions in profits for U.S. companies. The lesson: marketing works!

From car companies that sell a new brand of SUV, to a principal who sells an idea to his staff, the premise of marketing is the same. When done right, marketing primarily does two things. First, it inspires people. For a company, it inspires consumers to spend money. For a school, it inspires educators and students to act differently. Second, marketing creates a symbol that stands for something and prompts a specific thought. As we see with Nike, their powerful swoosh logo makes us think of sports or maybe exercise. For students who attend a No Excuses University, our logo reminds them that their paramount goal is to graduate from college. Many would argue that marketing is simply a form of brainwashing. While there may be some truth to this, I would suggest that marketing is more about the power to persuade people. Granted, it can certainly be used to encourage individuals to make poor decisions. However, it can also be used for good. The work of promoting college readiness to students is, at its core, noble. When you blend this nobility with a commitment to market a college readiness message in schools, you get what we refer to as *powerful symbolism*.

What Is Powerful Symbolism?

Powerful symbolism is the visible marketing of a school's number one goal. In short, it makes a school's purpose come to life. While this symbolism may express many ideas, such as character traits or academic expectations, the message that ties them all together is the same. For some schools, that message may be the exposure to the arts, technology, or a thematic focus on literacy. However, we find that the best, all-encompassing purpose is that of promoting college readiness to all students. The beauty of this college readiness focus

UNM

WE'RE COLLEGE BOUND

MICHIGAN STATE

Hello, Brutus!
Hello, Big Jay
Hello Big Al!

KINDERGARTEN BEAVERS
OSU
OREGON STATE

We're going to college!
University of Denver
Michigan State
PATHWAYS TO SUCCESS

COLLEGE-
BOUND
SCHOOLS

is found in how well it lends itself to marketing powerful symbolism.

Powerful symbolism unites teachers, excites parents, and motivates students. It can be implemented on any campus across the country no matter the demographics of a school or budget of a district. Unlike other reform efforts, the implementation of powerful symbolism can be affordable and swift. As you read of the many ways that No Excuses Universities expose their students to powerful symbolism, ask yourself, "How can we modify these ideas to meet the needs of our school's purpose?" If your purpose is in line with a mission to promote college readiness for all, don't hesitate to take advantage of the ideas listed throughout this chapter. As you read, you will find the letter E for elementary, M for middle or junior high school, and H for high school placed next to each concept. These indicate the levels where more than twenty examples of powerful symbolism are currently flourishing at No Excuses Universities across the nation.

E **Classroom Bulletin Boards:** One of the greatest experiences for students is the creation of a college bulletin board within their classroom. Classroom teachers work with their students to find facts about their particular university that spark interest and fuel continuous conversation. The best boards are those that are always changing throughout the year as a result of new information found by students, parents, and teachers or sent to the classroom by representatives of the university.

E M H **College-Bound Bulletin Boards:** Many schools have found that motivating students about college is as easy as a map, a few pictures, pushpins, and some string. The process could not be simpler. Gather individual pictures from every staff member who has earned a college degree. Post them on a centrally located bulletin board in a hallway, office, or school entrance with heavy foot traffic. Place a U.S. map in the center of the board and have teachers connect a string from their pictures to the locations of the universities from which they earned their degrees. You will be amazed at how many conversations take place in front of boards like these.

E M H **Monday College-Bound Gear:** Most schools offer spirit wear with the school slogan or logo printed on the front or back for students to purchase. When it comes to the promotion of college readiness, however, there are three simple changes that can be made in order to create powerful symbolism. First, create t-shirts with a college readiness focus that markets your message. Second, ask all students, staff, and parents to wear their shirts every Monday in an effort to set the stage for the week ahead. Finally, ensure that every student receives a shirt no matter his or her socioeconomic background. The value of having all students display powerful symbolism and wear their shirts on the same day far outweighs the cost of purchasing t-shirts for those who cannot afford to do so on their own. ***(Please note that only schools that have officially been accepted into the No Excuses University™ Network of Schools and received written consent are allowed to use the trademarked No Excuses University name and logo. Find out more in Chapter 19.)***

E M **Friday University Gear:** End your week by encouraging students to wear the apparel supporting the university that their classroom has adopted. Some classrooms that have been adopted by their university may be fortunate enough to have shirts donated to them, while other classes may have students make their own spirit wear as part of an art project. Still others may simply ask students to wear the school colors. Wearing university apparel every Friday is another display of powerful college symbolism that sends a school community into the weekend with high spirits.

E M H **Character Traits:** The promotion of college readiness must be done in such a way that focuses not only on the academic skills necessary for a student to be successful, but also on the life skills needed to make wise decisions. Focusing on specific

Where are you going to college? Dream Big!
COLORADO BUFFALOS
KANSAS JAYHAWKS
Duke
WAKE FOREST
(3) LUNGES
NEU
no excuses
Dove Academy
A&M

GO
TROJANS
USC
TROJANS
USC

TEXAS TECH
5
TEXAS
TECH
RED RAIDERS

GO
U
UTES!

ISU
ISU
5
GO CANES

character traits helps to do just that. The key is to have schools choose traits that are wide-reaching and comprehensive in nature. With so many traits to choose from, some schools get carried away, selecting a dozen or more. In the end, the quantity produces little quality in learning; students become overwhelmed with too many traits. Within the No Excuses University Network, I have found our Bridge to College™ Program to be essential. This program, founded by Michael Josephson, focuses on six traits that are broad enough to include every major value that one can think of, but specific enough to act as a springboard for meaningful conversations between students and staff. Learn more about this terrific program by visiting www.charactercounts.org.

E M **Murals:** Experience shows us that hallways and playgrounds are the most likely locations for behavior problems with students. Because of this, many schools have spent time, and in some cases money, to paint murals in strategic locations that remind students of the high academic and social expectations that we have of them. If your school does not have the resources or time to make this happen right away, do what many schools have done by making this a yearly promotion gift to the school from fifth, sixth, or eighth graders. This value-added philosophy will create a substantial amount of powerful symbolism in just a few short years.

E M H **Signage:** As a successful Title I school, Los Peñasquitos Elementary receives hundreds of visitors a year from all over the country. Over and over, people describe how they "felt differently" the moment they stepped foot on our campus. This is thanks in large part to the signage that is displayed at every turn. When visitors drive up to the school, they notice our large No Excuses University logo. Upon walking through the office, they read the Los Pen Pledge, which is painted on the wall: "We are committed to creating a school that knows no limits to the academic success of each student." When they look up, they see carefully selected slogans that promote our belief in students and their ability to attend college. Don't get me wrong; I'm not suggesting that you make your school walls look like buildings in Times Square, but I do believe that strategically placed signage can stimulate the physical environment of any school. From inspirational quotes in the hallways of elementary schools to tote boards that tally the amount students have earned in college scholarships at our high school campuses, signage is easily adaptable and highly motivational.

E **Mascot Books:** In 2003, Naren and Aimee Aryal founded Mascot Books Publishing. This company creates and publishes books that tell the story of universities through the eyes of their mascots. To an elementary school librarian, this is a godsend. It provides exciting literature that is aligned with a school's college readiness purpose. Just as many librarians have experienced, you will find that these books are tough to keep on the shelves. Visit www.mascotbooks.com for more information.

E M H **Kickoff Assemblies:** Let's face it—shaping a culture dedicated to promoting college readiness for all is a major shift for most schools. The schools that choose to ignore the gravity of this transformation are the schools that are destined to make this into a one-year endeavor. If you are to go about making college readiness the heart of your school culture, you need to begin by giving it the attention that it deserves. Hold a kickoff assembly for all students and parents that explicitly delivers new expectations, explains the rationale behind the symbolism seen on campus, and inspires students through the use of data that explains why they should live by a new commitment to learning.

E M H **Student Goals:** No matter what level you teach, goals can be a conduit for success. As early as kindergarten, we teach our NEU students to set goals alongside their teacher. As they enter into middle school, those academic goals are transformed into personal BHAGs (Big Hairy Audacious Goals). Larry Elder once said, "A goal without a plan is just a wish." Unless we begin to foster such planning at an early age, the dream of college will never become a reality.

E M H **College Fairs:** Before we take students on field trips to college campuses, we bring the college campus to them through college fairs. From elementary to high school, our students are exposed to guest speakers who share their college experiences and how their degrees have helped them to pursue a fulfilling career. Students rotate between these lectures, as well as a variety of college readiness activities, as if they were a student on any college campus across America, changing classes. When volunteers from universities are hard to find, students can design college displays and pretend to be college recruiters as their peers tour multi-purpose rooms or gyms that have been transformed into convention-like surroundings.

E M H **Hanging of Degrees:** When was the last time you walked into a doctor's office and didn't see a degree hanging on the wall? In contrast, when was the last time you saw the degree of a teacher hanging somewhere prominent in the classroom? Most students don't realize that their own teachers have put in five, six, and even seven years of college on their path to becoming a teacher. It's our job to let them know this by taking pride in our hard work.

E M H **Morning Meetings:** You get only one chance to set the tone for the day. Because of this, many NEU schools participate in morning meetings that prep students for the schedule ahead as well as reinforce appropriate work habits and academic expectations and explicitly model character. Students of poverty need this support from an early age. Older students benefit from the relationships that are built through teaching and discussing what other educators simply assume is already known. An example of what this looks like at the elementary school level can be found in the appendix.

M H **Promoting the Success of Alumni:** All too often, we in education focus on the half-empty portion of the glass. This distracts us from spotlighting success stories that are both inspirational and motivating to our students. I have seen two great examples of how schools have sought to inspire the students of today by telling the stories of their alumni. Some of our middle schools have taken the effort to paint the name, university, and graduation year of individual alumni on the interior bricks of their hallways. Another high school has developed a complete marketing campaign that shows off the talents of their alumni through posters that read "Tascosa Produces ..." One poster might tell the story of a nurse and another a mechanical engineer. Each poster tells a short story about the alumni, where they went to college, what they are doing with their degree now, and details that include the average salary and employment rate for their particular profession.

H **Celebrating Acceptance Letters/National Signing Day:** Today, high school athletes are celebrated for which university they will attend during National Signing Day. This coverage, which often takes the lead on ESPN, draws attention to dozens of high school seniors as athletic prospects but fails to spotlight the tens of thousands of students who will be attending colleges in the fall based on their academic potential. NEU high schools take the time to post acceptance letters in the hallways, use tote boards to tally scholarships earned, and display the names of students and the universities that they will be attending on the school marquee.

E M **Dress for Success Day:** Every year, NEU elementary and middle schools choose a "Dress for Success Day" in an effort to express the importance of "looking the part." While many students may complain about the requirement to wear a tie or a skirt, deep down they feel a sense of pride in looking professional. To no one's surprise, their actions tend to follow as well!

H **Day in the Life of a College Student:** Season two of *The Cosby Show* aired an episode titled "Theo's Holiday." In the show, Theo, the teenage son, brags about how he plans to live extravagantly when he turns eighteen and can be on his own. While he's at school, the family hatches a plan to role-play a real-world experience for Theo when he gets home. During his 24-hour experience, he soon finds that it's not easy to survive without a job, bank account, and quality education. NEU high schools offer a similar experience as they provide a day in the life of a college student that involves students in an emergent experience that is entertaining, relevant, and revealing at the same time.

H **Posting of Relevance:** The idea of educational relevance is very important to our students, especially in high school. Because of this, many schools post the relevance of each lesson on the board so that students can make a connection between what they are learning and how it will help them in college and in life.

H **Technology:** It's time to embrace the role that social media can play in inspiring our students. Today, every high school student in America has a cell phone. In most cases, it's a smart phone. Because of this, we place QR codes throughout the school related to higher education. Some codes can be found on a poster that tells the students about a specific college, while others are placed prominently in a high-traffic area with nothing more than the QR code, which creates intrigue that eventually brings the students to a website of our choosing. Whether this approach is informational or a source for a technology scavenger hunt of sorts, we desire to embrace technology that has the power to engage our students.

E **College-Themed Incentive Programs:** Having an all-encompassing theme like college readiness makes it easy for schools to shift their powerful symbolism focus without having to do away with the successful programs that already exist on site. For example, there are many schools that participate in reading incentive programs. Los Pen used to organize a yearly program titled "Reading Olympics" in which students were encouraged to read a certain number of books in order to earn a gold, silver, or bronze medal. Upon the creation of the No Excuses University, we changed the name of this program to "Read Your Way to College" and instead awarded students bachelor's, master's, and Ph.D. awards. While we changed the name and the awards, we didn't change the focus of the program. Examples like these can be found in the numerous programs that exist in our schools today. Whether you make a change from "Olympic Field Day" to "College Field Day," or replace a field trip to a museum with a field trip to a college campus, the theme of college readiness is easily incorporated.

E M H **University Adoptions:** If I had to choose one strategy to promote powerful symbolism that affects students at every level, it would be for every classroom to adopt a different university. The process of selecting universities can be done in a variety of ways but in the end should ensure a wide exposure to many universities and colleges across the country. No school should have two classrooms that represent the same university, as the idea is to present as many options to students as possible. Schools are encouraged to garner the participation of the office staff, librarian, custodian, and all specialists to join in this process as well. Each staff member should select a university he or she would like to represent. Once every staff member has done so, college flags or banners should be hung outside their doors. This visual message conveys a powerful statement about your school's purpose and excites students, parents, and staff. This excitement, blended with the creation of the six exceptional systems, has the potential to produce sustainable positive academic and social success for all students.

In connection with marketing and powerful symbolism, establishing an affiliation with a university can grow into building strong community support. Creating partnerships with colleges and universities helps our schools move beyond the window dressing with a variety of strategies that are practical and simple for any school to develop as part of their own college readiness initiative.

Partnering with Universities

The creation of the No Excuses University endeavor prompted immediate interest from educators throughout the country. Phone calls and emails from those in search of information became a daily occurrence for us. Principals contacted me seeking strategies to help them begin the process at their schools. Teachers asked how they too could create meaningful partnerships with universities. On many occasions, it was the universities themselves that called to offer support. The response was overwhelmingly positive, which is why I was so stunned one day when I received an odd request from a gentleman named Craig.

It didn't take me long to sense his frustration. Immediately after I introduced myself on the phone, Craig voiced his distaste for what he was viewing on the Los Pen website. He said, "I went online today and looked at your website. After about five seconds, I was disgusted with what I saw on the home page."

Worried that I had somehow overlooked a glaring mistake and expecting the worst, I said, "Please, tell me what's wrong and I'd be happy to fix it."

"On your website is a picture of three really cute kids. Unfortunately, they're wearing the most offensive t-shirts I have ever seen in my life."

"Really?" I asked.

"Yes. Those kids are wearing shirts from the University of Michigan. I'm from Michigan State. How do I get that blue and gold off your site and Michigan State green on instead?"

After a huge sigh of relief, I laughed and said, "Hey man, if you want Michigan State represented, you need to come and adopt one of our classrooms."

Sure enough, Craig showed up a couple of weeks later with brand new t-shirts for Mrs. Gentry's third-grade class. He spoke to the students about his experiences, taught them the Michigan State fight song, and encouraged them to keep working hard. It was clear that his visit not only inspired the students, but excited him as well.

Before departing, Craig dropped by my office, placed his hand on my shoulder, and said, "OK, Mr. Lopez. What do I need to do to get you to stack the Michigan State class with the smartest kids in the school next year?"

I asked, "Why would I want to do that, Craig?"

"Because I want Michigan State to beat Michigan in everything they do."

I jokingly made an appeal for his understanding. "Michigan State is third grade; Michigan is second grade. I love your competitive spirit, but I think you need to relax a bit."

The partnerships that No Excuses University classrooms have built with hundreds of college representatives are as exciting as the one that Craig has forged with Mrs. Gentry's third-grade class. From Boise State football players dropping off a sample of their bright blue "Smurf Turf" at a school in Los Angeles, to the Illinois State University mascot "Reggie the Redbird" visiting an NEU campus in Chicago, the stories of successful partnerships are plentiful. Such exposure to tangible models of college makes the concept real to students and provides a source of encouragement for kids, allowing them to set their sights high on the goal of earning a university degree.

"The kids feel like they are part of something," said third-grade NEU teacher Debra Baadilla in a recent *Press-Enterprise* article. "They all know when they are going to college and what year they're going to graduate."

With dozens of No Excuses Universities participating as part of our official network of schools, we have been able to learn a lot about how to create beneficial partnerships between colleges and classrooms. As you seek to open the doors to collaboration with colleges and universities, take a look at the answers to some of the most commonly asked questions regarding university partnerships.

Are selections based on whether or not a teacher or staff member is an alumnus of a particular university?

No. We have found that a high percentage of schools have educators who have received degrees from the same university. Had Los Pen used this as a rule for teachers, San Diego State University flags would be hanging on the outside of about half of our doors. But because of the spirit that is associated with being a graduate from a specific university, we always let alumni choose their own schools whenever possible.

What do you do if two people want to select the same university?

Flip a coin or play rock-paper-scissors. Yes, I'm serious. I have heard stories of teachers getting into arguments over the selection of a university. This completely defeats the purpose. Make your selections and then move on to the important work of promoting college readiness for all.

Should we select community colleges and trade schools?

The view of No Excuses Universities is that elementary schools should focus on promoting four-year universities, middle and junior high schools should add community colleges into the mix, and high schools should blend in the possibility of trade schools as part of their support of students. To suggest to five- or six-year-olds that they should think about community college or trade school as an option is not only playing the role of fortuneteller—it makes unfair suggestions about their abilities to succeed at the same level as many of their peers. The next chapter will offer the details of how to bridge the transition of conversations from four-year universities to trade schools through what we call "The Success Equation."

Must a university adopt your class before you can adopt them?

After staff members select a university to represent, the goal is to get that same university to adopt their classroom back. That said, it is not a prerequisite for choosing your university.

What Makes a Good Partnership?

A quality partnership between a school and a college or university is one that is beneficial to both parties. Universities love partnerships because of the publicity and the ability to spread the word about the benefits of their campuses to future students. Teachers and students love the partnership because of the free college gear and visits from alumni. I would suggest that teachers first seek to build a collaborative link between a university representative and themselves. Calling or writing with the sole purpose of getting "stuff" is likely a turn-off and defeats the purpose. The best partnerships are those that are built over time.

Kerri Kutzner, a teacher in San Diego, began the partnership between her fourth-grade class and the University of Nebraska simply by sharing what NEU was all about. She corresponded with the university and was open-ended about the variety of ways that a partnership could help. What began as a box of pencils and information packets about the university has become something much bigger. To date, her students have received t-shirts, pennants, inspirational letters from staff members, signed books by famous alumni, and surprise visits from football players. While this was never the end goal, Kerri's continuous partnership with the university has grown in such a way that the employees of the university are as excited as the kids are about the process. Partnerships are made over the course of several months, not several weeks. Be patient as you go forward. In the event that you are unable to grasp the interest of a particular university, select a different one. With more than 4,000 colleges and universities across the country, there are more than enough to choose from.

How can we encourage universities to become partners?

The first step in creating a partnership is to inform universities about the work that you are doing. We chose to send letters to alumni presidents who lived in our area. Creating a partnership with alumni organizations is key; they are the most capable of supporting your needs. Some schools and classrooms have successfully partnered directly with a university, but those partnerships tend to be ones that involved local universities and colleges. While I would never discourage people from trying to find representatives at all levels, I would suggest you save direct university contacts as your last resort. My hope is that the NEU model will gain influence in the future and in turn garner more direct support from universities. Until then, it is best to disperse our requests in a variety of ways so as not to overwhelm any one sector of the university system.

Once you have selected your contact, a simple letter or email is always the best avenue to introduce your interest in a partnership. (A sample can be found in Appendix B.) Remember, as described in Chapter 13, only schools that have officially joined the NEU Network of Schools can use the trademarked NEU name and logo.

Which universities are the best to choose?

I couldn't be happier with the feedback that I have received from universities that are partnering with our NEU endeavor. Their generosity is beyond any initial hopes that I had when this work began. A shining example of that support can be found in the generous involvement of the Wake Forest Alumni Association. After experiencing a terrific partnership with one of our NEU classes in Hemet, California, a representative contacted me directly asking how the university could expand its support. Because of this, numerous classrooms throughout the nation are now experiencing the joy of learning about this terrific university and the options that are available to students who attend. Partnerships like these are not unique. Rather than suggest which specific universities a teacher should pursue, I would like to describe the types of universities that classrooms should seek to create partnerships with.

The work of exposing students to colleges and universities is one of the most enjoyable features of the NEU model. However, you should always be aware of the end message that you wish to send to students. No Excuses Universities have a plan to expose students to the right opportunities at the appropriate times. For elementary schools, we focus on promoting four-year colleges and universities. These universities are typically selected because of easy access to college flags, banners, and apparel, or due to a personal connection that educators have as alumni. The selection of four-year universities at the elementary level is purposeful. It is too early for us to suggest that students have any limitations on their potential to earn bachelor's, master's, or even doctoral degrees when they grow up. Might some of them take the community college track? Of course, and of course there is nothing wrong with them doing so. But when it comes to setting early expectations for students, you always want to place the bar as high as possible. The statistics, as you will see, show a much higher completion rate when students strive for a four-year degree.

When it comes to middle school or junior high, we encourage schools to begin featuring several community colleges throughout their campus. Why wait until middle school? Because the data support such a decision. In 2007, USA Today reported that only 51 percent of all students who enrolled in a community college for the first year returned for a second year. This is far less than the 69 percent of four-year university freshmen who returned for their sophomore year. In addition, among the community college students who did return, only 36 percent received an associate's or bachelor's degree after six years of attendance. The message sent regarding community college at any level should be one that focuses on utilizing this route as a means to a four-year degree. Junior high and middle school is the best time to help create this message.

The issue of trade schools comes up quite often. As a son of a blue-collar worker, I am fully aware of the ability of individuals to attend trade schools and make an excellent living for themselves. These people support their families and make up a section of our population that should be respected and appreciated. In no way should we thumb our noses at trade schools. That said, the time for such discussion should not take place until students enter high school. Five-year-olds who want to enter a welding school can make that decision when they are fifteen or sixteen just as easily. Should they decide to go this route after several years of information about the greater benefits of a college education, then we can support them with the knowledge that we exposed them to every possibility. The idea of attending college is one that must be planned out for many years, while the decision to attend a trade school can be made within a much shorter time span. This method is the safest way for us to keep all doors of possibility open for students from all types of backgrounds.

What is the impact of college partnerships on parents?

If you had asked me during the birth of NEU what my number

one concern would be in promoting college readiness, I would have shared my concern for how the parents would respond. I was worried that parents without college degrees would take offense and challenge my leadership. Boy was I wrong. In the many years that I have been involved with this endeavor, I have had only two negative opinions from parents. One of those opinions came from a wealthy parent who wasn't frustrated by the fact that we were discussing college, but instead was angry that we were allowing all of the students to participate. I guess she would rather that we only provide the opportunity to the most "gifted" kids in the school.

Loons like this parent aside, I cannot begin to count how many parents have come up to me and said, "Thank you for sharing this message with my child, one that I was not credible enough to deliver to them myself." The support has been overwhelming. The parents have just as much fun portraying the college spirit as the students do. On any given Monday or Friday, parents are just as likely to have NEU or college gear on as their children. When college football or basketball season rolls around, parents are more engaged than ever as they root for a particular university right beside their kids. This creates a unifying spirit, but more importantly brings students and parents together in ways that benefit the home environment as much as it does the school surroundings. No story exemplifies this better than one that involved a young first-grade boy and his grandmother.

The only son of Iranian immigrants, Navid was a first grader at Los Pen who actively sought to honor his parents by working hard in school. One Monday morning, I noticed Navid hopping up and down on one leg as a result of what appeared to be an injury over the weekend. After watching him struggle to make it from one end of the campus to the other, I called him to the nurse's office to find out what had happened. Navid, wearing his No Excuses University t-shirt, winced as he sat down on a chair.

"What happened?" I asked.

He said he had badly sprained his ankle while playing outside. When I asked if he had seen a doctor, he answered, "Yes. He told me that it would get better in a few days. I'm supposed to stay off of my ankle until Wednesday."

Proud of his tenacity to fight through the pain, I inquired, "If the doctor told you to stay off of your ankle, why did you come to school today?"

Immediately he exclaimed, "No Excuses, Mr. Lopez!"

As touched as I was by his loyal commitment to our motto, I explained to Navid that a doctor's recommendations trump those of a principal. I told him that I would need to call his grandmother, who took care of him during the day, and have her pick him up.

Navid's grandmother, who arrived within minutes wearing her No Excuses University t-shirt, came into the office with a concerned look on her face. Speaking only Farsi, she pointed her finger at Navid as if to scold him. After some back and forth conversation took place within their native language, I asked, "Navid, what is your grandmother saying?"

He said, "Mr. Lopez, she wants to know if it would be OK for her to carry me around school all day so that I don't miss class."

This kind of commitment by a grandparent is the definition of the effect that No Excuses University has on the families within our network.

What do we do after we have created partnerships?

As shared in previous chapters, there is an abundance of options to pursue when it comes to promoting colleges and universities. From each classroom creating a college chant, to grade levels visiting college campuses, the continued exposure to all things college is key. Many NEU schools have developed yearly college fairs that bring in local universities and guest speakers. This provides a wonderful opportunity for students to learn not only about their own adopted university, but also other universities as well. Highly collaborative classes that work together will certainly develop several ideas that take your partnerships to the next level. As you work toward your students developing a greater understanding about college, don't forget to focus also on what it takes to get there. The older students get, the more involved you should be in sharing the steps that one must take to apply, enroll, and qualify for acceptance into the university system.

Dr. David Conley's book *College Knowledge: What It Really Takes for Students to Succeed and What We Can Do to Get Them Ready*, while written with a secondary focus, is a wealth of information for parents and teachers seeking to set their students up for success. "Many students are unable to attend college not because of their grades, but instead because they have not been able to navigate through this very challenging system," Dr. Conley said in a recent interview with me. Because many young adults do not know the difference between two- and four-year colleges, he said, "It is the job of the adults to make this clear."

Dr. Conley's research has created a path for many students, especially high school students, to follow. His declaration that "educators and other adults have a profound impact on the success rate of college acceptance" aligns directly with our work with the No Excuses University. The partnerships between classrooms and universities spotlighted in this chapter provide insight into the possibilities that exist when post-secondary educators align their passions with K-12 staff members. The feedback I have received from university representatives convinces me that they are both willing and eager to lend a hand. With the successful collaborative relationships being built between NEU schools and university campuses today, I can only imagine where our movement will be several years from now.

None of what I have written about in this chapter is difficult to achieve. In fact, I'm often told by teachers and leaders that it is one of the most enjoyable steps that their school has taken as they transform into an institution focused on college readiness for all. As you participate in marketing the message of college to your students, be aware that the simplicity of this act has the potential to divert you from the most important work of creating the six exceptional systems that are spotlighted in the previous chapters. As educators, we must guard against all of this becoming window-dressing. This responsibility falls solely on the shoulders of one group: the adults on campus.

Chapter Fourteen

Theory to Practice

☑

Items for Articulation

- ❑ This chapter provides numerous examples of powerful symbolism that can exist on a school campus. Which ideas could be implemented tomorrow? Which ones might take more time?
- ❑ How is your school currently displaying powerful symbolism? How might you make adjustments so that your school reflects a spirit of college readiness?
- ❑ When was the first time you visited a college campus? How did that visit influence your view of higher education?

Items for Action

- ❑ As a school, create a "powerful symbolism" committee with members from each grade level. The job of this committee is to:

1. Gather inspirational signage and post it throughout the school.

2. Work with grade-level teams to select individual universities for each classroom.

3. Design a college readiness t-shirt for every student to wear each Monday.

4. Work with your PTA, foundation, community supporters, and district to generate the funds necessary to purchase powerful symbolism items.

Decide upon a timeline for implementing each step. Most schools set a target of two to three months to have all of their powerful symbolism in place.

Chapter Fifteen

Key Concepts

"Ninety-nine percent of the failures come from people who have the habit of making excuses."

— George Washington Carver

1

Those who wait for everyone to "get on board" will be waiting forever.

2

Failure to achieve results is never an indictment of the naysayers; it's an indictment of the *closet optimists* who lack the will to take a stand.

3

The Six Cs of an NEU Professional ensure that the promotion of college readiness is more than window dressing.

4

Every adult on campus has a duty to explicitly model appropriate behavior and character in a unified way.

No Excuses Begins with the Staff

San Jacinto Elementary School is located in an impoverished area of Amarillo, Texas, where more than 95 percent of the students are considered economically disadvantaged. Every year, one third of the students, who live primarily in the low-income rental properties adjacent to the school, move outside the San Jacinto attendance area as new families move in. For years, this steady mobility rate came with a consistent level of academic student achievement that matched the basic expectations of most schools on a lower socioeconomic level. Test scores in all subjects were either near or at the bottom compared to other schools within the Amarillo School District. But the silver lining in the existence of San Jacinto Elementary had always been the school's tendency to employ warmhearted teachers who cared for children and were professional with each other. Still, in spite of the efforts of this collegial staff, the learning that took place was never enough to provide any kind of hope for children who were in desperate need of escaping a life of poverty.

In the eyes of many, San Jacinto was doing as well as could be expected. The community, while supportive as a whole, still focused primarily on the basic needs of students and families: food, clothing, school supplies, etc. A pervasive attitude existed both inside and outside of San Jacinto: "these students" simply had too many problems to even care about learning. There were, at times, pockets of excellence, but these successes were never sustainable from one classroom or grade level to the next. In 2005, state assessments revealed that 70 percent of the students were proficient in reading, 78 percent in writing, 60 percent in math, and 40 percent in science. While much better than many of the scores earned by similar schools, these marks still kept San Jacinto in danger of being labeled an "academically unacceptable" campus by the state of Texas.

Fed up with the status quo, Principal Doug Curry and three teachers from his school attended a two-day institute about the No Excuses University model. As the San Jacinto staff members heard about the steps necessary to create a *Culture of Universal Achievement*, develop exceptional systems, and foster a learning environment focused on promoting college readiness for all, one teacher turned to another and said, "We would have been elated if our kids simply made it through high school."

Principal Curry, along with his teachers, left the conference with a clear understanding that the expectations for their students were much too low. With a newfound excitement for teaching and a courageous spirit to influence their colleagues, these staff members presented the lessons learned from the conference, hoping that a rebirth would take place on the San Jacinto campus. Their passion captivated the rest of the staff and created a movement that day that surprised everyone. After brief discussions among teachers during their lunch break, every single staff member proclaimed their desire to adopt the tenets of the No Excuses University model. Amazed by the immediate positive feedback, Principal Curry challenged the staff to consider the possible ridicule that would come from others when a school known for poor academic results suddenly declared itself to be a new kind of "college preparatory" school. The staff's fearless response was simple: "Bring it on!"

Since that moment, San Jacinto has undergone a transformation that rivals that of any similar school in the country. Within one year of becoming an official NEU School, student academic results skyrocketed: 92 percent proficiency in reading, 92 percent in writing, 95 percent in math, and 90 percent in science. For the first time in the history of San Jacinto, the school achieved "recognized" status by the state of Texas. During its second year, San Jacinto built on those results and earned the highest ranking in the state of Texas: exemplary.

By the third year of becoming a No Excuses University, the transformation was so great that the community of Amarillo not only noticed but rushed to provide support. San Jacinto Elementary was asked to participate in the ACE program (Achievement through Commitment to Education). Funded by local philanthropists, ACE ensures that students in selected schools (find out more by visiting www.amarilloareafoundation.org) who maintain a specified grade point average, attendance in school, and level of acceptable behavior will have their entire college tuition paid for if they choose to attend the local two-year community college (Amarillo College) or local university (West Texas A&M). With support like this, there truly are no excuses! If the San Jacinto story ended there, it would no doubt be an inspiration to all. Thankfully, however, that's just the beginning of their story.

The students and staff from San Jacinto Elementary have inspired educators within their community to the point where some of the best ideas nationwide for NEU are developed within the city of Amarillo. With eleven No Excuses University Schools in Amarillo ISD, nearly

20 percent of all students in the district attend an NEU. In fact, students from San Jacinto Elementary feed into a NEU Middle School, Sam Houston, and then go on to attend the first-ever NEU High School in the nation, Tascosa High. What happens when they finish their education in high school? They have the opportunity to attend the first-ever NEU college of course, Amarillo College. Five years ago, students from San Jacinto Elementary School didn't know that the No Excuses University concept existed. Today, because four people attended an NEU Institute, it's ALL they know as part of an NEU Neighborhood.

This NEU Neighborhood takes students from elementary and even preschool and supports them all the way through college. Parents within this NEU Neighborhood are offered support through GED programs that take place on their campuses. Today, dozens of parents have completed a GED thanks to the support of NEU schools and are enrolled at the local college. The example that they are setting for their children is beyond anything that we could have ever imagined. Consider examples set by one single mom in particular. During a recent trip to San Jacinto Elementary, I noticed a woman wearing a bright t-shirt that, on the front, read, "My Kid's Going to College." When she turned around, I saw the back of the t-shirt said, "… and so am I!" That same mom came up and hugged me with gratitude for sharing the NEU message with her daughter's school. To this day, I have never experienced anything more rewarding as an educator.

The Closet Optimist

The San Jacinto Elementary example is reflective of stories that are common throughout the No Excuses University network of schools. Like those at most NEU schools, the staff at San Jacinto recognized the need to embrace reality, challenge results, and ask, "Can we provide a better education for our students than the one we are currently giving them?" The answer may not have been abundantly clear the moment they began their journey, but it certainly is today. The results earned by the San Jacinto staff were not a product of casting blame or even dwelling on the past. The results came from their humble act of acceptance and willingness to change.

In my work with schools, I've seen my share of educators who swear that they are up against insurmountable odds. Some insist that their job duties are too large and their paycheck is too small; yet the funny thing is … they keep showing up to work! The reality is that they will continue to show up every day, with no plans to change. Educators like these place a tremendous responsibility on students and parents and demand a level of excellence from others that they don't from themselves. Do you see the hypocrisy in their attitude? What a waste of time for them personally. What a tragedy for kids. In the midst of their complaints, many of these same individuals talk about their desire to be a part of something special but suggest that they are dependent on others to make that happen. At best we can chalk up their view of such school transformation as skewed; at worst it can be seen as *blatant excuse-making*. Through my research and personal experiences, I have found that not a single school turned around until ***individuals*** made the decision to cast aside their beliefs of what *should be* and focus on *what is*. I have shared with thousands of educators: It's all right to be jaded by politicians and bureaucracy, but never at the cost of becoming apathetic about the potential of a student. The best defense of such apathy is to maintain an outlook that is open to change.

As we know, change is never easy, especially in the world of education. In fact, change may be the single biggest cause of fear for those within our profession. Whether certificated or classified, employees not only fear change, they fight it. You and I could name a dozen adults with whom we have worked who have made a career out of fighting change. Many have become so sidetracked by this fight that teaching becomes secondary. In the end, some of our most needy students are left out in the cold as the perpetual cycle of poor instruction continues from one year to the next. As shameful as this small group of educators is, there is actually a group that I find more disappointing. I refer to them as the *closet optimists*.

Several years ago, I began working with a school just outside Seattle, Washington. Located in a small rural community, this elementary school experienced results of low scores that depleted the morale among staff as it entered into program improvement status. Wanting to learn more about their challenges, I studied the results of a recent survey taken by the staff. This survey, which consisted of just two simple questions, told me everything that I needed to know about the school. When asked, "Do you believe that all students can learn?" 90 percent of the staff answered, "Yes." When given question number two, "Do you believe that all of your colleagues believe that all students can learn?" 90 percent answered, "No." The analysis was simple. Ninety percent of this staff believed that they were among the minority of believers with the view that all students could learn. It was amazing! So much so, that I decided to candidly—and bluntly—share the results with them. My conversation went something like this:

"Today, I have great news for 90 percent of you, and very bad news for 10 percent of you. First, the good news: Ninety percent of you believe in the potential of your students. That is incredible and it is something that we are going to capitalize on. Now for the bad news: Ninety percent of you think that you are alone in this belief. I am guessing that this is because 10 percent of this staff does all the talking, voices all the viewpoints, and somehow believes that they represent the opinions of this staff. If that is the case and you are in that 10 percent, here is my message to you … ***shut up****. If on the other hand, however, you are in the critical mass of the 90 percent who does believe in the potential of all students and their innate ability to learn, then my message is one that is even stronger to you …* ***speak up****! To allow the naysayers*

on this campus to voice a negative opinion about the students of this school while at the same time marginalizing the positive influence that the critical mass of you hold, is not an indictment on the negativity of the 10 percent. It is an indictment on the meekness of the 90 percent."

You could have heard a pin drop. As the faces of two or three teachers began to show frustration, the faces of twenty others began to break out with a smile. They had been liberated while being called to action at the same time.

The critical mass of this small school in Washington had been behaving like closet optimists. A closet optimist is someone who is very positive and driven on the inside, but incredibly quiet and submissive on the outside. They are the people who might share how badly they would like to take part in innovative practices, but only if "everyone is on board." The reality for a closet optimist is that he or she will end up waiting forever, because there is no such thing as a staff where everyone is on board. The reason for this is simple: The negativity of most naysayers stems not from their educational philosophy, but from personal issues that may haunt them outside of the school. Think about it for a minute. Have you ever met a teacher who was negative and rude within his or her classroom or on campus, but who, the moment he or she left the gates of the school, became hospitable and encouraging as a person? It doesn't happen! The reason why people do not get on board at school is because they are generally not on board in life. And as sad as this is for them as individuals, what is worse is when an entire staff becomes hostage to such behavior. If the critical mass of a staff is hesitant to charge forward with a "no excuses" attitude until everyone is on board, results will remain status quo at best, and student learning will suffer. And because No Excuses begins with the staff, this is a battle that must be won decisively at the beginning of a school's transformation process.

The Six Cs of an NEU Professional

Working in a cohesive manner as a staff intent on supporting all students, no matter the challenge, takes work. It's not something that you can just talk about. It requires action and a game plan. A house becomes a home because of the family that lives there. A school becomes a No Excuses University because of the remarkable adults who work there and are willing to take responsibility for the success of every student. Henry Ford said, "Coming together is a beginning. Keeping together is progress. Working together is success." Every adult who works at a No Excuses University is a valued contributor to the success of the students. We respectfully refer to every principal, teacher, secretary, custodian, lunch aide, and any other adult who works at a No Excuses University as an NEU Professional. After many years of working together as a network, we have found that our NEU staff members can best exemplify the movement by focusing on what we call the Six Essential Characteristics of the NEU Professional (a.k.a. the "Six Cs"). Created with strong support from my colleagues Frank Nardelli, Dan Lopez, and Miriam Kim, these six characteristics are expectations for how NEU Professionals are to behave on a daily basis:

Committed: We believe that all students deserve the opportunity to be educated in a way that prepares them for college if they so choose to attend. We also believe that we, the school staff, have the power to make this opportunity a reality.

Courageous: To display courage is to show strength in the face of fear. We do this by ignoring those who try to tell us that our dreams for students' futures are unrealistic and impossible. We ask for forgiveness instead of permission. We hold one another accountable, and we come together as a critical mass to confront the status quo.

Collaborative: Our collaborative spirit is grounded on the idea that we each have unique strengths as well as different weaknesses. We make the time to work with one another in a way that maximizes accountability while minimizing anxiety. This helps us to achieve greater success for students as a team, while at the same time promoting balance in our lives as individuals.

Creative: We are innovative and love to explore new ways to get results for students. Experimentation is not a suggestion, but rather an expectation of an NEU Professional. When we find success through our creativity, we celebrate as a staff and seek ways to replicate the results elsewhere.

Character Centered: Character is doing the right thing when no one else is watching ... this goes double for adults. We strive to further develop our own character while we are consistent with the rules and methods of teaching behavior, and, at the same time, we take responsibility for the character development of all our students.

College and Career Crazy: College readiness is a tie that binds us as students, parents, and staff. Because of this, we reveal the benefits of a college degree to all students in practical and achievable ways that offer hope for a better future. Our network exists to shatter the myths that a student has to be rich or privileged to go to college. Students have the fundamental right to choose what they want to do with their lives after high school. Instead of assuming what their future will be, we take responsibility for preparing every one of our students to make that personal, educated choice.

Unlike the beliefs shared in Chapter 5 that offer suggestions for how schools can develop a culture of universal achievement, the Six Cs of an NEU Professional are non-negotiable for schools that wish to be a part of the network. These are not recommendations, nor are they merely ideas packaged with a catchy title. The Six Cs express who we are and how we want to behave. After you and your staff develop a culture of universal achievement that helps to foster positive change, I urge you to take the next step to escalate your commitment by practicing the Six Cs of an NEU Professional.

Classified Staff Members Are Teachers Too!

In a chapter that focuses on the importance of "teachers," it's critical to explain the role of classified staff members in this equation. To me, anyone who works both directly or indirectly to affect the academic and social success of a student is a teacher. Adults committed to improving the lives of students while working on a school site fall into the category of "teachers." Granted, they may not be compensated or celebrated as much as a classroom teacher is, but that has nothing to do with the level of importance that they have on an NEU campus. Some of my most memorable observations of successful breakthroughs with some of our toughest students involved that of a classified staff member. Just like a teacher, specialist, or principal, a committed classified staff member is fundamental to the success of students. Because of this, leaders would be wise to do the following:

- ❖ Ensure that all classified staff members understand and are a part of the development of the six exceptional systems that you create as a school.
- ❖ Create opportunities for classified staff members to grow professionally side by side with classroom teachers.
- ❖ Hold classified staff members to the same expectations as all other staff members. In addition, celebrate their investments with students the same way as well.
- ❖ Share the results of your Exceptional Systems and the achievement of your students with your classified staff members at the same time you share these results with the rest of your staff.

- ❖ Provide opportunities for your classified staff members to develop their skills and knowledge as professionals.
- ❖ Establish a work schedule for your classified staff members that can be implemented consistently.

More Than Window Dressing

As displayed by the examples in the previous chapter that encourage the creation of powerful symbolism, the visible steps necessary to create a spirit of college readiness are fairly straightforward and simple. The power of a college readiness message that has been strategically marketed to students, parents, and staff is truly inspirational. But if not accompanied by concrete steps taken behind the scenes, this inspiration will be short lived and educators may be left asking themselves, "Where are the results?" As described by numerous NEU educators across the nation, the real work of our college readiness endeavor is not found in what is seen, but rather in what is unseen. As a school begins the process of hanging flags outside of doors and in hallways, staff members must assume the responsibility of bringing the concept of college to life within the classroom in ways that may not be immediately visible to a typical passerby. To assist your progress through your own college readiness journey, I have included "40 Next Steps for Schools" in the appendix section of the book. These steps include five steps for each of the six exceptional systems, as well as five next steps for developing both powerful symbolism and also a culture of college readiness on site. You will notice a theme throughout each of the "40 Next Steps for Schools" related to developing a common language, integrating college readiness into subject matter, explicitly modeling behavior and expectations to students, and continuously collaborating as a staff. Because of the importance of these themes, I want to be sure to offer greater detail for each in this chapter.

Theme One: Define a Unified Language That Promotes the Concept of College

While every school is unique, the idea of instilling a unified language that promotes college does not have to be. Depending on their levels (elementary, middle, and high), schools should unify and create a list of words that are infused in the daily conversations among teachers, students, and parents. From the word "college" that is taught to kindergarteners to the words "major" and "dissertation" that might be taught to sixth graders, to an all-out checklist of words that high school students should understand, students should be offered a college-bound language from their teachers the same way my kids learned their ABCs from Elmo on Sesame Street. It doesn't have to be difficult, nor should it become a point for contention or debate by staff members. Each grade level and department should decide upon a list of five to ten words to reinforce on a daily basis. Much like the expansion of an adult's vocabulary over time, exposure to a unified language that promotes the concept of college should shift and grow from one year to the next.

Theme Two: Seek Ways to Integrate the Concept of College into Existing Subject Matter

My brother-in-law is a gifted photographer with a keen ability to find great pictures in situations that others do not. Most of his pictures are snapshots of our family, but he often has an urge to focus in on the minute details that nature provides. During these times, he shifts from a standard lens to a macro lens that highlights the miniscule features of a tropical flower or a tiny hummingbird. A simple shift of his lens enables him to take pictures of activity unseen by the naked eye. I am always amazed at the product.

When it comes to promoting college readiness, our work within the classroom must be looked at through a different lens as well. Math problems that used to focus on calculating distances from one arbitrary place to another can be shifted to lessons that ask students to compute the driving distance between Duke University and Boston College. State history units that require students to write extensively about local landmarks can also be used to focus on the history of the universities within their community. No matter the grade or subject, integrating the concept of college into the curriculum is easily done when viewed through a different lens. Every grade level or department should create a plan at the beginning of the year that weaves college readiness into the daily work of teaching and learning.

Theme Three: Explicitly Model College Readiness Behavior and Expectations to Students

Explicit is an adjective that is defined as: *stated clearly in detail; leaving no room for confusion or doubt.* This word is used liberally but implemented much too rarely in our field. It's a shame, because the actions that accompany this powerful word have the potential to open doors for student learning. Rather than explaining in our teaching, we often assume that our students understand concepts that we are presenting. This is a huge mistake, especially when working with students of poverty. Schools within the No Excuses University network take the guesswork out of promoting college readiness as they explicitly describe the academic and life skills necessary to be successful in the present and the future. They explicitly model, practice, teach, and review these behaviors in a variety of ways on a regular basis. Each school takes the time to lay out a detailed plan for this process in an effort to unify the work of an entire staff. Some examples:

Unified Classroom Management Plan: Like most schools, each No Excuses University adopts a set of behavior expectations for students to observe. These expectations are centered on a limited number of character traits (no more than six) that coincide with the values displayed in a productive citizen. For us, our Bridge to College™

Plan for Character Development of fairness, integrity, dependability, courage, kindness, etc. (see Bridge to College page 129) offers a structure to teach appropriate behavior. And I do mean teach.

Too often, educators focus on discipline rather than behavior modification. They act with the assumption that students should innately know right from wrong and therefore deserve punishment when they cross the line. I agree that there should always be consequences when rules are broken, but those consequences should never be doled out without an adult taking the time to reinforce appropriate behavior. When we fail to teach appropriate behavior, we are destined to find ourselves in the same exact situation with the same exact student in the future. Think about it for a moment. Does your school have lunch detention for your students? If it does, are the same students showing up in detention over and over again? The likely answer is yes. If that is the case, it is not because these students are innately bad; it is because the act of detention does not work for them. We discovered that this was exactly the case for many students at Los Pen. After years of lunch detention with the same students, we asked ourselves, "Is this working?" The data clearly showed that it was not. Therefore our mindset changed from being reactive to proactive. Instead of dealing with negative behavior after it took place, we decided to seek ways to stop it before poor decisions were made. From this thinking came a unified classroom management plan.

Every teacher implements and every staff member supports a behavior management plan that is universal from one classroom to the next. (See Appendix.) All of our rules are based on six Bridge to College™ character traits. When students break the rules after being given one warning, they take time to participate in "re-thinking" letters that force them to review the results of their actions. These letters are never used as busy work for a student, but rather are the catalyst for quality conversations between the teacher and the student. As negative behavior progresses, parents are brought into the mix and steps are taken immediately to set high expectations from the beginning of the year. Conversations with students during these times are candid and serious, but always respectful. We let students know how much we care about them, and that we are disappointed in their choices rather than in them. This lets the students know that they are capable of making different choices in the future. Because of such conversations, we have seen far fewer "frequent flyers," as we call them, to the office. In fact, our eyes have been opened by the positive effects that have come as a result of caring adults collectively embracing a school-wide behavior plan.

In addition to the consequences found within the unified management plan, we also focus on the numerous ways in which a teacher can positively reinforce good behavior and character. This is crucial; we need to ensure that equal time is given to students who consistently exhibit appropriate behavior. These students are often overlooked and taken for granted. When our attention becomes consumed by the negative, many of our well-behaved students may veer off course in an effort to be noticed. Like all endeavors, no plan is perfect. There are certainly times when we reach the end of our rope in search of unique solutions for unique students. Still, we remain steadfast in our desire to find better ways to improve behavior. Any adult can discipline a student, but it takes a true teacher to help change behavior.

Exploration of College Entrance Standards: Along with the reinforcement of positive behavior, we also work to set lofty academic expectations. Each No Excuses University seeks to prepare students for what it takes to be ready for college. Conversations about college entrance standards begin to take place in the upper grades as teachers break down a list of expectations that are required of students seeking entrance into public or private universities within a particular state. Some classrooms receive college application packets from their adopters and participate in mock enrollment lessons. Others take trips to university campuses and meet with guidance counselors or students as they learn about the choices that they can make today in order to smooth the road to college tomorrow. From early on in elementary school until the moment students graduate from high school, teachers must invest time in providing clarity when it comes to expectations required of students who are college bound. A great book to help guide you in this journey is *College Knowledge* by David Conley.

College Readiness Celebration: In many of our poorer communities, there is a negative stigma attached to attending college. Often, this attitude is a defense mechanism for students who feel that the attainment of college is an impossibility. And for students who come from generational poverty, who can blame them when all they have seen is one family member after another fail to make this idea a reality? The best means of changing their attitudes is to make the concept of college exciting and engaging. Students at many No Excuses Universities participate in weekly pep rallies, monthly awards ceremonies, and yearly college fairs. These events vanquish the attitudes of those who think that failing school is "no big deal" as they make excitement about learning the norm.

Theme Four: Continuously Collaborate in Search of Innovative and Successful Practices That Strengthen Your College Readiness Purpose

The best gains ever achieved by No Excuses Universities have always come as a result of team members who work shoulder to shoulder. When educators believe that they are stronger together than they are apart, ideas seem to flow like water from a fire hose. An openness to seeking new ways to promote college readiness must be prevalent in order to experience consistent gains. Make this attitude a priority as you begin to implement your plan for promoting college readiness.

From an early age, I noticed that my parents' attitude set the tone for the perspective I had as a youngster. When they were positive, I felt happy. When they were stressed, I felt worried. When they believed in me, I believed in me. Parent and child, teacher and student, the same holds true. All of our endeavors to transform our schools begin and end with the tone that is set by the staff. This chapter was strategically placed in this book before the chapters about students and parents because your calling as a teacher is greater than that of any other stakeholder. Your actions will be scrutinized by observant children and, more importantly, modeled by them. When a student's behavior mirrors that of a positive adult, nothing is more rewarding. No Excuses begins with the staff, but when implemented thoughtfully, it touches the lives of the students and their families as well.

Chapter Fifteen

Theory to Practice

Items for Articulation

- ❑ Are you a closet optimist? Talk with your team about the times when you wished you had been more outspoken on behalf of students.
- ❑ Of the Six Cs of an NEU Professional, which one does your staff exemplify the most? Which one do you focus on the least?

Items for Action

- ❑ On a small piece of paper, during a staff meeting, have each staff member write down an excuse that he or she has been guilty of making. After doing so, have every member stand up, state the excuse, wad up the paper, and then throw it into a nearby trash can. As a staff, discuss the strategies that will ensure that reasons do not turn into excuses.

Chapter Sixteen

Key Concepts

"The greatest danger for most of us is not that our aim is too high and we miss it, but that it is too low and we reach it."

— Michelangelo

1

Students need to be taught the difference between a job and a career.

2

The development of individual goals for every student guarantees differentiated instruction.

3

We are not in the business of discipline. We are in the business of teaching behavior.

4

Subscribing to the Success Equation will support our desire to create the *next greatest generation.*

Chapter Sixteen

High Expectations for Every Student

From the time that I was eight years old, my Saturday mornings always began the same way. I would hear my father's footsteps enter my bedroom followed by the words "Wake up, it's time to go to work." My brother Dan and I knew that procrastination would lead to phase two of the wake-up process, when my dad would place his boot on the base of our bed and give it a solid shake that invoked a fatherly earthquake of sorts. With sleep in our eyes, we would put on our work clothes and rush downstairs for a quick breakfast before heading out to support the family business. Summer mornings were no different. When most of our friends were watching cartoons or playing outside, my brother and I were working with our father, Steve.

The family business, which was to service and install submersible pumps for the water wells throughout our backcountry area, began as a risky endeavor on the part of my parents, who invested what little they had in the business. Because there was no money to pay a helper for my father, I guess you could say that my brother, who was ten, and I acted like two halves that made for a whole. The work each day was simple mentally, but exhausting physically. Our job was to take hundreds of feet of steel pipe out of the ground in order to replace or fix the pump at the bottom of the well. Every 21 feet, we took heavy wrenches and used them to unscrew each link of pipe. When we were done taking out all of the pipe, we replaced the pump and put it right back in. By the end of the day, our bodies were covered with dirt, rust, and grease. Our bones were achy and hands were sore from "swinging wrenches," as we called it.

As tedious as our work was, what was more repetitious during our days with my father were his teachings. Not a day went by where my dad didn't try to convince us that it was better to work with our brains than our bodies, and the only way that we could achieve that kind of work was with a college education. In order to drive the point home, my dad would often have my brother and me extend a 10-pound wrench from one arm as we held a feather-light pencil from the other. The arm with the pipe wrench would begin to shake after about 15 seconds as the weight challenged the muscles in my tiny wrist. The other arm held the pencil steadily and effortlessly. My dad's lesson: "You can graduate from high school and work with your body, or graduate from college and work with your brain." His lesson was not lost on either of us.

My father's teachings spotlighted the difference between having a job and having a career. His responsibility to us was to teach us a trade to fall back on, and also to teach us exactly what awaited us should we choose to take over the family business. Any romance that my dad had in having a "father and sons" operation was always trumped by his desire for us to have more opportunities in life than he did. He knew that a college education was a ticket into a game that he was only able to watch from the sidelines. My dad has always been a hero to me. Not just because he worked so incredibly hard to support our family, but more so because he acted selflessly in his pursuit to change a cycle of under-education that was prevalent in our previous generations.

The lessons taught to NEU students across the country from their teachers are similar to the lessons that I learned from my parents at an early age. No lesson is greater than our focus on the definitions that spotlight the difference between a job and a career. Students learn that a job is something that a person must do to earn money in order to pay for the basic needs of their families. A career, however, allows a person to be paid for doing what they, ideally, love to do. Jobs are short-lived, but careers more often than not bring with them longevity of experiences that are personally as well as financially gratifying.

Make the Family Proud

Students who live in poverty rarely get to experience the types of routines and schedules at home that model what it takes to create a career mindset. Many times, routine and structure in their daily lives occurs only within the six to eight hours they attend school each day. While many might find this fact frustrating, NEU educators see it as a gift. It's amazing how much can be accomplished within a six-hour day when caring educators assemble around a consistent message. Students who attend No Excuses Universities get a healthy dose of structure as every adult on campus consistently and reliably communicates the same message. One teacher to another, one year to the next, the daily life of an NEU student is designed in such a way that he or she feels important as an individual, but also responsible for the overall success of a school community of their peers. We call that community "*the family*."

One of the first things that students learn is that they are not alone in their successes or their challenges. The unique value found in each student is always encouraged and built upon, as represented by the creation of individual student goals for all, but never at the cost of sacrificing the success of the family. NEU students learn that for every decision they make, both negative and positive, the effects will be felt by dozens of others as well. Because of this, students are always reminded that they are a part of a team that is bigger than themselves. As a reminder, the saying "*Don't embarrass the family. Make the family proud.*" is one that is often heard on many NEU campuses. Students who come from families with similar mindsets understand all too well the importance behind these words, and those who do not are sure to learn them over the course of their time as NEU students. I have found that no matter the background of children or young adults, they tend to embrace this family spirit. For some, it is because they thrive on being respectful and successful ambassadors for the school. For others, it is because they feel cared for even in the midst of being disciplined on occasion. And for others, quite simply, the school is the only family that they have. Just like families, the best schools display a certain level of love, discipline, challenge, celebration, loyalty, and support. All act as a strong foundation for the work that we do to engage students in the No Excuses University experience.

Beyond Rules

Every school in America has some form of a code of conduct that they give to students. Most contain a series of rules that let students know the expectations that adults have of them when it comes to walking in line, being respectful to adults, and exhibiting appropriate behavior to one another by keeping their hands and feet to themselves. Don't get me wrong; the fact that these rules are standard does not bother me in the least. In fact, I wholeheartedly agree and have enforced these very rules as a principal. What does rub me the wrong way, when it comes to generic student rule books, is the limitations found in many of them. Many read the same way they did when I was a kid. Some are so old that they are better written on stone tablets than they are on student tri-folds. They often maintain a limited focus on communicating the rules for behavior, completely bypassing the academic opportunities for teaching the habits of mind. Today, our profession has access to more information than ever about student behavior, what grabs their attention, and how to communicate our expectations in a way that motivates them, yet we lean on reactive rules instead of proactive procedures. Aren't we better than this? Don't you think that our students deserve better at this point?

When the No Excuses University endeavor began, we decided that the expectations for student behavior had to be taught in harmony with our school's one goal to create academic proficiency for all. This shift in thinking made us understand that the work of student behavior was about so much more than "rules." Instead, our expectations of students were really more about a contract with them than anything else. And since a contract speaks to the need for two parties to participate, we as NEU schools promote the idea of a meaningful partnership between students and staff.

Before people sign a contract, they are informed about the expectations required of them to fulfill their obligations. Most of us have been involved in many of these situations, either as new employees signing a district contract or as new homeowners agreeing to pay back a loan. No job has ever been given to us, nor money granted on our behalf, without our signatures. Furthermore, we would never allow anyone to sign us to a contract without careful consideration on our parts. But that, unfortunately, is exactly the process that many schools use when developing a code of conduct for students.

In most cases, a *beginning-of-the-year packet* is sent out to parents containing a form about the rules that require a student's and parent's signature. These forms are returned to the school and placed in the student records file never to be seen again, unless the student misbehaves. At which point we place the form in front of the student and parent and for all intents and purposes say, "We told you so." Sure, we do a great job conveying our own liabilities with the use of forms like these, but really we do nothing to create meaningful understanding in the minds of students about the academic and behavioral expectations that we have of them. NEU schools do things differently.

During the first week of school, every grade level is asked to attend an assembly that addresses the expectations of an NEU student. We discuss the role that character plays in our school, the importance of "making the family proud," and the need for every student to live by the *Code of Conduct* found in the NEU handbooks given to each student. (See Appendix.) After the assembly, teachers return to class and discuss all components of the student handbook. From learning about the consequences that may come as a result of poor character to understanding our academic habits of mind to charting progress in a variety of assessments, this handbook acts as a guide for a student's college readiness journey. After students have been thoroughly informed about the handbook, they are asked to sign our NEU Three-Way Pledge. (See Appendix.)

This process of developing a foundational understanding in the area of expectations is certainly more involved than some might like. However, we find that the amount of time that has been invested proactively with students at the beginning of the year saves us tenfold in reactive measures that need to be taken by the end of the year.

Student Goals

The term "differentiated instruction" may be the most overused cliché in the business. When asked how a teacher supports the individual needs of each student, the response is almost always that they "differentiate instruction." For many, this may be true, but for far more it is not. It has nothing to do with teachers not knowing how to differentiate or even being lazy. It is incredibly hard to differentiate instruction for every student in a class. The more our pedagogy evolves, the more we understand just how important it is to capitalize on the strengths and adapt to the weaknesses of every student. In a classroom of twenty or thirty students, the chances that all children are performing at the same level with the same strengths are nearly impossible. Because of this, No Excuses Universities create individual goals for every student in the school.

What began as an idea to help support the most at-risk students in our school quickly became a comprehensive effort to promote academic growth for each student. The teachers at Los Peñasquitos Elementary led an effort that became one of the, if not the most, substantial reason for our school's success. Teachers decided that as part of a school-wide assessment commitment, we would use formative assessments to hone in on the individual needs of students. No longer would we discuss a student's weakness in the subject of "math"; rather, we talked about their lack of growth in the area of problem solving. Instead of saying that students were "below grade level" in reading, we sought to find better strategies to bring them up to par in the area of literal comprehension. The fine-tuning of our efforts to spotlight the subcategories within the curriculum made all the difference in the world.

As part of an assessment commitment endorsed by the entire staff, students create individual goals with their teachers at least three times a year. These goals are data-specific and representative of a partnership between the student and the teacher. No longer do teachers call students to the back of the room to participate in an assessment that the kids know nothing about. The student goal process requires that teachers share the details about the assessment, how it is scored, and why it is important in the creation of an individual goal. Through this process, students begin to learn about the importance of assessment and how to analyze the data.

After quality assessments have been given, the teacher works to spotlight the greatest learning need that exists for each student. Teachers then hold conferences with the students to create goals. Each conference may look a little different depending on the grade or the teacher, but every goal should include the following components:

1. ***Students should create only one goal at a time.*** We have found that more than one goal gets forgotten by students and teachers. Teachers are often tempted to create goals for students in each subject area; however, we must remember that the student goal process is about quality, not quantity.

2. ***Each goal must contain tangible steps that help students improve in their goal areas.*** Steps such as "try harder" or "read more" do nothing to support kids. Teachers are encouraged to generate ideas collaboratively as a team in an effort to accumulate an abundance of strategies to pass on to students. Quality goals offer three to four different strategies or ideas that students can use to improve, but no more.

3. ***Students should be given visible access to their goals on a daily basis.*** Some classrooms post goals on the wall, while others have designated goals folders. Many primary-aged students have their goals taped to the top of their desks. However you decide to display your goals, remember that students will care about them only as much as you do. Teachers who rarely reference goals tend to have students who forget them.

4. ***Goals must be academic in nature.*** There may be a need for some students to have behavior goals, but this should be in addition to a well-thought-out academic goal.

As a principal, one of my most common conversations with students revolved around goals. During these conversations, I would ask the students three very important questions:

"What is your goal?" Students' answers to these questions showed their investment and commitment in the process.

"What are you doing to help achieve your goal?" These answers expressed their plans for reaching their goals.

"How will you know when you have met your goal?" These answers demonstrated that their goals were data-specific.

Of the numerous conversations that I had with students, I was always amazed at the ability of a six-, seven-, or eight-year-old to understand the concept of goal-setting. In addition, I was regularly astonished at how goals helped to improve the individual and school-wide achievement of our students.

Many educators wonder how to get students invested in the learning process. The answer is crystal clear: Create individual goals with them. When you do, you will do away with the cliché of differentiation and guarantee that every student in your school is being taught at his or her level. One of the greatest misperceptions about Los Peñasquitos Elementary's success is that the staff focused all of their efforts on "teaching to the test." The fact is that our teachers, and the teachers at successful No Excuses Universities, focus on individual growth for each student. When you maintain such a focus, test scores tend to take care of themselves.

The Success Equation: Passion + Talent = Gift

When staff members work closely with the individual student in mind, it breeds success that is cause for great celebration. As soon as those celebrations dissipate, however, many teachers are left feeling a greater level of concern for what might await their students in the years to come when they no longer have a say in the instruction for their kids. Whether you are a first grade teacher worried about the transition to second grade or a middle school teacher concerned about the transition to high school, your anxiety is all too real. As much as we know one teacher can change the life of a student, the reality is that it often takes far more than that. In fact, in order to make meaningful and sustainable progress, especially for students of poverty, it takes continuity not only from one year to the next, but one level to the next.

The No Excuses University movement began at the elementary school level with good reason. I felt, and the data confirmed, that the typical strategy to support college preparation in high school was not working for our neediest students. In fact, according to a Department of Education study released in February 2013, while graduation rates have slowly increased over the last 35 years, more than 20 percent of our high school students still fail to graduate on time. Because of this, it made all the sense in the world for us to begin our work at the earliest opportunity possible and let it grow from the bottom up. What began in elementary school has slowly and organically progressed to the college level. Students who were once preschoolers in our movement are now college students. As they have grown, the way in which we provide continuity in our message has as well. Before today, there was never a need to speak the same language from elementary to college because all of our schools were at the K-6 level. With more than two dozen secondary schools in our network today, that need has changed. With that change, we have developed a system that ensures a progression for students under the same NEU umbrella. It's called the Success Equation.

The success equation, simply stated, is to take a student's ***Passion***, add it to his or her ***Talent***, and then get his or her ***Gift***. In elementary school, we focus our message on inspiring a passion for learning about college to all students. As they enter middle school, we want to combine that passion with the talents that students are displaying in sixth, seventh, and eighth grade. Students in our middle school begin to understand that there is a big difference between what you love to do, your passion, and what you are really good at doing, your talent. As they enter high school, it is the job of our high school teachers to find a way to combine a student's passion with his or her talent in order to find a student's gift. Now I'll be the first to admit that not everyone sees things the way that we do in our network. As for me, I just innately believe that every child was born with a God-given gift and that it is our job as adults to find out what that gift is and help him or her shape it somehow into a bright future. Luckily, there were adults in my life who believed the same for me.

When I was young, I was passionate about baseball. I decided at a very early age that I wanted to be a major league baseball player. Without question, this was my passion. The only problem with this was … I sucked at baseball. I couldn't hit a curve ball, I was too slow, and I rarely had the power to hit the ball deep into the outfield. While baseball was and still is a passion of mine, it certainly was not my talent. Fortunately for me, I also had another passion that aligned with what was a talent, working with young students. From my earliest memories of caring for my baby sister Aubrey, to my work as a teacher's assistant for third graders when I was in high school, I knew that I loved affecting the lives of younger students. More importantly, I knew I was good at it. It was my gift, and knowing that changed my life forever. As a network of schools, we want the same for all of our students. We want them to discover their passion. We want them to celebrate their talents. And, most importantly, we want them to take pride in the fact that they have a gift that they can turn into a fulfilling career in the future.

There are no doubt a number of ways that schools can define what this success equation means to them. As for us, in typical fashion, we have simplified our approach in an effort to ensure that all NEU staff members both understand and embrace this progression from one level to the next. I've offered the images below to convey what it looks like for us.

SUCCESS EQUATION
PASSION + TALENT = GIFTS

ELEMENTARY SCHOOL

1. Develop a ***passion*** for learning and for a future that includes college.
2. Promote an introduction of college by focusing on four-year universities.
3. Offer an instructional foundation dedicated to a strong focus in literacy.
4. Teach students about the importance of setting high expectations for themselves by creating individual student goals.
5. Utilize powerful symbolism and explicit instruction that develop a student's character.

MIDDLE SCHOOL

1. Create opportunities for students to identify their ***talent***.
2. Expand a college readiness message that includes community colleges and is accompanied by college tours by the students.
3. Broaden the curriculum in a way that shapes a student's academic success beyond the core of literacy.
4. Have students write personal and professional goals that go beyond the classroom.
5. Develop comprehensive ways to share real-world life literacy lessons that develop a generation of productive citizens.

High School

1. Combine students' passions and talents to help them discover their ***gifts***.
2. Add trade schools to a message that is both college and career centered.
3. Enroll students in a program where the default is college prep classes and where a student must opt out in order to take the high school diploma track.
4. Commit to having every teacher show relevance between each taught lesson and how it pertains to a student's college and career success.
5. Offer internships that expose students to careers aligned to their gifts.

As you can see, none of this is rocket science. It's just a very simple way of going beyond our work with the six exceptional systems in order to ensure that we support a student's success by speaking the same language from one level to the next. When one teacher affects the lives of hundreds throughout his or her career, it has the potential to shape scores of productive citizens who can make our communities better. When thousands of teachers come together, speak the same language, and provide continuity in their message from one level to the next, it has the potential to change a generation. If asked by someone about the greatest generation, most people would agree that the fine men and women who shaped our world during World War II would hold that honor. But as that generation slowly passes on, a new one must fill the void. What we want to do as a movement is create the next greatest generation. Unless we find a way to develop that generation, today's students, from preschool all the way through 12th grade, we will forever struggle to produce a community of citizens with the same potential to change the world the way our grandparents did.

The dreams that NEU staff members hold for our students are often bigger than the students themselves can comprehend. I, like many of you, am living proof of the importance of having others help stimulate those dreams throughout a lifetime. For me, it was my parents. The conversations that took place in my childhood about college eventually led to a very real *rite of passage* when I was eighteen. I will never forget the first day that my parents moved me into my dorm room. A young small-town boy with the propensity for being homesick, I stood in a 10×10 room and asked myself, "Will I even make it past the first semester?"

As I said goodbye to my parents, the answer to that question could not have been clearer. While other students were handed keys to brand-new cars as a gift for their hard work in being accepted to college, my father pulled from his pocket an equally special offering to me. It was a small, and very rusty, version of the same pipe wrench that my brother and I used to "swing" growing up. It moved me, not because of its tangible nature, but because of my father's words accompanying the tool. He looked me in the eyes and said, "If you ever decide that college isn't for you, I will support you 100 percent. But be sure to let this wrench act as a reminder of what waits for you when you come home." He hugged me and waved good-bye. That was all he needed to say. To this day, the wrench hangs proudly in my office.

Chapter Sixteen

Theory to Practice

Items for Articulation

- ❑ Talk about the Success Equation. What are you doing to ensure that your sister schools know your students, your belief in them, and how they can continue the success that is taking place on your campus?
- ❑ The key to getting students invested in the assessment process is to work closely with them. As a team, discuss specific examples of how you have made students your partners in the area of assessment. Ask yourself: "Do my students understand the nature of each assessment, why we give them assessments, and what each score means to them?"

Items for Action

Creating individual goals is vital to our commitment to differentiate instruction for each student. Schools should experiment in this process through the following steps.

- ❑ *Step One:* Have each teacher select three at-risk students and create one student goal with each.

- ❑ *Step Two:* Take the time over the course of six to eight weeks to discuss the progress of your students with your team.
- ❑ *Step Three:* As a team and a school, decide upon a timeline for rolling out the goals process so that it affects every student on campus.

Note: Most schools take between six months and a year to experiment and learn about the goals process before they implement it school-wide. This is not to say that it can't be done in less time; it is simply to advise schools to take time to implement the process in a quality manner from the start.

Chapter Seventeen

Key Concepts

"If kids come to us [educators/teachers] from strong, healthy functioning families, it makes our job easier. If they do not come to us from strong, healthy, functioning families, it makes our job more important."

— Barbara Coloroso

1

Demanding responsible parenting from those who were never taught such skills is futile.

2

Schools need to focus on the individual needs of families through differentiated parenting support.

3

The more secure parents are in the relationships they have with teachers, the more likely they are to take advice from the school.

Partnering with Parents

I have learned over time that no matter how convincing I think I may be when offering professional development to educators, there's always at least one person who finds a flaw in the message. While working with an elementary school staff in California, I saw this firsthand. As I presented information about the beliefs associated with creating a culture of universal achievement, a young teacher raised her hand and shared her frustration: "I would have 100 percent proficiency in my class if it weren't for just one of my kids!"

I asked her why this one student was not at grade-level standards. She simply said, "Because of the parents."

The voices in the room cried out with approval as heads nodded up and down to share their agreement with the teacher. I went on to inquire, "What is it about these parents that cause this particular student to fail?"

Among her litany of reasons were "they never help him on homework, they never read with him at home, they never volunteer in the classroom, they never drive on field trips...."

I stopped her and asked, "Why don't they do any of those things?"

She replied, "Because they are both addicted to drugs; they're methamphetamine addicts."

There was silence in the room before I finally said, "Let me ask you something. Why do you want two meth addicts driving on a field trip? How are two meth addicts going to fundamentally change the way a student completes their homework? Do you really want two meth addicts helping out in class? Maybe while they're tweaking they can do things really fast, but is that really what you want?"

She had nothing more to say. My candor forced her to look inwardly for the lack of results that she was getting from this one young boy. She had rationalized his lack of success based on a number of excuses with a victim mentality that, in the end, did nothing to improve the academic status of her student. In doing so, she pointed her finger squarely at the parents, an act that is easily done by many educators experiencing frustration. This blame game is exactly why the view of public education in society is on the decline. When we, professionals who are specially trained to teach students things that they don't know, don't embrace that responsibility, we dumb down our profession as a whole and put our entire existence in question. To decide to teach some students, but not all, is no different than a dentist who says, "I'll clean your teeth, but I'm not interested in fixing any of your cavities." Can you see the absurdity in all of this excuse making?

As a former teacher, I remember the challenges that went along with teaching students who came from home environments that were less than ideal. As a principal, I have worked with dozens of abused children who live challenging existences that most of us will never truly understand. In both roles I have found that blaming parents for lackluster performance, both academically and behaviorally, is one of the easiest things in the world to do. I have experienced times when these excuses made educators feel better about their own limitations for garnering results, but didn't do a damn thing to change the reality of the current situation for the student. Is it true that poor parenting makes our job harder? Of course it is, but dwelling on this fact without seeking timely solutions is a luxury that we simply do not have in public education. You and I could name a child who went from one grade to the next where teachers used the same excuse for why he or she was failing. Before we know it, six, seven, eight years pass by in this student's career with the same excuses … and the same results. How do we move beyond our frustrations and into proactive solutions regarding parenting support? We make them partners in our college readiness endeavor.

The term "parents as partners" has become an overused pledge in our profession. Such a term is now expected to be part of district mission statements and school improvement plans. I question whether or not those who write such statements truly seek to implement the goals associated with them. I have visited many schools that had value statements regarding parents as partners that were upbeat and supportive, but attitudes about parents that were negative and critical. I have no doubt that these schools would like nothing more than to have their deeds match their words. They just don't know how to connect with parents in a way that unifies their support with the purpose of the school.

The No Excuses University endeavor makes it easy for parents to understand, support, and participate in the goals of a school. This is done in two very important ways. First, we publicize our expectations to parents in a way that is respectful, timely, and clear. Second, rather than demand participation from parents, we seek to get them more involved in the workings of the school by reaching out to their basic needs. Both steps have helped us to create a more positive climate for students, parents, and staff members.

COMMUNICATING OUR PLAN TO PARENTS

When I became the principal of Los Peñasquitos Elementary School, there were two looming concerns involving the parents within our community. The first had to do with attendance. Not unlike those of other schools, the numbers showed that our attendance on Mondays and Fridays was significantly lower than that of the rest of the week. While the majority of our parents did an outstanding job of getting their children to school on time, others did not view their son's or daughter's education as a priority, and it showed in the extended weekend plans that were made with little to no regard for what the students were missing at school. Because the school is close to the Mexican border and had a large Hispanic population at the time, many of our parents were going home to visit families and returning at their own pace. While we could not judge the rationale for or the necessity of taking these trips outside of the country, we as a school determined that it was harming the success of our students.

The second concern in regard to parent involvement had to do with the safety of our campus. Like many campuses, ours was an open campus that allowed anyone unfettered access to our school grounds. Sure, there were signs informing all visitors to check in through the office, but more times than not, people ignored them. It was the culture of the school to allow our parents to roam freely. But the tragic events of September 11, 2001 changed everything, and modifications were not only necessary; they were required. Immediately, we began locking the gates to our school, allowing only one entrance to our campus, which went through the school office. In addition, all visitors were required to show ID to the school secretary. To my surprise, this measure infuriated some parents who had left their identification in the car. They felt inconvenienced by the fact that they were asked to return to the parking lot to retrieve their driver's licenses.

Both attendance and school safety concerns became the only two non-negotiable items that I had with parents. I went out of my way to publicize this fact to each parent in writing, phone calls, and face-to-face conversations. When a parent began to show frustration to my office staff members, I stepped in and candidly explained our check-in procedure without apology. When students consistently missed school due to reasons other than illness, I did everything in my power to let the parents know that this was unacceptable. From walking to apartments and homes in order to speak with parents directly, to involving our district truant officer, I would stop at nothing to create a cultural shift in the eyes of our community. After about a year, I realized that my efforts were paying off. Attendance numbers began to improve, but, more importantly, the attitudes of parents began to change. While walking across the street in one of our apartment complexes, I overhead a parent say to another, "Whatever you do, don't mess with Lopez when it comes to getting your kid to school. It's not worth it." The parent went on to describe how I filled up her voicemail box with messages and finally called her at work to talk about her son's attendance.

These examples represent mountains that are worth climbing. Unfortunately, some schools pick far too many issues to focus on with parents. Some demand that homework is completed appropriately, placing the burden on both the student and the parent. Others decide that classroom participation or financial support must take place in order to fund school projects or even parties. These demands come with great opposition from parents who are simply trying to make it through the day. After hearing numerous complaints from the school over a variety of items, our words become little more than background noise to parents, who inevitably throw up their hands and say, "Forget it!" I've learned along the way, sometimes the hard way, that picking your battles is a virtue that proves to be invaluable as a principal.

Just as important as picking your battles is knowing when to make your stand. From the beginning of our No Excuses University endeavor, we have made it a point to have every parent attend an NEU Parent Forum. These forums present the work that we are doing about college readiness, how parents can participate if they wish, and what is expected of each of them when it comes to our two non-negotiables. In our first year conducting these forums, parents were given five different opportunities to attend. The meetings took place on campus and typically lasted 45 minutes or less. After about 80 percent of our parents showed up, we scheduled two more forums in an effort to ensure that every student would have a parent attend. After this, we were left with a handful of parents who had yet to attend this mandated meeting. In a last-ditch effort to get parents involved, I sent out a letter along with voicemail messages that said:

Dear Parents,

As you may recall, we sent out a letter inviting you to attend one of the seven NEU Parent Forum meetings held over the course of the last several weeks. Because it is a requirement to attend, we wanted to schedule these meetings during a variety of days and times so that you might be able to join us. Unfortunately, your child has yet to be represented by a parent at one of these meetings. In an effort to go the extra mile, we have scheduled one more meeting for you to attend on September 23rd at 6 pm. If you cannot attend, please know that we will be scheduling a home visit with you in an effort to present this important information to you face to face. The No Excuses University endeavor is one that is exciting for all involved. We know that greater success will be realized if all students, parents, and staff have a true understanding about this work. I look forward to seeing you at our next meeting!

Sincerely,
Damen Lopez
Principal

To no one's surprise, the vast majority of remaining parents showed up to that final meeting. However, I do recall making several visits alongside our school counselor, Fran Hjalmarson, to apartments and houses with my laptop in hand. This took a lot of time, but it was well worth it as we laid the groundwork for publicizing our college readiness initiative. As part of our NEU Parent Forum, we focused our message on ways that parents could be encouraged to support their children and the school. In turn, we also shared ways that the school would support parents.

Just as every teacher created an individual goal unique to each student, we encouraged parents to create unique parenting goals for themselves. These goals would speak directly to the ways that parents would help support their child's academic progress. In addition, every goal would note ways in which moms and dads could continue

Take Five

1. *What is your student goal?*
2. *What did you do today to help achieve your student goal?*
3. *How did your character make a difference today?*
4. *What can you do tomorrow to conduct yourself as a No Excuses University Student?*
5. *Encourage your child in a very specific and genuine way.*

to grow as parents. When parents create goals for themselves, they assume a level of accountability in a manner that mirrors that of their own child. And because they are seeking ways to improve as parents, they model supportive behavior that connects directly with our college readiness initiative.

In addition to parenting goals, we encourage all parents to take part in a daily conversation with their children referred to as "Take Five." This conversation, focusing on five questions, is designed to be simple and last no more than five minutes. Some parents begin their Take Five conversation while walking home from school, while others engage in dialogue on their ride home in the car. Still others use the Take Five template to guide their talk at home. After attending the NEU Parent Forum, each family is given a magnet with our five key questions on it to put on their refrigerators. This small gift both encourages parents to have daily conversations with their students and also reinforces a similar culture at home that we try hard to instill at school.

Finally, when it comes to publicizing our college readiness focus to parents, each grade level creates Parent Assessment Guides that offer detailed information about the types of tests that students will be taking. In addition, they provide the contact information of every teacher should a parent wish to seek further information regarding assessment. For years, we hesitated sharing such information, not because we wanted to hide it, but more so because we assumed that our large second-language parent population would not understand. This assumption may have been correct in many cases, but it was no excuse for not doing our best to communicate the value that we placed on using data-driven assessments to target the individual needs of students. These guides were simple to create and easy to distribute. Some parents read them, others did not, but most of them appreciated our attempt to go the extra mile in an effort to provide better communication.

Differentiated Parenting Support

The second major way that we make parents our partners in the NEU endeavor is through what we call "Differentiated Parent Support." This style of support acts as a form of outreach to our parents, who bring with them a plethora of needs based on their individual circumstances. The brainchild of Fran Hjalmarson, author of the book *Differentiated Parent Support*, this method of supporting parents is actually an exceptional system of sorts that has affected the culture of our school in significant ways.

The idea of Differentiated Parent Support came as a result of 25 years of unproductive efforts to engage our parent community in the goals of our school. For years, we demanded that parents participate in homework, volunteer on site, and exemplify our definition of "parent." The problem was that many of our parents were either so incredibly busy keeping their heads above water that they couldn't do any of these things, or had come from environments where they were not taught the skills that you and I find second nature as parents. Of course they loved their kids; there was no doubt about that. But they did not grasp the obligation that a parent has as a partner with the school.

For years, I, along with several other staff members and fellow parents, pondered why this was the case. It wasn't until Fran joined our team in 2003 that we finally understood the answer. We had been trying to treat every parent the same way, when all along we should have been treating them as individuals. I remember one day in my office Fran saying, "We differentiate our support for students; why aren't we doing the same for our parents?"

It was an "aha" moment for all of us. Immediately, Fran began working with a small team of staff members, seeking to systematically support parents in a whole new way. Instead of waiting for parents to come to the school in search of support, we began to go directly to them. When we found out that a family was struggling financially, we would partner with faith-based organizations in order to provide essential items like food or clothing. When we learned that dozens of families could not afford a Thanksgiving meal, we worked with a sister school to provide a feast with all the trimmings. When Christmas came and there was little chance of some of our students having presents under the tree, we leaned on our local police unit to put together a party for our most needy children. No matter the need or the reason, Fran and the staff found a way to reach out to our parents. Through it all, we never got caught up in the frustration of the circumstances that came as a result of the poor decisions that some of our parents made in their lives. We focused on the fact that these parents needed a friend in the school. The volunteers and staff members who did not offer their support for the sake of the parents were instead compelled to do so out of their love for the kids.

As extraordinary as this shift in thinking was, what was more exciting was the outcome of our work. Parents who never used to show their faces on campus came often to seek support for various reasons. And because they were on campus more, they were more in touch with the academic and behavior status of their children. If their children were having difficulties, these parents were far more eager to be supportive. Many times, however, because of our outreach, parents found out about positive results that were taking place with their kids and about the amount of care that the school had for the individual wellbeing of their children. This made them swell with pride and encouraged them to be more invested in the partnership that we were trying to promote.

The more parents became comfortable with the school, the more likely they were to learn and take advice from staff members. Fran and her team took advantage of this newfound interest within our parent community and created the No Excuses Parent University.

This collection of courses was a form of professional development for parents. As we used to say, "Come and get your master's in parenting." The Parent University offered free sessions to adults, and sometimes their children, that took place on campus in the evening. Several staff members taught courses such as Family Math Night, where parents learned ways to enhance and support math skills with their children at home. Other sessions, like Developing Capable Young People (based on the work of H. Stephen Glenn), were taught by trained individuals like Fran who dug deeply into meaningful strategies that parents could use to promote lifelong success skills for their kids. From police officers who taught safety courses, to specialists who supported literacy development, the courses that made up the Parent University program were well received. But it wasn't just the variety of options that we offered to parents that made it successful; it was the way in which we reached out to parents to encourage them to participate.

I've met some educators who believe that parents lacking basic parenting skills should be required to go to classes like the ones we offered through the Parent University. Those who force this requirement on parents are likely to get a negative and defensive response. And who would blame the parents? No adult wants to be told that he or she needs to improve in the area of parenting. It's humiliating. We understood this at Los Pen and took a different approach to filling the seats of our classes. Instead of telling parents that they needed to participate, we publicized our events by asking parents to attend alongside staff members. One of the classes we offer was created by an outstanding advocate for children named H. Stephen Glenn. Glenn created a groundbreaking concept titled Developing Capable Young People that teaches adults how to shape children in a way that fosters what he calls The Significant Seven. (It's well worth your time to visit www.capabilitiesinc.com to find out more.) Knowing that I planned on attending a Developing Capable

Young People (DCYP) workshop, I went around school beforehand sharing my plans with other parents whom I felt could benefit as well. I would walk up to one of the parents and say something like, "Because I have kids of my own, I'm going to attend DCYP classes. You should join me and we can learn together." On other occasions, I might encourage parents to attend by saying how their parenting experiences could add a lot to the conversation. We found that any anxieties or defensiveness that parents might feel in attending classes like these were neutralized when staff members were inviting and made the choice to associate with parents not as teachers, but as fellow parents.

The work of the Parent University at Los Pen can be found in similar formats throughout the NEU Network of Schools. Educators within our network understand the need to reach out to our parents in unique and different ways. Schools like the No Excuses University at Vermont Elementary School in San Bernardino, California have made amazing steps forward to shift their school culture. An exemplary model that supports parents, Vermont Parent University (VPU) has an abundance of learning opportunities featured in a yearly course catalog. This catalog offers engaging classes that are free to every school parent. The effects of this program were felt immediately. Liz Atkinson, principal of NEU at Vermont, offered her thoughts about VPU: "I have noticed several significant changes to the culture of Vermont School since the creation and implementation of Vermont Parent University. First, parents have built a stronger rapport with our teachers through a common understanding of what is expected in our classrooms. They aren't afraid to ask questions or admit that they need help in a particular area. Second, parents feel much more confident in their abilities to help their children with their homework. Finally, our students show pride in their parents' interest in life-long learning. Our parents wear VPU shirts on the VPU class days to emulate their desire to be better-educated adults. In our inaugural year, we graduated 120 parents from Vermont Parent University who are now equipped to facilitate learning for their children at home."

Schools that wish to embrace parents as partners must first choose to shift their own thinking. The Vermont Parent University is a perfect example of productive change as a result of such a shift. There are always times for us as educators to be firm in our expectations of parents, but we must choose our stances wisely and do so with respect. Our understandings about the circumstances that many parents deal with on a daily basis should always be taken into account when sharing expectations with our parent community. We have found that there is a middle ground between enabling and commanding our parents. That middle ground is found in the way that we reach out to support the needs of our families.

In my career thus far, I have had the privilege to hear many very kind words from educators who have attended my conferences or visited schools in the network. Even so, the nicest thing that was ever said to me came from a complete stranger in one of the most unexpected of places. One day while sitting on the beach with my wife and kids, a stranger noticed the collective work that we were engaged in as we were playing on the shore. My girls were multi-tasking, both building a sand castle and dumping the leftover sand on my wife's legs and in my hair. As this stranger came upon us, she stopped briefly, looked me in the eyes, and said, "You have a really nice family."

I thanked her and she continued her walk down the beach. After she left, my heart was filled with gratitude for her words and pride in my family. I did not know this woman, but the words that she used to compliment my kids were enough to make me feel honored. Those of you who are parents know that when someone says kind things about your kids, in many respects, they're saying kind things about you. In fact, if given the choice, most parents would rather hear compliments about their children than receive accolades about themselves. As we work to strengthen our partnership with parents, we must never forget that no matter how unqualified we perceive some parents to be, in their heart of hearts they love their kids far more than any of us ever could. We must never, ever assume that we know better or care more for children than their own parents do. The best defense against such an attitude is to show a level of caring toward parents that is akin to the commitment we show to students in the classroom. When we do this, parents will not only learn the values that we promote through our No Excuses University endeavor; they will embrace them as well.

Chapter Seventeen

Theory to Practice

Items for Articulation

- ❑ Think about your families living in poverty. When was the last time your teammates or you visited the homes or apartments of these families? Why might this be important?

Items for Action

- ❑ As a school, choose a day to visit the homes or apartments of some of your neediest families. During your brief visits, say a kind word to the parents about their children, drop off a small treat as part of a holiday, or deliver information about an upcoming event. No matter how you choose to reach out to parents, make this a time that your staff displays a unified spirit of caring and stewardship.
- ❑ The ideas in this chapter related to supporting parents only scratch the surface of what we are doing throughout the network as a result of Fran Hjalmarson's work. For schools seeking to strengthen their relationships with parents and develop strategies that result in greater success for students, schools should make plans to read the book *Differentiated Parent Support* as part of a book study.

Chapter Eighteen

Key Concepts

"I do not believe in a fate that will fall on us no matter what we do. I do believe in a fate that will fall on us if we do nothing."

— Ronald Reagan

1

The NEU endorsement acts as a playbook of sorts that helps to guide a school's path.

2

Every system created by a staff is displayed in a practitioner-friendly way.

3

Schedules, strategies, and agreements within the endorsement are explicit.

4

The endorsement is revised and signed by the staff each year in an effort to meet the changing needs of students.

The NEU Endorsement: A Staff's Promise

Like many who grew up in a small town, I found the experience to be enjoyable as a young boy, but challenging by the time I entered high school. The romance of living in an Andy Griffith-like community became tainted by the reality of the trials that I faced as a teenager. The greatest challenge of all was the fact that I attended school with very few individuals who had a like-minded perspective about the future. Normally, students who face such challenges take comfort in the support that they receive from their teachers. For me, however, that demographic happened to be the one that presented most of the challenges.

I did have, like most students, a handful of highly supportive adults in high school who genuinely cared for me and actively sought out the good in me when my attitude or work habits were not all that they should have been. Among the best was my typing teacher, Mr. Wynn. His structured teaching and flexible attitude got the best out of me without breaking my spirit. As great as he was, the subject matter that he taught was not exactly what universities were looking for in future alumni from their schools. Absent my ability to type 85 words a minute, I partook in a high school education that left me ill-prepared academically and under-encouraged socially. Enter Ms. Leystan.

Ms. Leystan, whose name is fictional but whose presence was all too real, left a mark on my high school career that has yet to be forgotten. Her demeaning treatment of the young adult in me created a motivation out of spite for her that in many ways helped shape me into the man I am today. Ms. Leystan and I were about as different as they come. The personal beliefs about education that she openly shared with my classmates and me were nowhere near the ones that I held as an individual. I cannot recall a time when she mentioned the word "college," and if she did, it certainly was not used as a suggested path for any of us to follow. And while I can think of a dozen reasons why Ms. Leystan represented everything that I dislike in a teacher, it was her view of education itself that makes me cringe to this day.

Ms. Leystan had a simple perspective when it came to delivering instruction. She felt that it was her job to teach and it was my job to learn. Strategies of motivating students to learn or building on the individual strengths that they possess must have been taught in a course that she chose to sleep through in pursuit of her own college degree. When I was challenged by the content, the best feedback I received from her was the red markings on my graded papers. When I challenged her thinking in class, she degraded me in front of my peers. In fact, the only meaningful conversation that she ever had with me took place just two days before I graduated from high school. At the end of the period, she asked to speak with me alone at the back of the classroom. I thought to myself, "Finally, after four years she's going to apologize." I could not have been more wrong.

As I stood in her back office, she spoke words that to this day are ingrained in my memory. She said, "Damen, I want to tell you something that I have been wanting to say for four years now. I question your potential because I think all you are is just a big weenie."

Looking back, I'm surprised at her choice of the word "weenie" when she had so many other demeaning words to choose from, but nevertheless I understood her message. Not surprised at all by the feelings that she shared, I said, "Ms. Leystan, if I cared a bit about what you thought about me, I would be really disappointed, but the fact is I don't."

What hurt me as I left that classroom was not that she didn't like me, nor that she didn't believe in me. As you have read, I had parents who took on that role and supported me plenty. What saddened me was the fact that if she had had such a conversation with me, I could only imagine how many other students she had talked to in the same way.

Ms. Leystan's behavior was and is representative of a person who completely lost sight of her purpose as a teacher. I believed then, as I do now, that she entered the profession with the best of intentions just like 99.9 percent of the educators who do across the country. Her flaw, however, was not just that she lost sight of the real work of teaching, but more so that her colleagues and the school did as well. They never joined together in any way, shape, or form to endorse a model of promoting an educational experience that would enhance the lives of students. In fact, they never even decided exactly what they stood for as a school. Every teacher worked privately, with a level of independent thinking that exuded an aura of selfishness that would make Paris Hilton look like Mother Teresa. In turn, this selfishness put students into a cycle of academic and social failure that continued for many years to come. The word sad does not even begin to accurately describe this kind of culture. What is the best defense from such a culture? How do we ensure that we don't lose sight of the commitments that we all made as inspired new educators entering the profession? We pledge our commitments to each other through a comprehensive endorsement of best practices.

The NEU Endorsement

The NEU endorsement was purposefully created with simplicity in mind. It is the result of a staff's work on the exceptional systems, commitments, schedules, and strategies that have been developed to promote school-wide success. Never a byproduct of any kind of mandate from the top down, this endorsement is genuine, practical, and referred to often as a guide to support student learning for all. Every documented system within the endorsement includes the strategies, commitments, and schedules that play a part in promoting the kind of unity that instills accountability from one classroom to the next. This endorsement, which is seen in its entirety in the Appendix, is representative of the collective work of a staff's ideas.

It is crucial that staff play a major role in the development of an endorsement and the systems within it. Remember, when a principal creates systems, they will remain in place for as long as that principal continues as the leader of the school. However, when created by a staff with the guidance of a principal, these systems will remain far beyond the tenure of their leader. And because of the constant state of flux in which administrators often find themselves, we are better served to develop our endorsements with this in mind.

Endorsements can contain anything that is deemed to be critical to the success of a school. NEU endorsements go beyond most by including agreed-upon plans to promote college readiness on site. While there is no checklist for the specific items that must be included, each endorsement should have the following components:

1. ***Documentation of your school's pledge:*** Some schools refer to this as a mission or purpose statement, while others call it a school-wide promise. What you call it is not important in the least. What is important is whether the words can be recalled and, more importantly, lived by a school's stakeholders. I have worked with many schools that spent hundreds of man-hours developing statements that were a mile long and an inch deep. The result of their work may have ended up in a frame or on a poster that is strategically hung on the wall in the front office, but more often than not they were too long for anyone to recall, much less act upon.

   Many schools write statements like these either because they have to or because they think it's just something that they are supposed to do. It's time for all of us to say what we mean and live by what we say. And because I have yet to meet an educator who can reflect, recite, or even remember a 100-word mission statement as they teach, let's try to keep our words simple and to the point. The 18-word pledge of Los Pen has always been something that is at the top of every important document produced by our school. From letters to parents, to staff meeting agendas, the words "***We are committed to creating a school that knows no limits to the academic success of each student***" are a preamble of sorts that precede any message that we wish to send. These words, which are used by many NEU schools as well as other, non-NEU schools, describe our deep desire to find the potential in all of our students and prepare them for the future.

2. ***Explanation of your school's one goal:*** I have seen the results when schools set out to create goals for everything under the sun. I have met educators who had so many goals that they could not recall a single one of them. Definitions for goals are numerous, but I personally enjoy the definition of a goal as "the object of

a person's ambition." The word "object" is both singular and targeted. Because of this, I don't believe in schools having more than one goal. Of course there may be numerous things that a school needs to work on, but in my opinion, I don't think this automatically warrants the creation of additional goals. Rather, I would suggest that we seek not to make more goals but instead to develop different strategies to meet our school's top goal. Our one goal is simple: *Every student, without exception and without excuse, will be proficient or advanced in reading, writing, and math.* Everything else that others may describe as a goal is really just a strategy to help us achieve our one goal.

Depending on your level, your one goal may very well be different from the one that I have described. This is because the priorities of every school are diverse, especially when comparing the needs of elementary schools to that of secondary schools. In the end, your staff must decide what is most important to the success of your students and create one goal to follow as you move forward.

3. ***Systems and commitments that promote unity:*** Each of the six exceptional systems must be documented within a school's endorsement. Any additional exceptional systems should also be documented and endorsed by the staff. Some examples within our endorsement are the collaboration commitment, the assessment plan, student goals, the primary intervention model, the code of conduct, and many agreements in regard to the strategies that will be implemented as a part of a No Excuses University.

4. ***Schedules:*** Schedules are nothing if not abundant in schools. Because of this, NEU endorsements should include every important schedule that a teacher needs to refer to throughout the year.

5. ***Accessibility***: Every NEU endorsement must be accessible. At the end of each school year, our school's leadership team finalizes all of the components within our endorsement and then forwards the entire document to teams for review. In an effort to both save paper and create appropriate access, the endorsement is never placed in a master file or binder; rather, it is developed into a PDF document that is placed on the desktop of every computer in the school. Staff members refer to the document often to guide them in planning throughout the school year.

6. ***Signatures:*** Finally, every NEU endorsement is signed by each member of the staff. This is not contractual in nature. It is a promise that comes from the heart to support the content within the endorsement. If someone chooses not to sign, that is absolutely his or her choice. What most schools find, however, is that 100 percent of a staff takes pride in the work represented in an endorsement and eagerly signs this last page, which is framed and placed in a prominent area of the school. This is because the work is representative of their plans and strategies, not ideas that have been mandated.

The act of having an endorsement in writing is so important because it grounds us as a staff. Endorsements remind us of our beliefs on a daily basis and guard us from the trap of falling into the habits of teachers like Ms. Leystan and her colleagues. NEU endorsements make note of what we stand for and act as visual reminders of the commitments that we have made to our colleagues next door or across the campus. They are more than words on paper; they are expressions of the ideals that have the potential to turn our schools into great academic organizations.

Chapter Eighteen

Theory to Practice

Items for Articulation

- ❑ In order for a staff to unify around one endorsement, they must first build relationships based on respect and professionalism. Which areas of strength can your staff build upon in these two areas? What areas of challenge still exist, and how might you work to address them?
- ❑ Take a look at the "40 Next Steps for Schools" in the Appendix of the book for ideas as you begin to create your staff's endorsement.

Items for Action

- ❑ One of the most valuable activities a school can participate in is the creation of a document like the NEU endorsement. As found in the Appendix, the sample endorsement includes all of the systems and schedules that are used to unify a school's commitment to students. As a school, begin the work of creating your own endorsement. Your goal should be to improve your endorsement each year so as to become more explicit in your unified work as a staff.

- ❑ Endorsements should be worked on during the last few months of each school year, as opposed to the first few months when school begins. Such proactive planning will allow your staff to come back to school from summer vacation having schedules and systems in place and knowing exactly what they stand for as a school community.

Chapter Nineteen

Key Concepts

"Build for your team a feeling of oneness, of dependence on one another, and of strength to be derived by unity."

— Vince Lombardi

1

There is a big difference between schools that promote college readiness and No Excuses Universities.

2

Schools must apply for No Excuses University status before they can use the trademarked name and logo.

3

Not every school that applies is granted NEU status.

4

Every school within the NEU Network of Schools must communicate, collaborate, and show continuous improvement in order to remain in the network.

Chapter Nineteen

Joining the No Excuses University Network of Schools

In January 2004, a small southern California elementary school became a source of inspiration by creating a college readiness initiative known as the No Excuses University. In just a few short years, that inspiration has motivated educators and schools across the country to take a similar path. As of January 2013, there were more than 162 official No Excuses Universities in twenty-two states across America. The thousands of educators at these very diverse schools (K-5, K-6, K-8, middle, junior high, high school, college, and charter) collectively support more than 100,000 students, many living in challenging environments where poverty is the standard. No Excuses University staff members understand that we are in a race against the clock where the stakes could not be higher. (See how our network is growing by visiting www.noexcusesu.com.)

There's a difference between schools that promote college readiness and schools that are officially accepted into the No Excuses

University Network. Because of this, we go to great lengths to protect the integrity of this model. Everything that you have read in this book about promoting college readiness can be done within your classroom and your school with only one exception; only schools that have been recognized as official NEU campuses are allowed to use the trademarked No Excuses University name and logo associated with this endeavor. While the rewards of being a part of this movement are great, the expectations for the schools that are accepted are extremely high.

The act of being granted official No Excuses University status should not be looked at as an award. Participating as a No Excuses University is so much more than that. It is a way of life. Schools are not asked to pay a membership fee, nor are they required to pay dues of any kind. The purpose of creating a network like ours is to connect like-minded educators with a passion to learn from one another, work collaboratively, and participate in an educational reform effort that has the potential to change the face of public education as we know it.

As the founder of this endeavor, I take this responsibility very seriously. Schools that wish to join the network must participate in an application process that is reviewed by a committee of NEU educators and supporters. Not every school that applies is allowed into the NEU Network. In fact, not every school that has been accepted as an official No Excuses University is allowed to remain in the network. A yearly reapplication process takes place, as schools are held accountable for continuous growth in the development and implementation of exceptional systems that focus on promoting college readiness for all. Finally, schools are also judged on their collaborative contributions to the network. Schools who wish to join must continually ask themselves, "What value do we add to the No Excuses University Network of Schools?"

Joining the Network

Schools seeking membership into the No Excuses University Network can participate in the application process after a team attends a No Excuses University Institute. That team must include the principal. It is imperative that each team, including the principal, represent all grade levels or departments. After attending an institute, schools apply through a written submission that focuses on seven specific questions about the implementation of the six exceptional systems, as well as a video submission that displays a school's college readiness commitment at work. A committee, which selects only schools that show extraordinary passion and drive for the NEU model, reviews each application. This application, which can be found and completed online at www.noexcusesu.com, guides interested parties through the process. The guidance for a successful application is vague for a reason. Our desire is to select schools that are already displaying the ideals of the NEU model, not schools that have written to a rubric to receive a specific score.

Entrance into the No Excuses University Network is granted to schools for one year. Each year, schools take part in a short reapplication process to give evidence of the growth that they have made from one year to the next. Schools that do not continue to meet the declared expectations or that show a lack of desire to make improvements are dropped as official NEU schools.

Our ambition is to be associated with the best and brightest in our profession, but this does not mean that we seek to be an elitist organization. Many of our schools are far from being the top performing in their districts. In fact, some of our schools are challenged by a looming status of *program improvement* that makes others wary of forming long-term partnerships. We are different. We initially select schools based on potential and retain them as official members based on performance. This endeavor can be successful at any school that is willing to participate in innovative practices that promote college readiness. The most successful schools are the ones that step out unafraid as they eagerly seek to meet the expectations placed on every official No Excuses University.

Expectations of NEU Schools

Far more important for a school than being accepted into the network is its ability to meet the day-to-day expectations that come with being an official NEU school. We have observed several schools that made the mistake of thinking that their No Excuses University status was some kind of an award. They thought that their work was over after the application process. In reality, that's when the work really begins.

The No Excuses University Network is not for everyone. Both the organization and I have no desire to partner with educators who do not share the same core values that we do. Even though every NEU principal must sign an agreement that carefully describes the expectations of participating schools, there have been several who, frankly, just don't get it. Because of this, many schools have been asked to leave the network as quickly as they were asked to join. The seven agreements listed here clearly lay out the expectations that principals are asked to sign on behalf of their school in order to become a No Excuses University.

1. I/We will not authorize the use of the trademarked No Excuses University name and/or logo to any individual or organization other than our school, without the express written consent of No Excuses University.

2. Any speaking engagements that include a significant discussion about the No Excuses University concepts for which any staff member or I receive compensation must be

booked through No Excuses University and the president, Dan Lopez.

3. I/We understand that should the principal of our school retire, resign, transfer, or be terminated, the new principal must attend a No Excuses University Institute within one year of their appointment to our school. Failure for a new principal to attend an institute may result in the dismissal of our school from the No Excuses University Network of Schools.

4. I/We commit to having our school's principal and at least one representative from our school attend an NEU National Convention a minimum of once every two years.

5. I/We understand that should our school be dismissed from the No Excuses University Network of Schools, it is the responsibility of the principal to cease all use of the trademarked No Excuses University name and logo school-wide within 90 days of a written request on behalf of the No Excuses University.

6. I/We understand that the use of the No Excuses University name and logo, and acceptance into the No Excuses University Network of Schools, is granted on a yearly basis. I/We understand that all No Excuses University Schools must participate in a yearly webinar and provide a completed reapplication in order to retain membership and use of the NEU name and logo. Reacceptance into the network is contingent on each school living up to our NEU Promise and following the Six C's of an NEU Professional.

7. I/We understand that the principal is responsible for ensuring that all current and future members of the staff agree to all of the above terms.

No Excuses University Testimonials

As you can see, this endeavor is only for the most bold and passionate among us. Most schools do not typically seek the expectations that we place on those within the network. However, because of their desire to step away from the status quo, No Excuses Universities are realizing results that are exciting their entire school communities. After reading what some of our principals have said about their participation in the No Excuses University movement, I think you'll find that they would have it no other way.

Becoming a No Excuses University has brought the staff of Lowrie Elementary together to celebrate successes and plan together for challenges. Reflecting on our experience, the most powerful aspect so far has been the camaraderie that shared accountability has provided us. To begin with, a handful of teachers attended a workshop and returned to share their unbridled enthusiasm with colleagues. Next, we moved forward, as the staff attended training together and came to the realization that we certainly do have something special happening at our school! Documenting the exceptional systems that make Lowrie a special place to learn gave everyone a chance to dream big. Recording our application video gave us a glimpse into the excitement that our students hold about their futures. Finally, celebrating collaboratively with our students when we were accepted as a No Excuses University on May 25, 2009 made us realize our journey is just beginning.

Kelly O'Brien
Principal
Lowrie Elementary
Elgin, IL

The power of the No Excuses University experience is far reaching and brings opportunities to teachers, school staff, parents, students, and the community that were not present before. Prior to our school's dedication to the No Excuses ideology, our school's sense of collaboration and community were weak. Over the past three years as a No Excuses school, the growth and progress our school has made for students and families is priceless. The commitment teachers, staff, families, and students have made to excellence and high quality education will last our students a lifetime. During this period of growth, we have added a Heritage Wall to the center of our school, which showcases various tiles made by families at our school. As part of the partnership with parents and families, we were also fortunate enough to take students and their family members on a field trip to USC this past year. The experience and journey of No Excuses has shown teachers and school staff the ways to get students to succeed and how the greatness of a school truly does come from within.

Lucy Medina
Principal
Agua Caliente Elementary
Palm Springs, CA

No Excuses University has given our school structure for all the beliefs we have about our students. Using this structure to motivate our students towards excellence has made a measurable difference. The vocabulary is just a jumping-off point for our students. Fifth-grade students would ask at what age they could quit school. Now they are planning on where they will go to college! More of our parents are also going to college and thinking about the opportunities they could have with a post-high school education. NEU gives our students opportunities they never knew they had!

Cheryl Dixon
Teacher
Moffitt Elementary
Springfield, OR

The No Excuses University philosophy has created a paradigm shift at Kenyon Woods. The university focus has given relevance in the eyes of the students to the assessments they are required to take. They are not only excited about the prospect of going to college, but feel empowered to take control of their education. MAP scores are no longer just numbers; they are indicators to the students of what areas they need to strengthen in order to reach their goal of a higher education. As we integrate our existing programs into NEU and develop new exceptional systems where they are needed, support for both students and staff is strengthened. This framework, combined with focused leadership and boundless enthusiasm, has created our "culture of universal achievement," which is felt throughout the building. Our daily morning mantra "We are Kenyon Woods, and we dream big!" is more than just a saying; it's a philosophy our entire building works to embody.

Sue Welu
Principal
Kenyon Woods Middle
Elgin, IL

A little kindergarten boy at our school walked up to his teacher's desk with the question, "Can I borrow your stapler?" The teacher responded by handing the stapler to the boy, who immediately tried, without success, to cram it into his pockets, which were already bulging with pencils, erasers, and other school supplies. As he waddled back toward his desk, he was asked by his teacher, "What are you going to do with all that stuff in your pockets?" His answer was instant, and far-reaching. "I'm going to college, Mrs. Burrell." The power of No Excuses University is the undeterred, genuine hope it creates in the life of a child. The gift of No Excuses University is that it is not concerned with where a child comes from; it is focused only on where they are going.

Burke Staheli
Principal
Washington Elementary
Washington, UT

I have been blessed and honored to become the principal of Los Peñasquitos Elementary School *following* Damen Lopez *and* Jeff King, *former co-principals. I can personally attest to the uniqueness of this revelation. I am often asked what is at the foundation of this amazing elementary school and I easily reply, "The staff." At the heart of this extraordinary experience is an exemplary staff that breathes passion for student success. The common core belief is that collectively we are responsible and accountable for student success and achievement. This group constantly implements strategies to set aside the "baggage" children often bring with them, allowing instruction to reach students. If a child does not respond, they look to adjust instruction with a never-give-up attitude. They continually set high expectations for themselves and our students. The exceptional systems serve as a framework for excellence, providing a clear direction and momentum of this unique culture. This recipe for success withstands the transition of personnel. A climate exists where commitment to excellence grows and the staff works to inspire, motivate, and nurture individuals to exceed their potential.* WELCOME TO NEU!!

Deanne McLaughlin
Principal
Los Peñasquitos Elementary
San Diego, CA

No Excuses University inspired me to establish a pen pal program with Illinois State University for my intermediate classroom of students with emotional disabilities. The assistant women's athletic director was incredibly supportive as she recruited the perfect mix of college students who became positive role models for my class. After our class earned 1,000 Reggie (ISU mascot) grams for displaying positive behavior, our pen pals took it upon themselves to travel three hours to make a surprise visit with Reggie in tow. The bond between pen pals and students reached beyond pencil and paper. Their connection helped my students realize the importance of their own goals, both immediate and long term. Now my students can visualize themselves going to college. Many students, parents, and pen pals said they are better for having gone through this experience. As a teacher I couldn't agree more!

Stephanie Kovarik
3-6 ED Teacher
Whitley Elementary
Hoffman Estates, IL

My second-grade bilingual teacher called me to her classroom to see what one of her students was wearing. I was thinking—what it could be? She brought me one of her students, who is a second language learner and a struggling student. I saw that she was wearing a Texas Tech lanyard. I asked the child why she was wearing it, thinking that she would tell me that it was because her teacher went to school there. She told me that her father bought it for her because this was where she was going to go to college. When she goes to college, she will be the first in her family to attend college.

Haidi Appel
Principal
Mitzi Bond Elementary
El Paso, TX

We have developed a Culture of Universal Achievement at Dove Academy that challenges our students, staff, and parents to look beyond an elementary school, middle school, or even high school education. Our No Excuses University Program is driving the evolution of our school from a good academy to a great one. As a charter school, we are a school of choice. Our funding is based upon our enrollment. For our school to exist, we have to distinguish ourselves from the variety of educational programs offered in the metro Detroit area. We have to give the families in our community a reason to select our academy as their elementary school. The development of our No Excuses University Program has furthered our efforts to become a school of substance. We are becoming a school of "first choice" for our community. The results from our efforts this school year are pouring in. We cut our grade level retentions in half and on average we beat the Detroit public schools on every state test that we administer. More than 96 percent of our students re-enrolled for next school year and we surpassed every Adequate Yearly Progress (AYP) Target that we had to meet. This year, Dove Academy was recognized by the Michigan Department of Education for Beating the Odds, achieving 80 percent proficiency on the state math test and nearly 70 percent proficiency in English Language Arts —even though nearly 60 percent of our students are "economically disadvantaged." Working with Damen and developing our No Excuses University Program has helped us realize that for our students to prepare happy and successful lives, they need to learn about college now. All of our students will be proficient in reading, writing, and math. All of our students must build their character. Our students are college bound and they know it!

Frank Nardelli
Principal
Dove Academy K-7
Detroit, MI

As educators, our dream is to make a real difference for all kids, inspiring all students to persist to graduation with the skills and confidence to pursue post-secondary education and training. No Excuses University sets us up for achieving our dream. Working together to accomplish a K-16 goal means we are better preparing our kids for the future challenges they will face. As a staff, self-reflection and candid conversations allow us to continuously evaluate our school and determine our strengths and weaknesses. The six exceptional systems gave us the framework to improve our effectiveness in all areas. As one of the first No Excuses High Schools we are looking forward to a growing network of secondary schools with which to collaborate and share ideas. No Excuses University promotes relationships, collaboration, and change, all of which have positively impacted our school climate.

Kandy Frazier
Principal
Carthage High School
Carthage, MO

Kenda Parkey, a kindergarten teacher, was having her students participate in math centers. One of the centers for the day was free choice with math manipulatives. Kenda was instructing her math lesson at the back table with a group. During her lesson, she could hear the words "college," "teaching," and "going to school" coming from another center. When the bell rang to change centers, she went to the manipulative center and noticed an amazing arrangement on the carpet and asked her students what it was. Her students told her the kangaroos were all going to college and the bears were teaching them. The group insisted on leaving their college up for the next group. Each group continued to add more to the "college." Wow. It is amazing, when you open up the world to children, what five-year-olds can see! No Excuses University really is awakening hope, determination, and persistence in all of the students at Prince Elementary School.

Tassi Call
Principal
Prince Elementary
Tucson, AZ

As I reflect on this year there have been great accomplishments and others still to conquer. We began with attending the TurnAround Schools NEU retreat two years ago and I was eager to jump on board. However, I knew we had work to do at Rosemary Kennedy Elementary in order to receive the honor of truly becoming an NEU school. Many of my teachers wondered why we were moving slowly and why we didn't order shirts for everyone because it was such a great concept. Today I had a conversation with someone and shared with them that now we had earned the privilege of wearing the NEU logo. This has been a great beginning to our journey. The concept of NEU infused energy needed to move forward and not just face challenges but overcome them. We have implemented School-wide Intervention for all students and this has yielded great benefits in many different aspects because we are all responsible for our students' academic gains. The year closed out with grade levels having conversations about students and honesty to be forward with concerns as well as accountability to each other. Often accountability is thought of as a "district concept." Today at RMK, it is our job to not just teach our children but ensure that if something isn't happening we will have the conversation as to why and how can we make it happen. I am pleased to say that we are all in make-it-happen mode, which is key to success, and look forward to the new chapter of success we will write in the upcoming school year.

Jackie Casillas
Principal
Rosemary Kennedy Elementary
Riverside, CA

Because the testimonials from energized and passionate NEU Professionals are far too numerous to publish in this book, I encourage you to visit www.noexcusesu.com to view many more first hand accounts of how the No Excuses University endeavor is generating results for schools across our country. By visiting our website, you can also search for a No Excuses University nearest to you and schedule a site visit through the principal. Finally, I invite you to subscribe to our various social networking pages. The sharing that takes place daily by thousands of NEU staff members will feed your soul with inspiration and stimulate you with ideas and strategies that you can use on your campus immediately.

Chapter Nineteen

Theory to Practice

Items for Articulation

- ❑ In Chapter 1, you were encouraged to create a checklist of the reservations that you may have about promoting college readiness to all students and place it inside of an envelope. Take that envelope and open it with your teammates. Which reservations have been alleviated? What challenges or questions still exist for you personally in regard to the promotion of college readiness?

Items for Action

If you and your colleagues are interested in creating a No Excuses University environment in an effort to join the NEU Network of Schools, consider some of the following suggestions:

- ❑ Assemble a No Excuses committee to help implement the strategies and ideas necessary for schools to be invited into the NEU Network.

- ❑ Create a comprehensive plan to promote a spirit of college readiness at your site that is in line with the six exceptional systems found in Chapter 4.
- ❑ Take the time to examine the Appendix. Many of these items offer tremendous examples for schools to follow.
- ❑ Review the NEU application found in the Appendix. This will help guide your own journey in discussing the benefits that your school can offer to the network. Schools that apply for official NEU status typically take several months to implement the strategies, ideas, and suggestions offered in this book before submitting their application.

CHAPTER TWENTY

EXTRAORDINARY

When I was a new staff member at Los Peñasquitos Elementary, the bell that rang at the end of the day acted as a reminder that the second part of my day was about to begin. Several times a week, I would leave campus around 3:30 p.m. in order to work the 4 p.m. to midnight shift as a bellman at the Radisson Hotel in San Diego. For many months, especially in the summer, the job was filled with meeting interesting people who offered plenty of tips. However, as the years went by and the economy began to dip, the tips went from filling the pockets of my uniform to barely filling the palm of my hand. One night, while working alone, I pulled from my pocket three one-dollar bills and lined them in a row on the top of the bell desk. These fruitless symbols of my labor inspired me to make a decision that I had been putting off for several months. I decided right then and there that the job had nothing left to offer me.

As I began to make plans to talk with my boss about resigning, a gentleman summoned me to his car and asked for my assistance with his bags. I loaded my bell cart and proceeded to lead the man to the elevators within the hotel lobby. After delivering the items to his room, I said, “Is there anything else I can help you with today, sir?”

Knowing that this was bellman language for “Could you please tip me?” the man pulled out a crisp five-dollar bill and a brand-new copy of a book. Thinking that he was going to give me a book and a five-dollar bill as a bookmark, I was surprised by his offer. He said, “Here’s the deal. You can have five bucks or you can have a copy of my brand-new book. But you can’t have both.”

I knew my answer immediately. I didn’t want some book that I knew nothing about. I wanted the five dollars! However, I was raised with enough manners to say to the man, “Sure, I love to read. I’ll take the book.”

I thanked him and headed downstairs. Exclaiming a few choice words under my breath, I walked to my bell desk with the same amount in my pocket as before, three dollars.

Out of boredom, I sat at the desk and opened up the book that the man gave me. Immediately, I became inspired by the collection of short anecdotes, poems, and writings within the pages. These stories were often about ordinary people who did extraordinary things. I can’t say that it was one specific item in the book that made such a profound impact on me, but I do remember being overtaken by a desire to somehow live a life that would influence others. As someone who has always considered himself to be quite ordinary, I finished reading the book feeling like I was very capable of doing something extraordinary. It wasn’t until many months later that I realized the significance of my experiences that afternoon. That man, Jack Canfield, had given me a book, *Chicken Soup for the Soul*, that would later sell more than 100 million copies and inspire people all around the world.

The message that I learned then is as relevant as the message that I try to share today. The No Excuses University Network of Schools is about *ordinary* people coming together to do *extraordinary* things. The strength that is found in the collaborative efforts of one another is immeasurable compared to the limitations of individuals acting alone. I wrote this book knowing that one person can influence a team. A team can influence a school. A school can motivate a collection of like-minded individuals. And like-minded individuals working together can change the world.

APPENDIX

NO EXCUSES UNIVERSITY

NO EXCUSES UNIVERSITY

ENDORSEMENT

NEU Commitment

In 1996, the staff of Los Peñasquitos Elementary School made public a commitment that was consolidated into one pledge and one goal. Today, our focus remains just as clear as it did when we first began.

Our Pledge

We are committed to creating a school that knows no limits to the academic success of each student.

Our One Goal

Every student, without exception and without excuse, will be proficient or advanced in reading, writing, and math.

Six Exceptional Systems

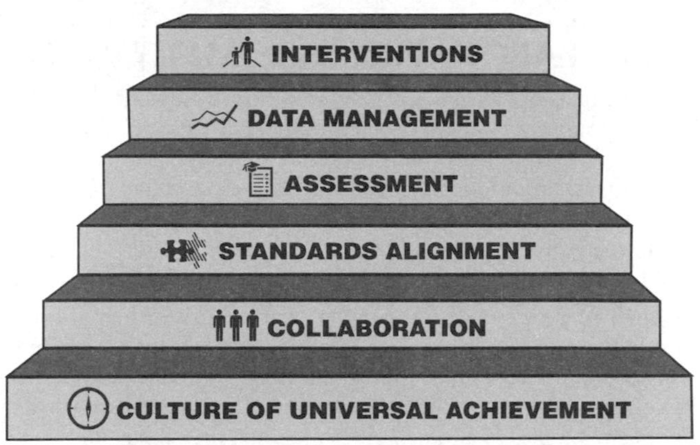

There is a difference between systems and "exceptional systems." Exceptional Systems are unique solutions to important challenges. They are created by the critical mass of a staff in a highly collaborative way. They are reviewed annually and driven by results. The six core exceptional systems that must be present on any successful campus should be visualized as a staircase. At the foundation is a culture of universal achievement that is grounded on the belief that every student is capable of meeting or exceeding grade level standards. When staff members believe that it is their responsibility to create success for every student, they collaborate as teams with that belief at their core. When they collaborate, they ensure that their work is aligned to standards. As they continue, they select common assessments that also align to those same standards. Data is then collected from common assessments in a way that is easily accessible, openly shared, and deliberately arranged. Finally, students are plugged into meaningful interventions that create academic results.

"We are committed to creating a school that knows no limits to the academic success of each student."

Collaboration Commitment

As staff members of Los Pen, we are committed to collaborating with one another in a variety of ways. We understand that the greatest academic and social gains for our students come as a result of quality instruction from the classroom teacher and highly effective measures of collaboration among team members. Los Pen staff members work interdependently with their teams in many ways. The following are examples of individual commitments that we are all willing to make as we collaborate as a staff:

Clarity of Purpose: Team members remain driven by our one goal to ensure that each student is proficient or advanced in reading, writing, and math. They meet with a purpose and devise agendas and timelines to ensure success at every collaborative meeting. They take the time to decide upon meeting topics in advance. After meeting, they follow through with collective agreements as a team.

Respectful of Time: Los Pen staff members are action-oriented professionals who value one another's time. They are prompt to staff and team meetings. They make the most of their time by collaborating during the school day with colleagues as they creatively group students in an effort to meet every student's needs.

Wednesday Time-Banking: Every Wednesday afternoon from 2:15–3:40, we set aside time for teams to work closely as they design instruction that translates into academic achievement for all. This time is held sacred by all members of the team, and should not be used for personal appointments or individual work time. This time may be used for staff meetings once every other month.

Professional Growth: Los Pen staff members are open to learning new methods, ideas, and strategies that will lead to greater academic success for all. They participate in on-site Thursday Collaboration workshops. They seek ways to learn from one another, and are committed to growing professionally together.

Building Candid Professional Relationships: Los Pen staff members are committed to developing strong professional relationships with each other. They praise one another during times of individual, team, and school-wide success. They are honest with one another as they respectfully confront concerns through "Candid Collaboration." They support one another during times that are challenging both professionally and personally. They celebrate with one another as friends and colleagues outside of the school community.

"We are committed to creating a school that knows no limits to the academic success of each student."

Standards Alignment

Our staff believes that we must continuously align our teaching to state standards. Standards alignment is not something that we've **done**, it's something that we do. In an effort to align our work in a practical way, we are committed to going through the process of dissecting each sub-standard. As we do, we ask ourselves four questions:

Specific Skills: What are the major skills that need to be targeted in order to effectively teach each sub-standard?

Assessments: What assessments will we use in order to offer summative and formative data for each sub-standard?

Instructional Methods: What strategies and ideas can we use to teach each sub-standard to our students?

Resources: What resources and materials will we use to ensure learning for all students? As we go forward, we understand that there are no shortcuts in doing this work. The best results will be realized when our teams work collaboratively together.

"We are committed to creating a school that knows no limits to the academic success of each student."

Assessment and Data Management

This assessment plan was generated by the Los Peñasquitos Elementary School Staff. It expresses a collective commitment to participate in specific assessments throughout each school year. The process of generating this plan started with individual commitments by teachers to specific assessments within the classroom. Grade levels later came together to endorse a plan that would address the detailed assessment needs that they have as a team. Finally the Curriculum and Assessment committee, composed of teachers, classified staff, and support team members, took a detailed approach to ensure that we as a school participate in assessments that:

- **Support the One Pledge and Goal of Our School**
- **Correlate to Academic Success for All**
- **Align with State Standards**
- **Encourage Student Participation Through the Development of Class and Individual Goals**
- **Focus on Assessments "FOR" Learning**
- **Facilitate Differentiated Instruction**

We believe that careful follow-through on the assessments and goals within this plan will result in higher achievement for all students. All student data will be stored in a site database that is easily accessible. Data will be openly shared through articulation meetings three times a year. The insightful interpretation of specific student data will allow teachers to tailor their instruction to the unique needs of each student. This document is more than words on paper; it represents the hard work and commitment of this staff as we continue to strive for academic excellence.

What Character Means for Students

Integrity

Be honest ◆ Don't deceive, cheat or steal ◆ Be reliable — do what you say you'll do ◆ Have the courage to do the right thing ◆ Build a good reputation ◆ Be loyal — stand by your family, friends and country

Respect

Treat others with respect; follow the Golden Rule ◆ Be tolerant of differences ◆ Use good manners, not bad language ◆ Be considerate of the feelings of others ◆ Don't threaten, hit or hurt anyone ◆ Deal peacefully with anger, insults and disagreements

Responsibility

Do what you are supposed to do ◆ Persevere: keep on trying! ◆ Always do your best ◆ Use self-control ◆ Be self-disciplined ◆ Think before you act — consider the consequences ◆ Be accountable for your choices

Honesty

Play by the rules • Take turns and share ◆ Be open-minded; listen to others ◆ Don't take advantage of others ◆ Don't blame others carelessly

Compassion

Be kind ◆ Be compassionate and show you care ◆ Express gratitude ◆ Forgive others ◆ Help people in need

Stewardship

Do your share to make your school and community better ◆ Cooperate ◆ Get involved in community affairs ◆ Stay informed; vote ◆ Be a good neighbor ◆ Obey laws and rules ◆ Respect authority ◆ Protect the environment

Bridge to College™

Plan for Character Development

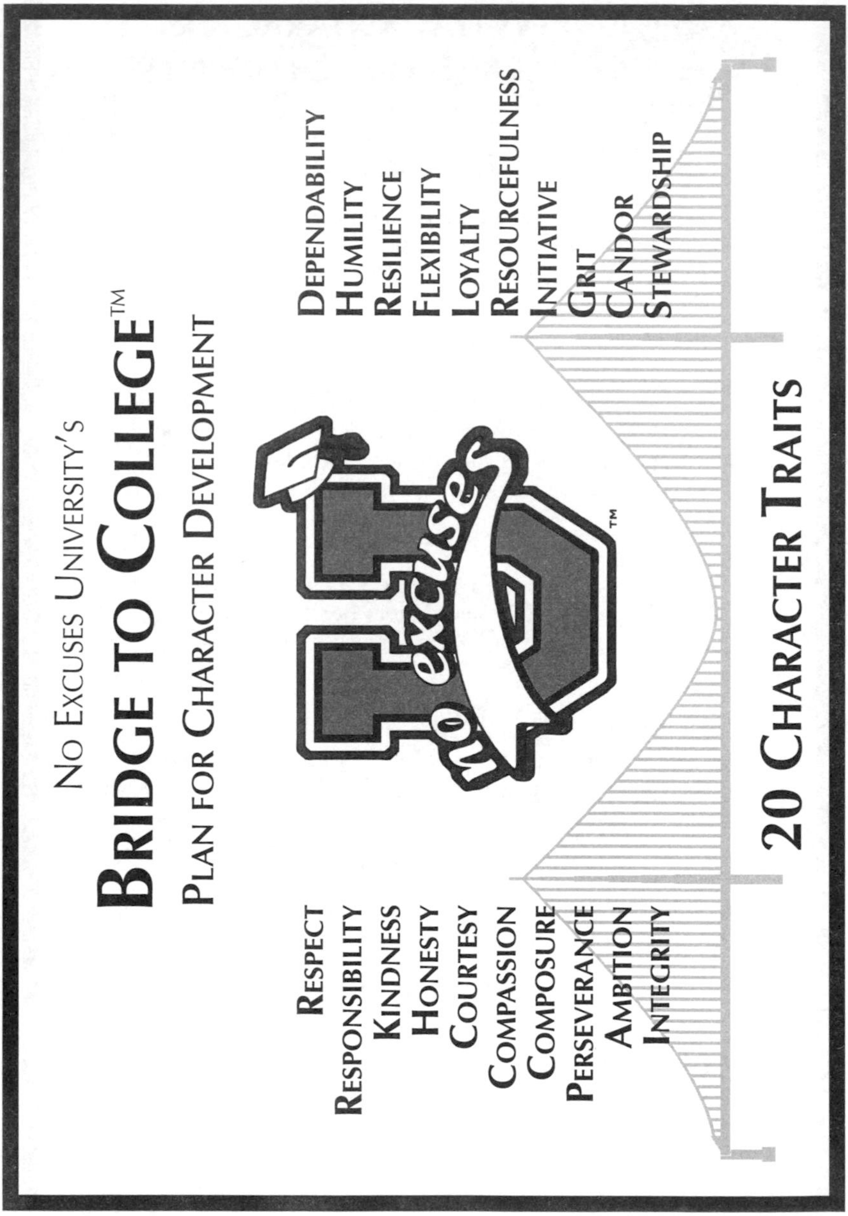

No Excuses University's
Bridge to College™
Plan for Character Development
no excuses
™
Respect
Responsibility
Kindness
Honesty
Courtesy
Compassion
Composure
Perseverance
Ambition
Integrity
Dependability
Humility
Resilience
Flexibility
Loyalty
Resourcefulness
Initiative
Grit
Candor
Stewardship
20 Character Traits

40 Next Steps For Schools

Culture of Universal Achievement

- ✓ Create a B.H.A.G, to endorse as a staff.
- ✓ Make a list of excuses you've made in the past and commit to fighting against them as a staff.
- ✓ Decide upon one clear set of rules and a common language that align with specific character traits and model them to students.
- ✓ Create one universal classroom management plan.
- ✓ Block off 15 minutes every day for morning meetings that educate and model expectations to students in every class.

Collaboration

- ✓ Create a one page, exceptional system for collaboration based on four to six commitments of how staff will treat each other and work as professionals.
- ✓ Establish routines of daily, weekly, monthly and yearly collaboration for staff as well as leadership teams.
- ✓ Devise a template for agendas based on action.
- ✓ Begin each collaborative effort by celebrating successes and laughing with each other and end with action steps for the future.
- ✓ Create a plan to practice candid collaboration as a staff.

Standards Alignment

- ✓ Create an exceptional system that aligns standards at each grade level.
- ✓ Generate a template for grade levels to use as they align their standards.
- ✓ Schedule opportunities for vertical articulation around standards.
- ✓ Ensure that all staff members agree on what mastery of each standard looks like and how it will be taught.
- ✓ Share standards daily with students in practical ways.

continued

40 Next Steps For Schools *cont.*

Assessment

- ✓ Create an assessment team made up of representation at each grade level or department.
- ✓ Determine which assessments you value and why.
- ✓ Devise clear schedules to both deliver assessments as well as analyze them.
- ✓ Implement a plan to develop individual goals for all students.
- ✓ Make sure that every assessment is aligned to a specific way of involving students in the process.

Data Management

- ✓ Create a database that is easily accessible to staff.
- ✓ Schedule at least 3 times a year to openly share data between the principal and individual teams.
- ✓ Design templates that are deliberately arranged to convey data in a way that encourages action.
- ✓ Post various data results throughout the school on a consistent basis.
- ✓ Ensure that data is readily available for students and parents.

Interventions

- ✓ Create an intervention support team packed with "doers" committed to results.
- ✓ Design an intervention master schedule that creatively lowers the student to teacher ratio.
- ✓ Shape routines that correlate the success of each intervention with a specific data point.
- ✓ Develop interventions that deal with social and emotional challenges impeding academic success.
- ✓ Establish a "community collaborative" that meets monthly to find ways to link organizations who want to give with families in need.

continued

40 Next Steps For Schools *cont.*

Powerful Symbolism

- ✓ Remove all clutter in classrooms and around campus.
- ✓ Establish Monday as "No Excuses" day where all students wear their school shirts and Friday as "college spirit" day where students and staff wear college apparel.
- ✓ Hang college flags and banners on every door in the school.
- ✓ Develop a list of inspirational quotes, have students vote on their favorites, and place them prominently throughout campus.
- ✓ Declare your commitments publicly and market your school in the press.

College Readiness

- ✓ Have every classroom adopt a university and refer to that class by the university name.
- ✓ Determine the years each grade graduates from college and refer to them as "class of 20--."
- ✓ Develop a yearly College and Career Fair that involves colleges and community members.
- ✓ Make a plan to take specific grade levels on yearly field trips to college campuses.
- ✓ Hold mandatory Parent Forums rolling out all of your college readiness plans and expectations as a school.

Classroom Management Plan
(Grades 2-5)

"Character is doing the right thing, even when no one is watching"

Code of Conduct:

I will display integrity ◆ I will be respectful ◆ I will be responsible
I will be honest ◆ I will be compassionate ◆ I will display stewardship

If you choose to break the code of conduct (consequences):

1st Time: Caution: Yellow
Sign in the book.

2nd Time: Stop: Red
Sign in the book. Fill out the rethinking paper

3rd Time: Time-Out:
Sign in the Book
Take a Break in another class
Fill out the time-out letter/home to parent
Possible Loss of Recess

4th Time or Severe Disruption:
Immediately sent to the office
Fill out character violation

Positive reinforcement:
Praise — Daily
Positive Notes Home — Random
Bridge to College™ Award
Individual Classroom Reinforcement

We have read and discussed this classroom management plan and will support and honor the plan throughout the year.

________________________ ________________________

Parent Signature Student Signature

Rethinking Letter

You are receiving a second warning about your negative choices. Please think about what you have done and answer these questions.

1. What did I do to receive my yellow warning?

    ____

    ____

2. What did I do to receive my red warning?

    ____

    ____

3. How did your choice affect others?

    ____

    ____

4. What caused your negative choice?

    ____

    ____

5. What could you do better next time?

    ____

    ____

Please check one:

______ I get the point. I will try harder in class.

______ I don't understand. We need to talk about my behavior.

_________________________ _________________________

Parent Signature Student Signature

Staff Code of Conduct

The Los Pen staff is committed to modeling character to students, parents, and each other. Based on work that was conducted by our staff during the 2004-2005 school year, we commit to focusing on the Bridge to College™ character traits in the following ways:

Integrity

- Return borrowed items in a timely fashion
- File own books in Book Room
- No using copy codes accidentally left on machine
- Promptness to all meetings and duties

Respect

- Resolve conflicts peacefully
- Every idea is important
- Showing Active Listening
- Please and Thank You!
- Embrace differences
- Consider each other's feelings
- Tolerance
- Less of: Put downs. Don't lose faith or temperament.

Responsibility

- Be on time
- Be organized
- Ownership of actions and consequences
- Accountable for learning
- Less of: Blame of others.
- No Excuses

continued

Staff Code of Conduct *continued*

Honesty

- Confidential with all
- Spotlighting fairness in our own lives
- Sharing work load among team/staff members
- Give people the benefit of the doubt

Compassion

- Greet fellow staff members
- Stop and have genuine conversations
- Mention and discuss caring interactions with other teachers to students
- Sign cards for staff members
- Greet parents
- Give compliments
- Less of: Rumors and gossiping

Stewardship

- Vote
- Take care of our classrooms
- Respect for our school community
- Reach out to our community partners
- Teach citizenship to students
- Involvement at Canyon Rim Community Center
- Less of: Complaining about evening school-sponsored events.

NO EXCUSES

"We are committed to creating a school that knows no limits to the academic success of each student."

INTERVENTIONS

Good schools are able to take interventions and analyze their effectiveness through the use of data. Great schools, however, are able to take data and translate it directly into the creation of appropriate interventions. Our school is committed to providing interventions that generate academic and social success for all students.

ACADEMIC SYSTEM

Intense, Individual Interventions (1-5%)

Increased group time and smaller teacher/student ratios

- Fluency
- Comprehension
- Phonics

Targeted Group Interventions (5-10%)

Small Groups

- Fluency
- Comprehension
- Phonics

Increased Instructional time

Universal Interventions (80-90%)

Core Curriculum

Differentiation of Instruction

Master Schedule

Assessments

Articulation

Class Placement

BEHAVIORAL SYSTEM

Intense, Individual Interventions (1-5%)

Behavior Intervention Plan

Possible Referral to IAT

Targeted Group Interventions (5-10%)

Social Stories

Referral to Counseling/ Caring Connections

Behavior Support Plan

Referral to SST

Universal Interventions (80-90%)

Code of Conduct/School Rules

Universal Classroom Management Plan

Morning Meetings

Resource Manual

Reinforcement System

Visual Schedule

Whole Class Social Skills

Behavior Contracts

Staff Development

Admin Connections/ Check-ins

Student Services

Recess Alternative

Class Placement

My Goals

____
Student (Name)

____
School Year

Subject: ______________________________

My Goal for the trimester is: ____________________

____

Three things that I can do to help me achieve my goal are:

1. ______________________________
2. ______________________________
3. ______________________________

____
Parent Signature

____
Student Signature

____
Teacher Signature

California State Fourth Grade Reading Standards

1.0 Word Analysis, Fluency, and Systematic Development

Students understand the basic features of reading. They select letter patterns and know how to translate them into spoken language by using phonics, syllabication, and word parts. They apply this knowledge to achieve fluent oral and silent reading.

Components of the Standards	Specific Skills	Assessments	Instructional Methods	Resources
Word Recognition				
1.1 Read narrative and expository text aloud with grade-appropriate fluency and accuracy and with appropriate pacing, intonation, and expression.	◆ Pacing ◆ Accuracy ◆ Intonation ◆ Expression	◆ IRI's ◆ DIBELS ◆ Fluency Timings ◆ Fluency Rubric	◆ Informal observations ◆ Anecdotal notes during guided reading ◆ Conferences ◆ Lit Circles ◆ Poem of the week ◆ Books on Tape ◆ Oral Presentation	◆ DIBELS ◆ Words Their Way ◆ 6-Min. Solutions ◆ Phonics They Use ◆ Rewards
Vocabulary and Concept Development				
1.2 Apply knowledge of word origins, derivations, synonyms, antonyms, and idioms to determine the meaning of words and phrases.	◆ Base Words (s,es,ed,ing,er,est) ◆ Idioms ◆ Synonyms ◆ Antonyms	◆ Theme Skills Test-HM (pages 14,15,44,60) ◆ HM Practice Sheets ◆ CA Summative Test (pages 4,25,47) ◆ Conferences ◆ Guided Reading ◆ Observation	◆ Guided reading ◆ Think aloud ◆ Idiom a day, discuss, post on chart ◆ Kids raise hand ◆ Games ◆ Use idioms in writing	◆ The King that Reigned ◆ Boss of the Plains-HM ◆ Internet - Google ◆ Book of Lists ◆ Frindle ◆ Wordly Wise Lesson

1.3 Use knowledge of root words to determine the meaning of unknown words within a passage.	◆ Roots (tele, rupt, sign, spect, graph, tract) ◆ Compound Words	◆ Theme Skills Test — HM (Pages 39,58,127) ◆ Use in Writing ◆ HM Practice Pages	◆ Root word trees (involve parents) ◆ Word Splash (Kids make dictionaries in journals) ◆ Games memory ◆ Teach physical signals ◆ Compound Word Pics	◆ Words Their Way ◆ Writer's Express ◆ HM ◆ puzzlemaker.com
1.4 Know common roots and affixes derived from Greek and Latin and use this knowledge to analyze the meaning of complex words (e.g., international).	◆ Roots- See Above ◆ Prefixes (re, mis, pre, con, com, dis, un, inter) ◆ Suffixes (ment, less, ly, y, er, or, ist, able, ible, ion, ness, ful)	◆ Theme Skills Test — HM (Pages 40, 59, 82, 84, 104,126,) ◆ Spelling Tests ◆ Guided Reading ◆ Meaning of Prefixes and Suffixes	◆ Spelling Book ◆ Word Sorts ◆ Prefix/Suffix Trees ◆ Word Hunt Prefix | Root | Suffix	◆ Red Hot Root Words ◆ Words Their Way ◆ Scholastic-Prefix/ Suffix Cards ◆ Rewards
1.5 Use a thesaurus to determine related words and concepts.	◆ Teach all about how to use a thesaurus		◆ Use Thesaurus ◆ HM-Overheads ◆ Make overhead of words — ask questions — mini lesson	
1.6 Distinguish and interpret words with multiple meanings.				

Los Peñasquitos Elementary Assessment Grid

	September	February	May
Kindergarten	• Letter I.D. • Phonics Skills • Running Record • Math Skills Checklist	• Letter I.D. • Phonics Skills • Word Recognition • Phonemic Awareness • Sentence Dictation • Running Record • Math Skills Checklist • On Demand Writing	• Letter I.D. • Phonics Skills • Word Recognition • Phonemic Awareness • Sentence Dictation • Running Record • Math Skills 1 Prob. Solving • On Demand Writing
First	• On Demand Writing • Spelling Inventory • Running Record / IRI • Math Skills Assessment 1 • Math Problem Solving	• On Demand Writing • Spelling Inventory • Running Record / IRI • Math Skills Assessment 2 • Math Problem Solving	• On Demand Writing • Spelling Inventory • Running Record / IRI • Math Skills Assessment 3 • Math Problem Solving
Second	• On Demand Writing • Running Record / IRI • Everyday Math Beg. Assessment • Math Problem Solving • Spelling Inventory • Fluency • MAPS (Read, Writ., Math)	• On Demand Writing • IRI • Everyday Math Mid-year • Math Problem Solving • Spelling Inventory • Fluency • MAPS (Read, Writ., Math)	• On Demand Writing • IRI • Everyday Math End of Year Assessment • Math Problem Solving • Spelling Inventory • Fluency • MAPS (Read, Writ., Math)

THIRD	• On Demand Writing • Spelling Inventory • Spelling (No Excuses Words) • Everyday Math Beg. Assessment • On- Demand Prob. Solving • MAPS (Read, Writ., Math) • Fluency	• On Demand Writing • Spelling Inventory • Everyday Math Mid-year • MAPS (Read, Writ., Math) • Fluency	• On Demand Writing • Spelling Inventory • Everyday Math End of Year Assessment • On- Demand Math Prob. Solving • MAPS (Read, Writ., Math) • Fluency
FOURTH	• On Demand Writing (Response to Lit) • GATES – Form S (Acad. October) • Everyday Math Beg. Assessment • Spelling – Word Journeys • MAPS (Read, Writ. , Math) • Fluency (students under 150 wpm)	• On Demand Writing • Everyday Math Mid-year • Spelling – Word Journeys • MAPS (Read, Writ. , Math) • Fluency	• On Demand Writing • Everyday Math End of Year Assessment • Spelling – Word Journeys • Fluency • MAPS (Read, Writ., Math)
FIFTH	• On Demand Writing (Persuasive Essay) • GATES – Form S (Acad. October) • Everyday Math Beg. Assessment • Spelling – Word Journeys • MAPS (Read, Writ. , Math) • Fluency (students under 150 wpm)	• On Demand Writing • Everyday Math Mid-year • Spelling – Word Journeys • MAPS (Read, Writ. , Math) • Fluency	• On Demand Writing • Everyday Math End of Year Assessment • Spelling – Word Journeys • Fluency • MAPS (Read, Writ., Math)

Student Involvement in Assessment

The staff at Los Peñasquitos Elementary believes that one of the best ways to increase student achievement is to involve students in the assessment process. Below is an example of the ways that third grade teachers will involve students in the process. Each grade level has made a similar commitment based on the assessments used by their team.

3rd Grade's Commitment to Involving Students in the Assessment Process	
On Demand Writing	Teachers will share the "six traits" child friendly rubrics with their students. We will involve the students in the scoring process, starting with the whole class and working towards individual peer scoring. Teachers will continue to guide students toward mastery in the first three traits, "ideas, organization, and conventions." Teachers will add "word choice" as a new area of focus.
Problem Solving	Teachers will also share "Problem Solving" child friendly rubrics with their students and involve them in the scoring process. Students will practice scoring with their peers.

Spelling Inventory	Teachers will share scores with their students. We will explain the spelling stages and make the students aware of their current stage. Teachers will help students set individual goals for themselves based on their needs and group accordingly.
Math Skill Assessment	Teachers will meet with students individually to discuss results of the Math Basic Skills Test. All students will receive a check-off sheet highlighting the test items that they have not yet mastered. Teachers will assist students in setting goals for the future.
Fluency	Teachers will receive training from Gail Adams in "Fluency Timings." Students will participate in fluency timings at least three times a week. Students will score themselves and chart growth. Teachers will instruct students on how to make individual goals for themselves.
IRI	Teachers will share IRI results including miscues, retelling, and comprehension. We will communicate students' strengths and weaknesses and help students create goals for the future.
MAPS	Teachers will share scores with their students and will set goals with them. Teachers will share Lexile ranges with students to use at home. We will work towards involving parents as we gain experience with MAPS.

No Excuses University Three-Way Pledge

Teacher Pledge

I am committed to creating a school that knows no limits to the academic success of each student. The following represents my personal commitment to the academic success of every student at Los Peñasquitos Elementary School:

- Accept no limits on the learning potential of any child
- Meet the individual learning needs of each child
- Create serious classroom learning environments
- Treat students, parents, and colleagues with courtesy and respect
- Hold students, parents, and each other to the highest standards of performance.
- Collaborate regularly with colleagues to seek and implement more effective strategies for helping each child to achieve his or her academic potential
- Do whatever it takes - go the extra mile - to ensure that every student achieves or exceeds grade level expectations based on state academic standards

______________________________ _______________

Teacher Signature Date

Teacher + Student + Parent = Success

No Excuses University Three-Way Pledge

continued

Student Pledge

I understand that my education is very important to my future. It will help me develop the tools I need to become a successful and productive person. I know that my education now will prepare me for college in the future. Because of this I am committed to following the requirements found in my No Excuses University Student Handbook. In addition, I commit to:

- Arriving at school every day on time unless I am ill
- Following the rules and the six Bridge To College™ character traits of our school
- Completing and turning in homework on time every day
- Returning letters, corrected work, and other school materials to my parents

____________________________ ______________

Student Signature Date

Teacher + Student + Parent = Success

No Excuses University Three-Way Pledge

continued

Parent Pledge

I understand that my child's education today is essential for their success in life. This experience will support him/her to become a successful and productive person. It will also prepare them for college if they so choose to attend. Because of this I am committed to following the requirements found in my No Excuses University Parent Handbook. These responsibilities are found in the:

- Mission, Vision, Shared Commitment, and Goal of Los Peñasquitos
- Parent Code of Conduct
- "Take Five" Commitment
- Parent Goals Commitment
- Commitment to ensuring my child attends school on time every day unless they are ill

Each of these responsibilities speaks to my commitment to support Los Peñasquitos in order to ensure a bright future for my child.

______________________________ _______________

Parent Signature Date

Teacher + Student + Parent = Success

"We are committed to creating a school that knows no limits to the academic success of each student."
No Excuses University Pledge

College Vocabulary by Grade Level

Below are the words that each grade level has committed to using in their classes as we promote college readiness for all. Please work with your team to continuously expose students to the college vocabulary within your grade's column, as well as all the grades before you.

Grade:	Vocabulary Words
K	College
1st	Achieve, Career Graduate, Goal
2nd	Major, Mascot Professor, Scholarship Dormitory
3rd	Advisor, Alumni Application, Bachelor's Degree Dean's List, Finals GPA, Grants Loan, NCAA Research
4th/5th	All words K-3 Focus on College Entrance Requirements for your state

"We are committed to creating a school that knows no limits to the academic success of each student."

No Excuses University Pledge

2012-2013 College Readiness

Grades: K-3

The planning committee came to the understanding that instead of strictly promoting the A-G requirements, we will focus on promoting awareness about college. We believe that this can and should look differently across the grade levels. See below for the ways that each grade will be asked to promote this awareness.

- Utilize college vocabulary in each classroom
- Participate in a college readiness kick-off assembly
- Promote college readiness at Friday Flags
- Add questions to the yearly school climate survey
- Continue to promote the idea of college in creative ways deemed appropriate by each grade level

---

- Change Olympic Field Day to College Field Day
- All classes have a chant for their university
- All classes participate in individual student goals conferences where they explain data and assessment to students.

continued

2012-2013
College Readiness *continued*

Grades: 4-5

- Participate in a college readiness kick-off assembly
- Discuss the importance of students being on the college requirement track in high school
- Display state college entrance requirement posters
- Talk about different college options
- Help students understand that if they want to work in a specific profession that there are decisions that they can begin to make now as they choose their track to college
- Decide upon specific strategies that will be promoted at each grade level to support college readiness (Cornell notes, use of planners, etc.)
- Support the idea of students being accountable for their learning
- Introduce authentic college readiness tools that students will see in high school (Enrollment packets, etc.)
- Continue to take field trips to college campuses
- Encourage parents and students to attend the yearly college fair at the convention center

---

- Change Olympic Field Day to College Field Day
- All classes have a chant for their university
- All classes participate in individual student goals conferences where they explain data and assessment to students.

"We are committed to creating a school that knows no limits to the academic success of each student."

No Excuses University Pledge

NEU Parenting Goals

Every family plays a key role in supporting the academic and social growth of a No Excuses University Student. Just as students set academic goals, parents should also set goals to support the success of their child. Below is a template used for parents to develop two very important goals. First, parents should develop one goal to support the academics of their child. Second, plans should be made to continue to support the social and emotional growth of their student through a goal to enhance parenting skills. Both goals should include specific steps that will be taken to ensure success.

Academic Goal	Goal to Enhance Parenting
Goal: ________________ ________________ Steps for Success: ________________ ________________ ________________	Goal: ________________ ________________ Steps for Success: ________________ ________________ ________________

No Excuses University at Los Peñasquitos Student Handbook

This book belongs to:

____

The year I graduate college:

____

Dear Students,

Welcome to the No Excuses University at Los Peñasquitos. This year you will learn like never before as we prepare your path to college. Each and every one of you has very special academic and social gifts. These gifts are seen on a daily basis in the way that you work hard in the classroom in reading, writing, and math. They are also seen in the way that you display character by focusing on the six character traits described in this handbook. As you read through this handbook, you will learn about the expectations we have for all students of the No Excuses University at Los Peñasquitos. I promise that you will be successful if you remember these two words, **No Excuses**. "No Excuses" is not just our motto, it is our commitment as students, parents, and staff to do whatever it takes to be successful in school. I know that you are capable of being a great student. I am proud of you and I look forward to celebrating your successes throughout the 2005 – 2006 school year!

Sincerely,

Mr. Lopez

Mr. Lopez
Principal

Bibliography

Alliance for Excellent Education. (2006). *Saving futures, saving dollars: The impact of education on crime reduction and earnings.* Washington, D.C.: Alliance for Excellent Education.

Baum, S., & Ma, J. (2007, January). *Education pays 2007: The benefits of higher education for individuals and society.* Retrieved August 11, 2009 from College Board Web site: http://www.collegeboard.com/prod_downloads/about/news_info/cbsenior/yr2007/ed-pays-2007.pdf

Bureau of Labor Statistics. (2006). Average number of jobs started by individuals from age 18 to age 42 in 1978-2006 by age and sex. *National Longitudinal Surveys.* Retrieved August 11, 2009 from http://www.bls.gov/nls/y79r22jobsbyage.pdf.

Bureau of Labor Statistics. (2007). *College enrollment and work activity of high school graduates.* [Press release] Retrieved August 11, 2009 from http://www.bls.gov/news.release/archives/hsgec_04252008.htm

Bureau of Labor Statistics. (2008). *Volunteering in the United States.* Washington, D.C.: The U.S. Department of Labor, Bureau of Labor Statistics.

Bureau of Labor Statistics. (2009a). *Education pays.* Retrieved August 11, 2009 from http://www.bls.gov/emp/emptab7.htm

Bureau of Labor Statistics. (2009b). *Labor Force Statistics from the Current Population Survey.* Retrieved August 11, 2009 from http://www.bls.gov/cps/

Conley, D.T. (2005). *College knowledge: What it really takes for students to succeed and what we can do to get them ready.* Hoboken, N.J.: Jossey-Bass.

Day, J.C., & Newburger, E.C. (2002, July). *The big payoff: educational attainment and synthetic estimates of work-life earnings.* U.S. Census Bureau. Washington, D.C.: U.S. Government Printing Office.

Federal Trade Commission. (2008, July 29). *FTC report sheds new light on food marketing to children and adolescents.* [Press release]. Retrieved August 11, 2009 from http://www.ftc.gov/opa/2008/07/foodmkting.shtm

Harlem Children's Zone. (2009). *Harlem children's zone.*

Retrieved August 11, 2009 from http://www.hcz.org/

Henderson, P. (2009, February 10). U.S. judges seek massive California prisoner release. *Reuters*. Retrieved August 11, 2009 from http://www.reuters.com/article/topNews/idUSTRE5190CB20090210

Johnson, M.C. (2008, December 10). Prepping for college — in elementary school. *The Press-Enterprise*. Retrieved August 11, 2009 from http://www.pe.com/localnews/inland/stories/PE_News_Local_S_nexcuses11.4702b37.html

Kinsey, T., Jemal, A., Liff, J., Ward, E., & Thun, M. Secular trends in mortality from common cancers in the United States by educational attainment, 1993–2001. *Journal of the National Cancer Institute*, 100, 1003–12.

Lopez, D. (2009, January/February). College readiness for all: What's the alternative? NAESP's *Principal Magazine*, 50-51.

Marketing Charts. (2008, January 23). *Super Bowl ad spend totaled $1.84B over 20 years, rates quadrupled*. Retrieved August 11, 2009 from http://www.marketingcharts.com/television/super-bowl-ad-spend-totaled-184b-over-20-years-rates-quadrupled-3153/

Marklein, M.B. (2008, August 1). U.S. community colleges at a 'turning point.' *USA Today*. Retrieved August 11, 2009 from http://www.usatoday.com/news/education/2008-07-22-comcol-main_N.htm

Meara, E.R., Richards, S., & Cutler, D.M. (2008). The gap gets bigger: Changes in mortality and life expectancy, by education, 1981–2000. *Health Affairs*, 27(2), 350–60.

Ransdell, E. (1999, December). The Nike story? Just tell it!. *Fast Company Magazine*, 31. Retrieved August 11, 2009 from http://www.fastcompany.com/magazine/31/nike.html

Reinberg, S. (2008, July 8). College-educated fare better when cancer strikes. *U.S. News and World Report.* Retrieved August 11, 2009 from http://health.usnews.com/articles/health/healthday/2008/07/08/college-educated-fare-better-when-cancer-strikes.html

Riemer, J. (2001, February 10). Perlman makes his music — the hard way. *The Houston Chronicle*, E8.

Riordan, J. (2008, February 28). *Pew report finds more than one in 100 adults are behind bars.* [Press release]. Retrieved August 11, 2009 from the Pew Center on the States Web site: http://www.pewcenteronthestates.org/news_room_detail.aspx?id=35912

Rupert, P. & Stepanczuk, C. (2007, March). Women in the workforce. *April 2007 Economic Trends.* Retrieved August 11, 2009 from Federal Reserve Bank of Cleveland Web site: http://www.clevelandfed.org/research/trends/2007/0407/03ecoact.cfm

Safer, Morley. (Correspondent). (2002). The mensch of Malden Mills. [Television series episode]. In D. Hewitt

(Producer), *60 minutes*. New York: CBS.

Smalley, L. (Director). (2008). Darius goes west. [Motion picture]. United States: Roll With Me Productions.

U.S. Department of Agriculture. (2009). *Supplemental nutritional assistance program.* Retrieved August 11, 2009 from http://www.fns.usda.gov/snap/

U.S. Department of Health and Human Services. (2009). *The 2009 HHS poverty guidelines.* Retrieved August 11, 2009 from http://aspe.hhs.gov/poverty/09poverty.shtml

Vock, D. C. (2006, August 3). Medicaid: Biggest insurer is a budget buster. *Stateline.org.* Retrieved August 11, 2009 from http://www.stateline.org/live/ViewPage.action?siteNodeId=136&languageId=1&contentId=131622

A sincere and special thanks to my design and editing team for all their hard work — for offering candor that did not break my confidence and suggestions that did not ruin the substance of this book. It has been my pleasure to work so closely with each of you.

Shendl Diamond
LikeMindsPress.com

Kaitlin Barr Nadal
Editor
kaitlin.n.barr@gmail.com

Catherine Perry
Cover Design
CPerryDesigns.com

Katie MacLeod
Cover Portrait Photo
CandidsByKatie.com

Fran Hjalmarson
Supporting Editor
fran@turnaroundschools.com

Kim Melvin
Supporting Editor

Carolyn Ottoson
Supporting Editor

And

Michelle Lopez
Supporting Editor

I thank you all.